THE
FURNITURE
OF
HISTORIC
DEERFIELD

Frontispiece: The north parlor of the Sheldon-Hawks house contains many of Deer-field's best local treasures. The clock by George Holbrook (figure 514) was owned by the Dickinson family of Deerfield, and the Pembroke table at the right (figure 257) was made for the Sheldon family by Daniel Clay of neighboring Greenfield in 1805. While the looking glass, candlesticks, and carpet were imported, the side chair in the window was made in eastern Massachusetts between 1765 and 1795 (figure 95). In the entry is a local banister back side chair (figure 41), made about the same time for the Sheldon family.

THE FURNITURE OF HISTORIC DEERFIELD

DEAN A. FALES, JR.

Historic Deerfield, Inc.,
Deerfield, Massachusetts.

Published 1981 in the United States by Historic Deerfield, Inc., Deerfield, Massachusetts. First published 1976 by E.P. Dutton & Co., Inc., New York. No part of this book may be reproduced or transmitted in any form or by any means, electronic or mechanical, including photocopy, recording, or any storage and retrieval system now known or to be invented, without permission in writing from the publishers, except by a reviewer who wishes to quote brief passages in connection with a review written for inclusion in a magazine, newspaper or broadcast. Printed and bound by Dai Nippon Printing Co., Ltd., Tokyo, Japan. Library of Congress Catalog Card Number 76-25790. ISBN 0-525-11101-8.
Second Edition

HENRY NEEDHAM FLYNT
(1893–1970)

In his portrait by the Scottish artist, David Ewart, Henry Flynt is shown in the eighteenth-century manner with attributes revealing some of his many interests as a collector. Seated in a Massachusetts armchair (figure 115, page 64), he holds a letter of George Washington. On the stand next to him is a highly prized New York silver covered cup made by Gerrit Oncklebag in the 1690s. In the background can be seen the Ashley house in Deerfield, the first major house in the town restored by the Flynts between 1945 and 1948.

Blockfront chest of drawers, mahogany and white pine, Boston area, 1765–1790.
Brasses old but not original. See other blockfront chests on page 189, 190.
H. 30½″, W. 36″, D. 20½″.

Foreword

I am very pleased that this book is dedicated to my most dear and loving husband, Henry N. Flynt, with whom I had the privilege of collecting this furniture for Deerfield. I learned gradually, but he knew furniture because he grew up with it, and his judgment was excellent. Everyone speaks of him as a great man.

It was his wish that Dean A. Fales, Jr. would write this book and my good fortune that he accepted the task. To Virginia and Gilbert McCurdy we extend warmest thanks for their most generous contribution, making possible many of the pictures. My thanks go also to Cyril I. Nelson and to E. P. Dutton and Company, Inc., for publishing this book.

May it prove as fascinating to the reader as it has been to us.

HELEN GEIER FLYNT   *July, 1974*

Dressing table, walnut and yellow pine, New Jersey type, 1720–1765. Most of the brass pulls are original. The carved Spanish feet are highly distinctive. H. 31″, W. 33½″, D. 19½″.

Cupboard, pine, New England, 1750–1800.
Repainted red over original red paint. One
shelf and bottom gnawed by porcupine
and restored. Top molding restored.
Similar to large dresser shown on page 254.
H. 75″, W. 49″, D. 20″.

Preface

The purpose of this volume is to illustrate and bring into print as many of the fine pieces of furniture at Deerfield as possible. While basic information such as histories, woods, and dimensions are given in the captions and text, the pieces are treated as briefly as possible so that more types can be included. Rather than a catalogue raisonné, perhaps this work should be considered a catalogue illuminé. In addition to pertinent information on each example, an attempt has been made to include background material on the development of styles and use of forms so that the individual examples can be seen within a broader context. Since the furniture at Deerfield is mostly New England in origin, this area is emphasized, but not to the exclusion of other American or even foreign examples. Special emphasis is given to those pieces made in the Deerfield area, the upper Connecticut Valley of Massachusetts, since they form a most important core of the collection.

The furniture is shown by major forms, with the pieces within each category arranged as chronologically or stylistically as the transitional nature of much American furniture will allow. Great care has been given to the dates and places of manufacture of the examples shown, as well as to the attributions to particular makers. Since dressing tables (or lowboys) were often made to match or accompany high chests of drawers and are in reality case pieces rather than tables, they are included in the section on high chests (see pages 204–224).

Original colors and finishes are noted wherever possible. While wood identification is largely visual, microscopic examination has also been used. The term whitewood is used (as it once was) to describe woods such as cottonwood, basswood, and other lightish native timbers. White pine, the noblest of New England secondary woods, is listed as such wherever possible, although in some instances of uncertainty it may appear as merely "pine."

Measurements are in inches, since the examples here were made according to that soon-to-be-gone system, and maximum dimensions are given. In the section on looking glasses, the height precedes the width of each example. In the case of upholstered chairs and sofas, the upholstery is described when it is old and suitable for the piece it clothes. While approximately half of the furniture at Deerfield is shown here, hopefully all the most significant examples are included. Only a few of the pieces illustrated are not yet on permanent exhibition in the houses.

Footnotes are not used in the text, but pertinent references appear in parentheses. While they can be a bit jarring to smooth reading at times, it is hoped that they will prove more helpful to the reader.

The collections of Historic Deerfield, Inc., are amplified and complemented by those in Memorial Hall owned by the Pocumtuck Valley Memorial Association (indicated P.V.M.A. in the captions). Henry N. Flynt was the cofounder of the former and became president of the latter. Donors to both organizations are listed in the captions, and whenever no name appears, it can be assumed that the particular object was acquired for Deerfield by the Flynts.

Two large bequests are included. The first consists of the furnishings of the Frary house collected over seventy years ago by Miss C. Alice Baker. She bequeathed these with the house to the P.V.M.A. upon her death in 1909. In 1969, the house and its contents were transferred to Historic Deerfield, Inc. The second large group of furniture given to Deerfield was collected by Lucius D. Potter and Rowena Russell Potter of Greenfield. Mr. Potter had known Henry Flynt's father, and after the former's death, Mrs. Potter left the collection to Deerfield as a memorial to her husband.

The great majority of the examples shown were acquired by the Flynts. Their taste and love of collecting can constantly be seen in the extraordinary range of treasures they found for Deerfield. Combining the simple with the elaborate and the ordinary with the unusual, the furniture collections at Deerfield represent one of the biggest and best assemblages of early New England furniture in the country today.

DEAN A. FALES, JR.

Kennebunkport, Maine

Acknowledgments

In the writing of this book, the author has received much help from many persons, all of whom have made his own work easier and hopefully more precise.

To Helen Geier Flynt go my deepest thanks for her assistance in innumerable specifics and generalities from the very beginning. May this work be worthy of her tireless efforts at Deerfield.

Friends are always good to have, and when they really know something they are even better. The following have contributed to this work: Henry N. Flynt, Jr., Benno M. Forman, Miss Jennifer Furkel, Thompson R. Harlow, Benjamin A. Hewitt, Frank L. Horton, Patricia E. Kane, Bertram K. Little, Nina Fletcher Little, Amelia F. Miller, the late Richard Mills, Charles F. Montgomery, Charles S. Parsons, Richard H. Randall, Jr., Kenneth D. Roberts, Gordon Saltar, and Arthur Vitols.

The staff of Historic Deerfield, Inc. has worked hard in providing information to an often absentee author. To Donald R. Friary, Maude Banta, Mary D. Brooks, Edward A. Gritz, and Sylvia M. Wells go a thousand thanks. Natalie H. Whitcomb remeasured all the furniture in the book, thereby receiving yards and yards of thanks (to the nearest sixteenth of an inch).

David R. Proper, the best librarian of local history anywhere and Librarian of the Memorial Libraries at Deerfield, put on his other hat as a clock expert and provided detailed horologic notes of all the timepieces in the collection.

The person to whom most of the work fell and all the glory should go is Joseph Peter Spang III, Curator. With his enthusiastic knowledge of Deerfield, his long association with the Flynts, and his scrupulous recording of facts and ephemera, he embodies the best spirit of the true antiquarian and has added immeasurably to this work.

To my favorite proofreader go my everlasting thanks. While we old English majors come around to suggestions slowly and with great torment, there is no one anywhere who can read me better.

Finally, I would like to thank Henry N. Flynt—especially for himself. Aside from his prowess as a collector, he had a marvelous wit and always a warm twinkle as a friend. We had great enjoyment discussing the furniture at Deerfield, and the basic organization of this book was his idea. The result is longer than we expected, but then so were our conversations!

D.A.F., Jr.

Contents

Upholstered armchair, cherry, Massachusetts (probably Connecticut Valley, 1780–1810). Feet repaired where rockers were added. Similar to back stool number 120, page 66. Owned by Crafts family, Whately, Massachusetts (just south of Deerfield). H. 40½", W. 24", D. 19". Lucius D. Potter Memorial.

Slatback rocker, maple, probably Deerfield, 1800–1835. Painted red. Given to Miss C. Alice Baker by Mrs. Henry King Hoyt (Catherine Wells) and owned by her family in Deerfield. Two other local nineteenth-century rockers are shown on page 25, numbers 24 and 25. H. 44¾", W. 21½", D. 16".

Short Title Index

Since references are given directly in the text, the titles of the most frequently used works have been truncated, as listed below, in the interests of conserving space and preserving continuity.

Boston Furniture	WHITEHILL, WALTER MUIR, ed. *Boston Furniture of the Eighteenth Century.* Boston: the Colonial Society of Massachusetts, 1974.
Chamberlain and Flynt	CHAMBERLAIN, SAMUEL, and FLYNT, HENRY N. *Historic Deerfield: Houses and Interiors.* New York: Hastings House, 1972. (Earlier editions published in 1952, 1957 and 1965, the first two entitled *Frontier of Freedom*).
Comstock	COMSTOCK, HELEN. *American Furniture: Seventeenth, Eighteenth, and Nineteenth Century Styles.* New York: The Viking Press, 1962.
Cummings	CUMMINGS, ABBOTT LOWELL, ed. *Rural Household Inventories: 1675–1775.* Boston: the Society for the Preservation of New England Antiquities, 1964.
Dow	DOW, GEORGE FRANCIS. *The Arts & Crafts in New England: 1704–1775.* Topsfield, Massachusetts, 1927.
Downs	DOWNS, JOSEPH. *American Furniture: Queen Anne and Chippendale Periods.* New York: The Macmillan Company, 1952.
Edwards	EDWARDS, RALPH. *The Shorter Dictionary of English Furniture.* London: Country Life Limited, 1964.
Fales, *Essex*	FALES, DEAN A., JR. *Essex County Furniture: Documented Treasures from Local Collections 1680–1860.* Salem, Massachusetts: Essex Institute, 1965.
Fales, *Painted*	FALES, DEAN A., JR. *American Painted Furniture 1660–1880.* New York: E. P. Dutton and Co., Inc., 1972.
Greenlaw	GREENLAW, BARRY A. *New England Furniture at Williamsburg.* Williamsburg: The Colonial Williamsburg Foundation, distributed by the University Press of Virginia, 1974.
Harvard Tercentenary Exhibition	*Harvard Tercentenary Exhibition: Catalogue of Furniture, Silver, Pewter, Glass, Ceramics, Paintings, Prints, Together with Allied Arts and Crafts of the Period 1636–1836.* Cambridge: Harvard University Press, 1936.
Judd	JUDD, SYLVESTER. *History of Hadley, Including the Early History of Hatfield, South Hadley, Amherst and Granby, Massachusetts.* Northampton, Massachusetts, 1863.
Kettell	KETTELL, RUSSELL HAWES. *The Pine Furniture of Early New England.* New York: Doubleday, Doran & Co., Inc., 1929.
Kirk, *Chairs*	KIRK, JOHN T. *American Chairs: Queen Anne and Chippendale.* New York: Alfred A. Knopf, 1972.

Kirk, *Connecticut* KIRK, JOHN T. *Connecticut Furniture: Seventeenth and Eighteenth Centuries.* Hartford, Connecticut: Wadsworth Atheneum, 1967.

Kirk, *Early* KIRK, JOHN T. *Early American Furniture.* New York: Alfred A. Knopf, 1970.

Luther LUTHER, CLAIR FRANKLIN. *The Hadley Chest.* Hartford, Connecticut: The Case, Lockwood & Brainard Company, 1935.

Lyon LYON, IRVING W. *The Colonial Furniture of New England.* Boston and New York: Houghton, Mifflin and Company, 1891.

Montgomery MONTGOMERY, CHARLES F. *American Furniture: The Federal Period.* New York: The Viking Press, a Winterthur Book, 1966.

Myers and Mayhew MYERS, MINOR, JR., and MAYHEW, EDGAR DE N. *New London Country Furniture 1640–1840.* New London, Connecticut: The Lyman Allyn Museum, 1974.

Nutting NUTTING, WALLACE. *Furniture Treasury.* Framingham, Massachusetts, Old America Company, 1928–1933; reprinted New York: The Macmillan Company, 1948, 1954.

Palardy PALARDY, JEAN. *The Early Furniture of French Canada.* Translated by Eric McLean. Toronto and New York: Macmillan of Canada and St. Martin's Press, 1965.

Palmer PALMER, BROOKS. *The Book of American Clocks.* New York: The Macmillan Company, 1950.

P.V.M.A. *Catalogue* *Catalogue of the Collection of Relics in Memorial Hall, Deerfield, Mass., U.S.A.* Deerfield: Pocumtuck Valley Memorial Association, 1920. (Earlier catalogues published in 1886 and 1908).

P.V.M.A. *Proceedings* *History and Proceedings of the Pocumtuck Valley Memorial Association* (1870–1942). Deerfield: 1890–1950. 9 volumes.

Randall RANDALL, RICHARD H., JR. *American Furniture in the Museum of Fine Arts, Boston,* Boston: Museum of Fine Arts, 1965.

Sheldon, *Guide* SHELDON, GEORGE. *A Guide to the Museum of the Pocumtuck Valley Memorial Association.* Deerfield, P.V.M.A., 1920 (2nd edition).

Sheldon, *History* SHELDON, GEORGE. *A History of Deerfield Massachusetts.* Deerfield, 1895–1896; reprinted Somersworth, New Hampshire: the New Hampshire Publishing Company in collaboration with P.V.M.A., 1972. 2 volumes.

Warren WARREN, DAVID B. *Bayou Bend: American Furniture, Paintings and Silver from the Bayou Bend Collection.* Houston, Texas: The Museum of Fine Arts, 1975.

Wills WILLS, GEOFFREY. *English Looking Glasses: A Study of the Glass, Frames and Makers (1670–1820).* London: Country Life Limited, 1965.

NOTE: *The works listed above are those of most use in studying the Deerfield collection of furniture. Other equally important works on American cabinetmaking are not listed since they have no great bearing on the pieces at Deerfield. Certain works, such as Palmer, Sheldon's History, published Deerfield Vital Records, and many of the valuable articles on craftsmen published by the Connecticut Historical Society, are not cited every time in this text, but specific references are given in key places.*

D.A.F., Jr.

I. SEATS AND BEDSTEADS

1. Joint stool, oak base with hard pine top, eastern Massachusetts, 1660–1710. H. 18⅝″, W. 20″, D. 12¾″.

2. High stool, birch and maple with pine top, painted black, probably Quebec, 1700–1740. Ex coll. Vincent D. Andrus. H. 19″, W. 9⅜″, D. 9⅜″.

3. Form or bench, maple throughout, probably Massachusetts (Connecticut Valley), 1700–1740. H. 20″, W. 37½″, D. 12″.

Stools, Chairs, Couches, and Sofas

The first section of this work (pages 14–108) deals with objects in the Deerfield collections that were made to hold people, either in upright or recumbent positions.

The simplest type of sittable is the stool, a form popular in the Colonies from the earliest days. In the seventeenth century, stools appear in inventories with far greater frequency than do chairs, which were often beyond the means of many of the early settlers. In the inventory of Thomas Hawley of Roxbury, Massachusetts, taken in August of 1676, "5 joined Stooles" are listed in the kitchen (Cummings, p. 14). The term joint stool indicated that the piece was the work of a joiner—its quality better than the work of a turner or wheelwright (Edwards, pp. 502–504).

Figure 1 is an excellent example of an early joint stool. Made of oak, the most popular wood of the seventeenth century, and with a pine top with molded edges, the stool has the appearance of a small table. Its legs, with their varied ring-and-baluster turnings, splay outward at the bottom a bit for greater stability. This stool was found in Chiltonville at the southern reaches of Plymouth, Massachusetts, and represents the earliest type of New England joint stool. Its crisp stance and varied turnings result in a high quality.

The high stool (2) is a generation or two later, and while it was found in Connecticut, it probably filtered southward to New England from Quebec. A similar high stool came from the old Seminary of St. Sulpice, Notre Dame, in Montreal (Palardy, fig. 237).

Furniture can move about rather easily, and many Canadian pieces have been found in northern New England. While this stool is now painted black, its original color was a blue-gray.

Forms or benches were elongated stools capable of holding two or more persons. They were drawn up at tables (a feat requiring a certain amount of physical dexterity and teamwork), and forms appear in New England inventories from the 1640s on. The example at Deerfield (3) is an eighteenth-century form, made completely of maple and originally painted red. The simpler turnings of the legs lack the excitement of the stools. It was acquired in Greenfield.

In these first three examples, we can see how the web of the collections at Deerfield has been woven. Top priority has been given to pieces made in the area, while great emphasis has also been placed on examples from other areas that would have been used in Deerfield homes. Eastern Massachusetts and Connecticut quite naturally lead this procession, but we will also encounter examples from other New England states, New York, and points southward, and even occasional examples from Canada and England. The great strength of the collections will be found in the breadth of New England furniture—rural and urban alike—from the seventeenth to the early nineteenth centuries, with particular attention paid to those examples from the Deerfield area, the upper Connecticut Valley of Massachusetts, and western Massachusetts itself.

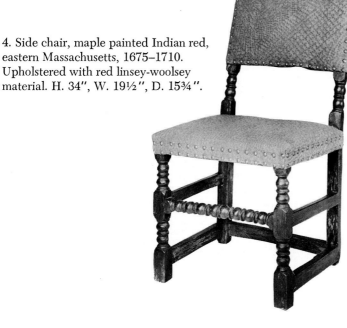

4. Side chair, maple painted Indian red, eastern Massachusetts, 1675–1710. Upholstered with red linsey-woolsey material. H. 34″, W. 19½″, D. 15¾″.

5. Side chair, red oak, Massachusetts (Connecticut Valley), 1680–1725. Upholstered with leather. H. 37″, W. 18″, D. 14⅞″. P.V.M.A., gift of Joseph N. Fuller.

Wainscot chairs with plank seats, turned chairs with rush or splint seats, and chairs with upholstered backs and seats were the three main types of chairs made in seventeenth-century Colonial America. Upholstered chairs are the rarest since comfort was a feature that came to the Colonies in the next century. Above are two so-called Cromwellian side chairs, based on English farthingale chairs of the early part of the seventeenth century. These low-backed chairs were very comfortable, and their original upholstery most often was turkey work or leather (see Lyon, pp. 147–153). The chair at the left (4) is a good example of an urban production, with very crisp ball-and-disc turnings on the front legs, front stretchers, and back supports. It has lost an inch or two of its legs over the years. The chair was found in Carver, Massachusetts, in Plymouth County, and was probably made there or in the Boston area.

The other chair (5) is upholstered in leather which was applied at a later date, covering the entire back. Originally, only the seat and upper panel would have been upholstered. This chair is the earliest chair with a Deerfield history known. It was owned by John Amsden (1721–1794) of the Bars, an agricultural area south of the town of Deerfield, and came from the house of Samuel Allen (1702–1746), built in 1739 at the Bars. Allen's father had lived in Suffield, Connecticut (Sheldon, *History*, II, 11, 12, 29 and P.V.M.A. *Catalogue*, p. 16). The chair was owned later by the nineteenth-century local artist, George Fuller, who used the Allen house as his studio. Made of native

American red oak, determined by microscopic analysis, the chair combines early hefty baluster turnings with simple rectangular stiles and stretchers. There was only a single front stretcher originally. The "kick" at the base of the rear legs is an unusual feature on an early New England chair. This combination of elements is found frequently in pieces made away from the larger population centers. Since Deerfield was an outpost until well into the eighteenth century —Samuel Allen was killed by Indians in 1746—its earliest furniture tends to be quite simple and conservative. This chair, then, is a rather stylish exception to the rule.

The largest group of early chairs is turned. These include Carvers, Brewsters, slatbacks, and banister backs. The early appraisers rarely differentiated between the various types, and "Chaire," "greate Chaire," and "old Chaire" are frequently the only descriptions in documents. In Deerfield, the term "Timber Chair" appears frequently in early inventories from 1698 (Thomas Wells) to 1746 (John Wells) and possibly indicates these early turned examples.

The most impressive of the early, turned great chairs are the Carvers and Brewsters, named (later) after examples owned by luminaries of the Plymouth Colony. Carvers have turned vertical spindles in their backs (6, 7), while Brewsters have an added row (or rows) of spindles under their seats or arms. Both types were made occasionally as side chairs, but they usually occur as massive armchairs of heroic proportions.

6. While turned Carver and Brewster chairs were made in the seventeenth century, this Connecticut great chair of the second quarter of the eighteenth century has well turned uprights that contrast delightfully with the rather languorous sausage-turned spindles and front stretchers. Made entirely of maple, it was painted dark red originally. H. 45½″, W. 21¼″, D. 15½″.

7. Great chair, maple and oak, probably Massachusetts, 1680–1715. H. 46″, W. 19″, D. 16″.

8. Great chair, maple and oak, eastern Massachusetts, 1645–1675. H. 46½″, W. 19″, D. 16¼″.

The two great chairs above are interesting to compare. The turnings on the Brewster type (8) are heavier and crisper than those on the Carver (7). In the world of the turner, a lack of definition is frequently a sign of a later date. The flattened single balls in the front and rear posts of 7 are similar to those on a slatback armchair at Deerfield (11), as are the finials. They both echo an earlier great chair of the slatback type found in Killingly, Connecticut (Lyon, fig. 57). Flattened ball turnings in the posts are often associated with the eastern Massachusetts area (see Fales, *Painted*, p. 14). The feet and bottom row of stretchers of 7 have been restored, and the chair has been repainted (see *Antiques*, October, 1945, p. 189). Such wear on early chairs is to be expected. The legs of the Brewster chair (8) are pieced out, and the knobs of the arm supports and some of the spindles have been replaced. Its magnificence warrants this restoration. It is similar to a Brewster chair at the Boston Museum of Fine Arts (Randall, no. 118).

The small child's rocker at the right (9) shows how the form survived. It closely resembles a nineteenth-century English chair of a type which was made as late as the 1920s as apprentice exercises by a furniture firm at Addingham (see Christopher Gilbert, *Town and Country Furniture*, Leeds, Temple Newsam, 1972, fig. 36).

9. Child's rocker, oak, American or English, 1800–1850. H. 23¼″, W. 11¼″, D. 10″.

10. The great hall of the Wells-Thorn house shows many of the early types of chairs used in New England homes. In the foreground is a heavy great chair of the Carver type, formerly owned by the Curtis family of Massachusetts. At the left of the chest and window are two cane-back side chairs. Most of these were imported from England and were popular in Colonial households early in the 1700s. At the far end of the table is a wainscot-type armchair, with a plank seat and back; and to the right of the window is a small slatback side chair made later in the eighteenth century. The room is from the earliest part of the house built by Ebenezer Wells about 1717 at the southeastern corner of the Street and what is now Memorial Street. The house is shown on page 265.

11. Great chair, maple and ash,
probably eastern Massachusetts, 1680–1715.
Painted black. H. 50″, W. 20½″, D. 17″.

12. Great chair, maple and oak,
probably New York, 1680–1710.
Ex coll. John C. Spring.
H. 36″, W. 17½″, D. 16½″.

Slatback chairs were one of the most popular types of chairs made. Their span extended from the busy hall of a seventeenth-century home to the drowsy piazza of a nineteenth-century resort hotel. The earliest examples had turned posts that were like the Carver and Brewster great chairs, but their flat slats were far more hospitable to the human back than were elaborately turned spindles. The posts of 11 (above) are similar to those on 7, a Carver type. The finials are well turned, with a ball surmounted by two varied discs and topped by an ovoid ball, the latter a replacement. The upper two inches of the front posts and the arms were also casualties to the years. The feet, interestingly enough, were never cut down. Often they were the first elements of early chairs to disappear when later generations fancied converting them to more comfortable rocking chairs.

Both chairs on this page were originally painted black. Lampblack was an easily available pigment, and most early chairs of the seventeenth and eighteenth centuries were painted black or red. Indian red (or Spanish brown) were both earth colors which were imported and available. Unfortunately, subsequent wear, coupled with the later rage for refinishing, has left few early chairs with their original paint.

The chair above (12) is a small great chair, but one of very staunch proportion. It would appear to have had finials originally, but the tops of the back posts are quite worn in their present state. The lined urn turning on the front posts and double discs on the rear posts are quite similar to those on a turned chair with quadrilateral back owned by the Stryker family of New York, now at The Metropolitan Museum of Art. This and a similar chair at the Connecti-

13. Armchair, maple,
probably Connecticut Shore, 1700–1725.
Painted green-black. H. 43″, W. 19″, D. 18¼″.

14. Armchair, maple and ash,
probably Connecticut Shore, 1700–1725.
Painted black. H. 47½″, W. 19½″, D. 15½″.

cut Historical Society were probably made in New York. (Both illustrated in Robert C. Bishop, *Centuries and Styles of the American Chair*, New York: E. P. Dutton and Co., Inc., 1972, p. 26). The bottoms of the feet have been restored.

The two slatback armchairs on this page have many similarities in their turned posts. The double ball elements that occur above the seat rail on the front posts and between the upper two slats on the rear posts are a feature generally thought to indicate a Connecticut origin. Many of the rules of regional characteristics are frequently broken, however, and this feature is also seen on an earlier Carver-type chair with a long Rhode Island history (*Antiques*, April 1927, p. 305).

The raking arms of 13, with their compressed ball turnings, are a startling feature. Originally, the chair

had finials, and these must have been very similar to those on its neighbor above. Figure 13 has been repainted a green-black with stripings in the nineteenth century. Frequently, local coach painters were called upon to repaint and "improve" the finishes on older pieces of furniture. This chair was formerly in the collection of J. Stogdell Stokes, a pioneer American collector (see *Antiques*, March 1934, p. 107, fig. 28).

The other chair (14) may not have the zooming glamour of diagonally soaring arms, but it is a fine example of high quality. The balance of the chair is perfect, and the varieties of its turnings—especially on the back posts and even the arms themselves—lend much to its dignity. The splint seat is a nineteenth-century replacement, and the chair has been repainted black. Both chairs have fine "mushroom" terminals on their front posts.

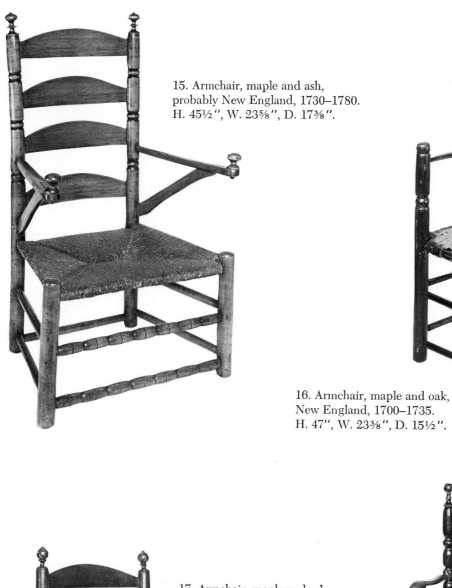

15. Armchair, maple and ash, probably New England, 1730–1780. H. 45½″, W. 23⅝″, D. 17⅜″.

16. Armchair, maple and oak, New England, 1700–1735. H. 47″, W. 23⅜″, D. 15½″.

17. Armchair, maple and ash, New Jersey, 1710–1780. H. 43½″, W. 20¼″, D. 18½″.

18. Child's chair, maple and ash, Massachusetts (Connecticut Valley), 1710–1780. H. 37″, W. 10½″, D. 11″.

The variations on the slatback theme can be endless. On the opposite page, 15 (top left) has the slightly lighter turnings of the eighteenth century. The crane-type arm supports are most unusual, and they permit the chair to be on the wide and deep side without appearing too cumbersome. The sausage turnings on the front stretchers are well executed. The chair has been refinished. However, the armchair to its right (16) was painted black originally (now it is a dark green) and is one of the few early chairs at Deerfield with an old splint seat. The flattened arms, shaped slats, and ovoid finials on discs give it an early appearance. It was owned by the distinguished American silver scholar, John Marshall Phillips, and many of its features relate to chairs from eastern Massachusetts.

The armchair at the lower left (17) is a New Jersey type of the eighteenth century. The "blunt arrow" turnings of the feet, the plain rear posts, the flattened arms, and the simple slats are all features of central New Jersey (see *Antiques*, July 1932, p. 40). The two sausage-turned front stretchers and the strong turnings on the front posts above the seat add oomph to what might have been a rather plain chair. It is painted black.

The child's high chair (18) has indeed a splay to its front legs! It is painted black, and the rounded bead-and-reel turnings of the posts—and especially the smaller turned ball elements on the stretchers—are very close to those on an armchair at Deerfield (page 287, no. 576) from the Bates house in Conway, a town just west of Deerfield. The lower two slats have lost their rounded tops over the years.

The two chairs on this page have good Deerfield histories and were made locally. Both have finials of a local type, and the armchair (19) has a turning more like a stretcher used for what might have been the upper slat. The chair was owned originally in the Stebbins or Wright families in the handsome brick house at the north end of the Street. The Wright house was built for Asa Stebbins, Jr. in 1824 and is now owned by Historic Deerfield, Inc. Dr. Edwin Thorn, who lived in the Wells-Thorn house, received this chair as payment for his medical services in removing a splinter from one of the Wright children in the early 1900s. Dr. Thorn was also an antiquarian and amateur cabinetmaker, and he probably pieced out the legs, added the missing lower stretchers, and stained the chair dark brown.

The side chair (20) has survived many vicissitudes in its life and is included here to demonstrate what fate will inflict and what loving care will fix. Owned in the Williams family of Deerfield, "EW" is stamped on one of its slats, as is "Mch 10, 1809," perhaps the date of the chair. The top slat probably became broken, and someone must have thought hard and long to come up with the decision to even off the top and third slat! The front leg on the left also must have vanished, and its replacement lacks the turnings of the other leg and posts. There are also the initials "EH" carved into the back of a slat, and one can only hope they do not refer to Eben Hart, a joiner in nearby Shelburne, who advertised in the *Greenfield Gazette* in 1806 for apprentices to "the Joiner's and Carpenter's business." The chair has been restained a dark brown.

19. Armchair, oak,
Deerfield area, 1780–1820.
H. 44″, W. 20½″, D. 15½″.

20. Side chair, maple and hickory,
Deerfield area, 1780–1820.
H. 40¼″, W. 16″, D. 13⅛″.
Gift of Elizabeth Fuller.

22 (right). Side chair, maple and hickory,
Massachusetts (Connecticut Valley), 1785–1820.
H. 45½ ", W. 16½ ", D. 13⅛ ".
Gift of Elizabeth Fuller.

21 (below). High side chair, maple and ash,
New England, 1800–1860.
H. 56", W. 17", D. 14¼ ".

The side chair above (22) is a most satisfying slatback. Its verticality and balance, coupled with its bowed top slat and the urnlike elements in the turnings of the back and front legs, result in a chair of great refinement. The taper at the base of the rear legs indicates a date normally after 1800 in New England chairs. Repainted olive green, it was owned by the Williams family of Deerfield. Three generations of this illustrious family ministered to the medical needs of the townspeople of Deerfield from 1739 to 1850. Dr. Thomas Williams (1718–1775) came to Deerfield in 1739, and he was succeeded by Dr. William Stoddard Williams (1762–1829) and Dr. Stephen W. Williams (1790–1855) (Sheldon, *History*, II, 381–385). While the chair has an early eighteenth-century appearance, it was owned by one of the later two physicians.

The tall chair at the left (21) was probably used by a weaver or a bookkeeper. The seat is a lusty 31¼ inches high, and the front legs are sharply raked for stability. It has been repainted red, and its main distinction is its unusual size.

23. Wagon seat, maple and ash, New England, 1810–1860. H. 26″, W. 35″, D. 14¾″.

Wagon seats or wagon chairs were removable small benches, usually of the slatback type, that could convert a farm wagon to a pleasure vehicle (see Ada Hemstreet, "Ancestral Rumble Seats," *Antiques*, June 1931, pp. 464, 465). The front center post is invariably thicker than the others. Many of these seats were rather crude, homemade affairs in the nineteenth century. The example above (23) has been refinished. In its embryonic finials and swelled turnings under the arms on the outer front posts, there is an attempt to give this simple form a modicum of stylishness.

Rocking chairs were made in the eighteenth century. As early as 1762, Eliakim Smith of Hadley charged Elisha Porter "To putting rockers on a chair,

3/" (*Antiques*, May 1928, p. 409). In the later examples shown below, it appears that 24, with a single front stretcher, was made as a rocker, while on 25 rather clumsy rockers have been grafted to an armchair form. Joseph Griswold, a cabinetmaker of nearby Buckland, charged a dollar for making "Chairs great & rocking" between 1804 and 1813 (Ms. price list, the Henry N. Flynt Library). The use of the term great chair is interesting at this late date. Both chairs have short arms with their own supports, a later feature than the arms continuing to the front posts. The turnings are more flaccid than earlier ones. Figure 24 was owned by the Henry Bates family of Conway, and 25 by the Allen family of Deerfield.

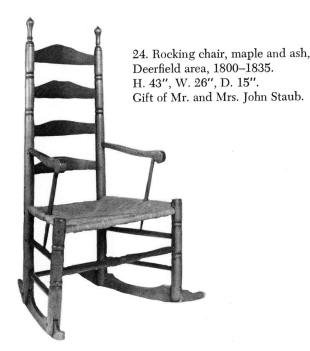

24. Rocking chair, maple and ash,
Deerfield area, 1800–1835.
H. 43″, W. 26″, D. 15″.
Gift of Mr. and Mrs. John Staub.

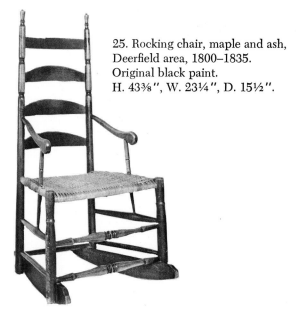

25. Rocking chair, maple and ash,
Deerfield area, 1800–1835.
Original black paint.
H. 43⅜″, W. 23¼″, D. 15½″.

26. Side chair, European beech and cane, England, 1685–1710. Painted black. Found locally. Similar to 27 (right). H. 49″, W. 18½″, D. 14″.

27. Side chair, European beech and cane, England, 1685–1710. Painted black. Acquired from Mrs. Natalie Ashley Stebbins, with a long Deerfield history. Stiles flanking caning and bottom back rail replaced in nineteenth century. They probably resembled those on 26 (left). H. 50″, W. 18″, D. 14⅜″.

28. Side chair, soft maple and cane, probably Boston, 1710–1725. Originally painted black or grained. Owned by Ashley family. Applied toes of Spanish feet missing. H. 45″, W. 18″, D. 14½″. Gift of Mrs. Dorothy Blatchford Pettit.

Cane-back chairs appear in Massachusetts inventories as early as 1689 (Lyon, p. 153) and continue to be listed as household possessions frequently into the mid-1700s. Most of these chairs were imported from England, and they were usually made of beech stained dark to resemble walnut. The chair at the left above (26) was found near Deerfield, and it closely resembles chairs owned by Richard Lord of Hartford, who died in 1712 (Lyon, fig. 68 and *Connecticut Chairs*, Hartford, Connecticut Historical Society, 1956, pp. 8, 9). The chair above at the right (27) was originally quite similar to 26, the main differences being in the feet and turnings of the rear posts. Cane chairs are rather fragile, and the later repairs demonstrate both a love and sense of preservation—and thrift—in Deerfield.

The side chair at the left (28) is one of a small number of American examples probably made in Boston. It was owned by the Reverend Jonathan Ashley, whose house (see p. 108) is one of Historic Deerfield's proudest possessions. It came from his wife Dorothy's family, the Reverend William Williams family of Hatfield. Several identical chairs exist in other collections, as do a small group of similar chairs with scalloped seat rails. Two of these were traditionally owned later by Nathaniel Hawthorne in Salem (*Harvard Tercentenary Exhibition*, no. 215).

There are four other types of American maple cane chairs, all relating to each other and many with variations within their types. They range from fancy cresting rails (Comstock, no. 37) to rounded crestings (Randall, no. 127), and from open cresting rails (*American Antiques from Israel Sack Collection*, II, Washington: Highland House Publishers, Inc., 1969, 367) to a tighter, stepped cresting (Fales, *Painted*, no. 73). Owners of these chairs included John Hancock of Boston and Col. John Stoddard of Northampton. The chairs have been found throughout New England and as far south as

29. Armchair, European beech and cane, England, 1690–1710. Painted dark brown. Front stretcher replaced in nineteenth century. H. 53¾″, W. 22⅝″, D. 16¹³/₁₆″. Gift of John B. Morris, Jr.

30. Armchair, European beech and cane, England, 1690–1700. Painted black; banisters strengthened in back. Human head finials. H. 52¼″, W. 20″, D. 17½″.

Virginia and Georgia, indicating that, like the leather "Boston chairs" which were exported up and down the coast in the first half of the 1700s, these, too, were a part of our inter-colonial trade (see Richard H. Randall, Jr., "Boston Chairs," *Old-Time New England,* Summer, 1963, pp. 12–20). These cane chairs have many similarities to the leather "Boston chairs," and often the bases and arms are identical in both types. While some cane examples have been published as made in the area where they were found, circumstantial evidence points strongly to a Boston origin for the five main types. Some of these have punched initials on a rear leg. EE (conjoined) is seen on several types (including 28), and while it is tempting to hope they might signify Edmond Edes, a joiner working in Boston in 1709, there is no proof of this as yet (see Randall, no. 127). There is also the possibility these initials could signify owners, since initials other than EE are found on cane-back chairs.

On this page, the two English armchairs above have many features that were also used on Colonial chairs. The scrolled cresting of 29 appears on some highly developed American banister backs (33, page 28), as do the scrolled arms. Figure 30 is a regal prototype of the American banister back (pages 28–32). This armchair was owned by the Ayer family of Bangor, Maine, and was probably owned by earlier Rhode Island ancestors (compare with Edwards, p. 124, no. 34; and *Antiques,* September 1931, p. 157, fig. 4). The side chair at the right (31) is a very simple cane back example. While wood tests are inconclusive as to its beech being European or American, it has significant points in common with a chair owned by Nicholas Sever (1680–1764) of Harvard (*Harvard Tercentenary Exhibition,* no. 211), and to a maple and oak Boston leather armchair at Winterthur (see John D. Morse, ed., *Country Cabinetwork and Simple City Furniture,* Winterthur, 1969, p. 234).

31. Side chair, beech and cane, England or Boston area, 1700–1725. Brown stain. Double ball feet. H. 46¾″, W. 18″, D. 15″. Gift of John B. Morris, Jr.

32. Armchair, maple and ash, Boston school, 1710–1740. Originally painted Spanish brown. H. 46½", W. 20½", D. 16".

33. Side chair, maple and ash, Boston school, 1710–1740. Originally painted Spanish brown. H. 45½", W. 14¾", D. 13¾". Gift of Mrs. Ray Morris.

One of the most stylish types of early chairs made in the Colonies was the banister back. Based obviously on English prototypes (see preceding page), with a touch of Colonial baroque in their crestings, these chairs were originally referred to as banister backs (Lyon, pp. 165–166). They were made from the early eighteenth century well into the 1800s in both urban and rural areas. The split balusters forming their backs were usually flat on the side facing the sitter, and their outline usually conformed with the turnings of the stiles on side chairs. The fanciest examples (above) had carved scrolled crestings reminiscent of cane chairs, and these chairs relate to the leather and cane chairs made in the "Boston chair" area—from Boston eastward to coastal New Hampshire. Both chairs above have had their feet replaced. The crisp turnings and carving on the side chair (33) are executed with more finesse than on the armchair (32). The side chair also has ball-and-ring turned side stretchers which reflect the front stretcher, and the bottom rail of the back has a rounded tablet which adds to the upward thrust of the chair (see Kirk, *Early*, pp. 48–52).

The small child's chair at the right (34) has mushroom armposts, and its base resembles that of a slatback. The trumpet-turned back stiles and the double arch on the top rail are found on a high chair from the Little Compton area in Rhode Island (see Kirk, *Early*, no. 38).

34. Child's armchair, maple, possibly Rhode Island, 1710–1790. Originally painted red. H. 25¼", W. 12", D. 10½". Lucius D. Potter Memorial.

35. Side chair, maple, eastern Massachusetts, 1710–1740. Repainted black and gold. One of a pair. H. 47¾", W. 18⅝", D. 13½".

36. Armchair, maple, Connecticut, 1770–1820. Originally painted black. H. 42½", W. 21", D. 18".

37. Side chair, maple, Essex County, Massachusetts, 1740–1775. Dark red stain. H. 41½", W. 15¾", D. 13".

The side chair at the left above (35) is quite an ambitious one, with floridly carved cresting and double ball feet which occur occasionally in eastern Massachusetts chairs. The shapings of the balusters and stiles do not line up as they usually do on side chairs, however, and the turnings on the stiles do not quite match each other. "R S 1643–96" is carved on the back of the chair, and this must be some sort of later commemoration of an earlier family member, who must have been the father or grandfather of the original owner. The chair has been repainted black with gold stripings in the nineteenth century coach painter's tradition. The initials and date could have been added then.

The armchair above (36) has later turnings, and its banisters are flat strips of wood with beaded edges. The double ball turnings above and below the arms on the rear posts continue a tradition seen on earlier slatbacks from the Connecticut Shore (see 13 and 14). The side chair at the left (37) features a wavy cresting which has been likened to both the tail of a fish and the head of a wolf. Chairs of this type, invariably with a single ring turning on the upper part of the stiles, have been found with histories in Salem and Andover, Massachusetts, as well as in southeastern New Hampshire—pointing to an Essex county origin for this different type. This chair has been repainted black at a later date.

38 (left). Side chair, maple, eastern Massachusetts, 1725–1790. Old black paint. H. 44″, W. 17″, D. 13½″.

39 (below, left). Armchair, maple and ash, Milford/Fairfield area, Connecticut, 1725–1795. Repainted black. H. 47½″, W. 25½″, D. 18″. Gift of estate of Mrs. Walter Pritchard Eaton.

40 (right). Side chair, maple and ash, probably western Connecticut or Long Island, 1800–1825. Repainted black. H. 40″, W. 15½″, D. 14¼″.

The split balusters of banister backs, like split spindles on earlier case pieces, were turned from two pieces of wood lightly glued together which were then separated, the result being two shaped banisters. Thus, chairs with turned banisters usually have an even number (four or six). The chair at the upper left (38) shows how the turnings of the stiles are mirrored by those of the banisters themselves. The turnings on the back and those on the front legs are quite ornate on this chair, and the double arching effect at the crest are features seen on chairs with long Boston and Plymouth, Massachusetts, histories. This type is one of the few in the banister back realm without finials.

The heart-and-crown chairs of the Connecticut Shore have long been prized by collectors. Recent discoveries have linked them with towns and even some makers (see Benno M. Forman, "The Crown and York Chairs of Coastal Connecticut and the Work of the Durands of Milford," *Antiques*, May 1974, pp. 1147–1153). The armchair at the left (39) is of this type, and it closely resembles an armchair at the Wadsworth Atheneum (Kirk, *Connecticut*, no. 210), the base of the Deerfield chair being simpler. The elongated bulb on the rear stiles, above the juncture of the arms, seems to characterize this sub-type (see also Kirk, *Connecticut*, nos. 211, 212). The feet of the Deerfield chair were rockerized in the nineteenth century and have been restored.

The side chair above (40) has concave saddle cresting. The lack of definition of its turnings, its weak finials, and the treatment of the feet suggest a later date, in spite of the sausage-turned stretchers. A similar chair was found in New Jersey (*Antiques*, April 1928, p. 299) and a similar armchair is at the Suffolk County Historical Society in New York). Connecticut examples exist, and the Ashleys once owned a similar set in Deerfield. Another in the Frary house was found by Miss C. Alice Baker in Newport, Rhode Island, in the 1890s.

On banister back and slatback side chairs, the front posts invariably extend an inch or so higher than the seat. These posts can be finished with a boss effect (see no. 38, opposite), but more often they are slightly rounded off as on the chair at the right (42).

The chairs on this page all have Deerfield histories. The one at the right (42) was owned by the Ashley and Stebbins families. It has moderately successful turnings, and the bowed bottom rail of the back and the shaped cresting can be seen with variations on other chairs with local histories (see nos. 44, 45, next page).

The chairs below are of a type often encountered in Deerfield. Their finials are distinctive, as are their broad, curved crestings. The collar-and-urn turnings of the front legs are reminiscent of those on some of the Milford area heart-and-crown chairs (see Connecticut Historical Society, *George Dudley Seymour's Furniture Collection*, Hartford, 1958, pp. 70–71). Invariably, the banisters are reversed on these Deerfield chairs, the turned side facing the sitter. George Sheldon, the great local historian and founder of the Pocumtuck Valley Memorial Association in Deerfield in 1870, was aware of this in reporting the 1895 annual meeting: "the chairs of one or two centuries ago, about the room, prove the degeneracy of the New England back as men of 1895 strive for comfort in them" (P.V.M.A. *Proceedings*, III, 273). The side chair (41) was one of Sheldon's own family chairs. The feet of the armchair (43) have obviously lost several inches.

41 (left). Side chair, maple, Deerfield type, 1775–1800. Restained brown. H. 42″, W. 16¼″, D. 13¼″.

42 (above, right). Side chair, maple, Deerfield area, 1790–1820. Originally painted black. H. 43½″, W. 19½″, D. 14½″.

43 (right). Armchair, maple, Deerfield type, 1775–1800. Old mahoganized finish. H. 45½″, W. 19½″, D. 14½″.

44. H. 42⅛″, W. 16″, D. 13¾″.
P.V.M.A. Donor unknown.

45. H. 46¼″, W. 17″, D. 14¼″. P.V.M.A.
Gift of Mrs. Catherine W. Hoyt.

46. H. 41½″, W. 16″, D. 14⅛″. P.V.M.A.
Gift of Mrs. C. E. B. Allen.

The rather bedraggled trio of banister backs above are all examples of the simpler types used in Deerfield homes in the late eighteenth and early nineteenth centuries. Made of maple and ash, all three chairs are painted black and have their old splint seats.

The chair at the left (44) relates to 42 on the preceding page. It has an extra strut inserted under the front seat rail. The chair in the center (45) started out life as a side chair and had mini-arms added in the nineteenth century. At the same time, the legs were cut and rockers added. It was owned by the Hoyt family in the Old Indian house. This impressive, early house was built in 1698 by Ensign John Sheldon and was ravaged during the Indian massacre of 1704. Owned later by David Hoyt, who ran the house as a tavern, it was finally dismantled in 1848. The famous front door, besmirched and lacerated by many axe blows, is preserved in Memorial Hall, and a reproduction of the house, built in 1929, stands now on the Street (see Chamberlain and Flynt, pp. 64–65, 141).

The chair at the right (46) has a curved cresting reminiscent of that of 41 and 43 on the previous page. The definialization of the chair occurred just before 1800. The chair stood in the old meetinghouse in Deerfield, and the catalogue of P.V.M.A. tells us that "Rev. Rodolphus Dickinson, when a boy, fired a stray bullet through the meetinghouse window, which cut one of the knobs" (P.V.M.A. *Catalogue*, p. 161, no. 14). Dickinson went on to become a prominent theologian and author, living in South Carolina (Sheldon,

History, II, 148–149). Perhaps it was this chair that helped faith arrive.

George Sheldon was a staunch supporter of all strengths of earlier days. In writing of the 1897 annual meeting at Memorial Hall, he said, "And as for the straight back chairs in which the guests sat about the cheery fire in the kitchen . . . who shall say they were not made for backs young and erect rather than for the Grecian bends and rocking-chair curves of this later and more aged day" (P.V.M.A. *Proceedings*, III, 397).

The small child's chair (47) is an orphan. It is made of maple and was originally painted red. It has no history but was made in Massachusetts about 1800. The absence of a rear stretcher indicates it was made as a high chair and truncated at a later date.

47. H. 23″, W. 12¼″, D. 10″.

One of the joys of American furniture can be seen in successful transitional pieces which combine two or more styles effectively. After Queen Anne chairs with their solid, vase-shaped splats had been introduced to the Colonies in the 1720s, these newer backs were combined with the older, rush-seated block-and-vase turned bases that were popular on banister backs and "Boston chairs." New Englanders liked these chairs, and their popularity continued throughout the eighteenth century. The turnings of their bases is the key to their dating, like banister backs, and they were made with carved or plain top rails. There have been attempts to regionalize them (see *Antiques,* July 1932, pp. 6–7), but this is not always easy or successful.

The armchair at the right (50) has a strongly turned base, carved Spanish feet, rolled arms, molded stiles, and carved top rail—all well executed. The vase-and-ring turnings under the arms are similar to those on banister back armchairs. It seems very much an urbane production.

The two side chairs below are simpler and with lighter, less well-defined turnings that indicate a later date. Figure 48 has turned feet, while 49 has bold Spanish feet and turned stretchers. The latter was found in Franklin, New Hampshire. Considerable variations occur in the stretchers of these chairs, and the backs can be straight but are often shaped in the more stylish examples.

48 (far left). Side chair, maple, Massachusetts, 1740–1800. Refinished; originally painted black. H. 41″, W. 15¼″, D. 13¾″.

49 (near left). Side chair, maple, probably upper Merrimack Valley, New Hampshire, 1750–1800. Originally painted black. H. 42″, W. 15¾″, D. 13¾″.

50 (above). Armchair, maple, probably Massachusetts, 1720–1760. Repainted black. H. 43½″, W. 20″, D. 17″.

52. Side chair, maple and ash,
Massachusetts, 1720–1770.
Refinished. H. 42″, W. 15″,
D. 13¾″.

51. Side chair, maple, probably
Massachusetts (Connecticut
Valley), 1730–1780. Repainted
black. H. 40¾″, W. 15″,
D. 14″.

The chairs above all have Deerfield histories. The one at the left (51), with a broad flattened yoke on its top rail characteristic of the upper Connecticut Valley, has unusually square, brushlike Spanish feet. An extra reel turning is added below the usual vase turning on the upper part of the front legs. The chair was owned by Col. Israel Williams (1709–1788), originally of Hatfield, Massachusetts, a town south of Deerfield in the Connecticut Valley. Col. Williams was prominent in the French and Indian wars and was a most outspoken Tory at the time of the Revolution (see Sheldon, *History*, II, 378 and Judd, p. 603). He was an older brother of Dorothy Williams, who became the wife of Parson Jonathan Ashley of Deerfield.

The other two chairs (52 and 53) were more likely brought to Deerfield from eastern Massachusetts. With their narrower, well carved yokes and molded, shaped stiles these chairs have a good feeling of crispness. The one in the center (52) has been refinished and the lower three inches of its feet have been replaced. It was owned by the Sheldon family. The chair at the right (53) is very similar to 52, and its feet and paint are intact. It has lost its old rush seat, but the present leather seat has been on the chair for a long time. The woven splint seat of 51 is also an early replacement.

These chairs were all painted originally. Black and red were the most popular colors. Remnants of worn red can also indicate that it might have been the base coat for a grained finish.

The earliest couches (or day beds as they are now called) that were fashionable in Massachusetts were cane-backed, cane-seated examples very much like the elaborately carved chairs that were imported from England. Such a couch appears in a Boston inventory as early as 1696 (Lyon, p. 154). Their popularity was short-lived, however, and from 1718 on, the term "old couch" appears in these listings of possessions (Cummings, pp. 97, 120). While cane couches went out of style rather rapidly—this fate often befalls objects made in the most elaborate tastes—the form itself continued. Leather examples were made in the style of the "Boston chairs"; and transitional William and Mary/Queen Anne couches, like the example below (54), were produced. These were never made in great quantities, judging from surviving examples, and were used anywhere in an early eighteenth-century home, either upstairs or down. These couches were covered with an upholstered squab and usually had a pillow. The couch below features very crisp turnings, and its double-stile adjustable back is well carved (compare Downs, no. 210), as are the Spanish feet. While anyone who has tried to sit or recline on this form might achingly question this statement, the form shows the direction of upholstered furniture toward providing more comfort as the eighteenth century progressed.

53. Side chair, maple and ash, Massachusetts, 1720–1770. Painted black. H. 41½", W. 18¼", D. 14". P.V.M.A., donor unknown.

54. Couch, maple throughout, Massachusetts or Connecticut. 1720–1750. Painted black originally. Laced canvas sacking for squab or cushion. H. 39", W. 21½", L. 64".

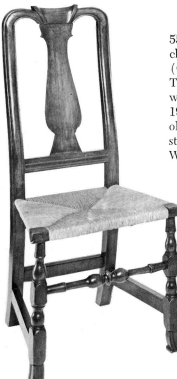

55 (left) and 56 (right). Side chairs, maple, Massachusetts (Connecticut Valley), 1730–1780. The splat on the chair at the left was inverted during repairs about 1900. The chair at the right has its old rush seat. Both have a brown stain. H. 39¾″ and 39½″, W. 15″, D. 14¾″ and 15″.

57. Side chair, maple, probably Massachusetts (Connecticut Valley), 1795–1825. Originally painted red or grained. H. 38″, W. 16¼″, D. 14¼″.

59. Side chair, maple, probably Connecticut Valley, 1790–1820. Old red paint. Turnings well executed. Only one front stretcher originally. H. 40″, W. 16½″, D. 14¼″.

58. Armchair, maple, probably Massachusetts (Connecticut Valley), 1785–1820. Painted black; originally painted red or grained. H. 43¼″, W. 24¾″, D. 16″.

The two side chairs (55, 56, opposite page, top) have the broad, flattened yoke seen so often on chairs with local Deerfield area histories. These were owned by the Williams and then Billings families. When the chair at the left (55) was repaired in this century, the splat was put back upside down. The moral of all this might be: even with antiques, he who fixeth should know which end standeth.

The six chairs at the bottom of these two pages (nos. 57–62) are all Connecticut or Connecticut Valley interpretations of the rural Queen Anne style. Two (57 and 59) are local variants of the so-called "Dutch chairs" of western Long Island and New York, a type characterized by broad vase-shaped splats, heavy turned members, and thick, tapering front legs that terminate in slightly offset pad feet (see Huyler Held, "Long Island Dutch Splat Backs," *Antiques*, October 1936, pp. 168–170). These were made in New York state throughout the eighteenth century, and their influence bounced across Long Island Sound to Connecticut. Shortly after the mid-1700s, the term "York chair" appears in inventories and accounts in the Stratford-Milford-Fairfield area of Connecticut (see Benno M. Forman, "The Crown and York Chairs of Coastal

Connecticut and the Work of the Durands of Milford," *Antiques*, May 1974, pp. 1147–1154). Other Connecticut towns felt this influence, and it was not long before variations of this type were made throughout the state—and even as far north in the Connecticut Valley as the Deerfield area. The side chair (57) was owned by Erastus Childs (1782–1858) of the Wapping section of Deerfield, and later by George Sheldon. The armchair (58) has no history; but the side chair (59) was owned by the Lane family of Northampton and Deerfield, as was 60. The turnings of 59 show definition and crispness that belie the notion that later turnings are always weak. Those on 60, however, seem to substantiate it !

The two chairs at the right below (61 and 62) are also late examples, their rear legs tapering in at the floor. They both revert to the earlier use of finials at the top of their stiles, rather than the overlapping and conjoining top rail normally associated with the vase-shaped splats. The top rail of 62 is well shaped, while that of the armchair lacks definition. The turnings of the front posts of the armchair, however, are successful. The "ringed" feet of 62 are unusual and a later feature.

60. Side chair, maple and ash, probably Connecticut Valley, 1800–1840. Repainted black; rear legs pieced out 1″. H. 39½″, W. 16⅝″, D. 13½″.

62. Side chair, maple, Connecticut, 1785–1820. Painted black with gilt decoration in coach painting tradition. H. 40¾″, W. 15¾″, D. 13½″.

61. Armchair, maple, probably Connecticut Valley, 1785–1820. Crackled red and black paint. Originally grained. H. 48½″, W. 20½″, D. 16½″.

Roundabout chairs had appeared in New England inventories by 1738 (Lyon, p. 168), and they continued to be made in the Queen Anne and Chippendale styles. No less than three are listed in the inventory of John Shirley, a victualler of Roxbury, Massachusetts, in 1773. They were located in the front room, the front chamber, and the kitchen (Cummings, pp. 255–257). For lengthy periods of sitting, they were one of the most comfortable of the early turned chairs. The example at the left is a gem (63). Its turnings, stance, high crest, and original finish all make it one of the best Spanish foot examples known. The old paint is a good example of eighteenth century "cedar graining," a fanciful rather than imitative emulation of richer, darker woods that was popular both on furniture and interior architectural trim and doors (see Fales, *Painted*, pp. 32–33).

The chair at the lower left (64) is an example of the splatless Queen Anne style, with a front cabriole leg and pad foot. The turned supports above the seat, however, are very similar to those of the other roundabouts shown here (especially 65). The treatment of the rear legs—button feet on discs—is seen on other Rhode Island chairs and tables.

Figure 65 is unusual in that it is made of cherry. It was

63. Roundabout chair, maple, probably eastern Massachusetts, 1720–1760. Original cedar graining (red) and rush seat. Four carved Spanish feet. H. 32⅜", W. 14¼", D. (diag.) 20".

65. Roundabout chair, cherry, Connecticut Valley, 1725–1780. Refinished, probably mahoganized originally. H. 31¾", W. 13⅞", D. (diag.) 19¾".

64. Roundabout chair, walnut, probably Rhode Island, 1730–1760. Needlework seat signed by Polly Wright and dated (underneath) 1757. H. 32¹¹⁄₁₆", W. 19⅛", D. (diag.) 26⅛".

probably mahoganized originally. Its turnings and carved Spanish feet are ably executed, and it is interesting that the rear stretchers are plain, while the front ones are intricately turned. It was owned by Miss Susan Hawks, one of the last of her family to live in the Sheldon-Hawks house (see 67). She ran an antique shop there in this century, and most of her things came from the immediate area near Deerfield.

The roundabout on this page was owned originally by Joseph Stebbins (1718–1797). It descended to George Sheldon from his mother's family, and on page 82 Sheldon can be seen in the Joseph Stebbins house reclining in this chair. The turnings of its base are similar to those found on Deerfield banister backs (see 41 and 43). This chair, with its history, helps date others with almost identical turnings.

One feature of early, turned roundabout chairs that should be noted is that the upper turnings of the front leg cannot match the corresponding members of the other three, due to the construction of the chair itself. The treatment of this area can be a guide to quality. On the grained chair (63), this transitional area is handled with great skill, blending in with the other three legs in a most subtle manner.

66. Roundabout chair, maple, Deerfield area, 1775–1800. Painted dark brown. Feet missing. H. 27", W. 14¾", D. (diag.) 21".

67. Built about 1743, the Sheldon-Hawks house is one of the most authentic early houses in Deerfield. The ell was added in 1802. George Sheldon, the historian, was born here, and his daughter married into the Hawks family. The weathered brown color and the handsome front doorway make it one of the most popular houses owned by Historic Deerfield, Inc.

69. Easy chair, maple (ebonized; secondary woods not visible), Essex County, Massachusetts or coastal New Hampshire, 1720–1730. Reupholstered in red moreen. The combination of cabriole legs and Spanish feet is unusual. H. 50″, W. 28″, D. 20″.

68. Easy chair, walnut (secondary woods not visible), Boston area, 1750–1780. Reupholstered in green leather. These graceful Queen Anne easy chairs were popular from the 1730s until after the Revolution. H. 46½″, W. 36″, D. 21½″.

Easy chairs were an eighteenth-century innovation and a landmark in the achieving of comfort in upholstered furniture. Recorded as early as 1712 in Boston (Lyon, p. 167), they were invariably used in chambers. (All eighteen references to easy chairs in Lyon and Cummings, between 1712 and 1773, locate the chairs in chambers). The earliest examples had high crestings, C-scrolled arms, and block-and-turned bases. When the cabriole leg became popular, a few easy chairs were made combining this new leg with carved Spanish front feet, retaining the cresting and arms of the earliest style (69; see also Fales, *Painted*, no. 37). The cresting soon became flattened, with the C-scroll arms and Spanish feet retained (see Downs, no. 72 and Morrison H. Heckscher, "Form and Frame: New Thoughts on the American Easy Chair," *Antiques*, December 1971, 886–893, especially fig. 2). About 1730, the mature Queen Anne style easy chair appeared in the Boston area, with cabriole legs, vertically rolled arms, and bowed top rail (68). This form became a classic and remained in favor until after the Revolution, although after the 1760s the carved claw-and-ball foot was more fashionable than the turned

pad foot. Pad feet on thick discs (like those on 68) were used on Chippendale chairs in eastern Massachusetts (see no. 81, p. 48), and modern scholars tend to assign later dates to pieces having this feature (see Randall, no. 154 and Greenlaw, nos. 66, 67). A chair at Colonial Williamsburg is very similar to the Deerfield example, with the exception of chamfering on the rear legs of the former (Greenlaw, no. 67).

Easy chairs were upholstered in the full range of domestic and imported eighteenth-century materials, from leather to needlework and woolens to silks. Slip covers were also used. A 1746 Boston auction notice for "fashionable crimson Damask Furniture" listed "one easy Chair and Cushion same Damask, and Case for ditto" (Dow, p. 111).

Imported furniture with American histories is not often encountered and has been paid little attention by collectors. These pieces provided the most direct method of bringing new styles to the Colonies. The couch (70) came from the house of Samuel Penniman, who was born in Mendon, Massachusetts, in 1717. It recalls the 1746 Boston advertisement for "Walnut Tree Chairs, India Back, finest Cane" (Dow, p. 111).

70. Couch, walnut (braces of beech), probably English or North European, 1710–1740. Caning replaced. Note the squared, shaped cabriole legs. Owned in Mendon, Massachusetts, in the eighteenth century. H. 37", W. 16", L. 62½".

71. Side chair, walnut and maple,
Boston, 1730–1760.
Japanning added, 1800–1820.
H. 40″, W. 20¼″, D. 14¾″.

The outline of these two side chairs is typical of the best of the Queen Anne style in the Boston area. Gentle, curved surfaces on the legs, skirts, backs, and splats result in a counterplay of delicacy and strength. Their simplicity adds to their timelessness. The only interruption to this flow is in the use of stretchers in the bases. New Englanders loved furniture with lightness and clean lines, but they loved stability as much. Thus, stretchers on chairs occur more often and for a longer period in New England than elsewhere.

While the form is satisfying, it is the decoration of these chairs that is fascinating. They are both painted black and decorated with late japanning in gilt decoration. The earlier japanning, which was popular in Boston from 1710 through the 1750s, involved a complicated technique of building up areas to be decorated with gesso, in a three-dimensional manner. Then, fanciful chinoiserie decoration was used to produce the final effect (see page 204). The later simplifications of japanning gave up the gesso, and the decoration was merely painted on the wood directly, as in these chairs. Floral forms, pagodas, people, and birds exist on the splats of these chairs in a Western depiction of Oriental make-believe. The grape borders of the stiles and legs of 71, as well as the scroll borders of 72, recall border decorations of Chinese export porcelain of the late eighteenth and nineteenth centuries, providing a clue to the date of the japanning itself.

There are six of these chairs known, the decoration differing on all. Two are privately owned (*Antiques*, January 1968, p. 76), and two are in the Bayou Bend Collection, the Museum of Fine Arts, Houston (Warren, no. 36; Fales, *Painted*, no. 94—one in color). All these chairs have a history of ownership in the Winthrop-Blanchard families of Boston, with a tradition of having been sent to China to be decorated about 1795. However, it appears that the chairs probably never left Boston, and the decoration was added at home sometime in the early nineteenth century. The arms painted on the skirts under the seats are those of the Gardner family. Samuel Pickering Gardner (1767–1843) was a prominent Boston merchant who was guardian to his grandniece, Eliza Blanchard, after her parents died. She married Robert C. Winthrop in 1832 (see Lawrence Shaw Mayo, *The Winthrop Family in America*, Boston, 1948; and Frank Augustine Gardner, *Gardner Memorial*, Salem, 1933). The crest over the arms is a griffin's head, not the turbaned head shown on the bookplate. Both were Gardner family crests appearing on silver and needlework coats of arms (see Charles Knowlton Bolton, *Bolton's American Armory*, Boston, 1927, reprinted Baltimore, 1964, p. 65). The fact that few Colonials had the right to bear arms did not diminish the American appetite for them at all.

72. Side chair, walnut and maple, Boston, 1730–1760. Japanning added 1800–1820. H. 40″, W. 20½″, D. 15″.

73. Bookplate of Samuel Pickering Gardner, Boston, paper watermarked 1809. The Gardner arms were painted at the center of the seat rails on these chairs.

74a

74 (above). Side chair, walnut, Boston, 1730–1760. One of a set of six. In 1748, "six black Walnut Chairs, with work'd Cloth bottoms" were sold at auction in Boston (Dow, p. 112). H. 40″, W. 19¾″, D. 14⅞″.

74a (above, left). Detail of original needlepoint seat from chair at right. Wrought by Jane Brown in the Boston area about 1760. One of six. W. 18⅞″, D. 14¼″.

75 (left). Side chair, walnut, Boston, 1740–1760. One of a pair, with III and IV carved on the inside of the seat rails. This was done on the slip seat frames also, so the proper seat would be used with the right chair. H. 40″, W. 21″, D. 14¾″.

76 (left). Stool, walnut and pine (maple seat frame), probably Boston, 1740–1760. Seat recovered with eighteenth-century English crewelwork. H. 18½″, W. 19″, D. 15″.

77 (right). Side chair, mahogany and white pine, Boston, 1750–1780. Old embroidered cover, ivory ground with polychrome flowers and vines. H. 38½″, W. 19½″, D. 14½″.

Walnut veneers had come into use in the early eighteenth century in case pieces, and by the Queen Anne period, walnut was used as the basic wood for fine chairs, tables, and case pieces. Until mahogany became the fashionable wood around the middle of the century, walnut reigned supreme.

Slip seats, which could be upholstered, and the shaping of the backs of chairs to conform more with those of their occupants were two major strides toward comfort realized in Queen Anne chairs.

Figure 74 is very similar in form to the japanned chairs shown on pages 42 and 43. Jane Brown, born in 1743, made the handsome needlework seats for these chairs, as well as a family coat of arms. She married John Gulliker, a sea captain, in Boston; and the chairs descended in the Gulliker-Barnard-Root families, being taken to Mexico, Maine, about 1800 (see *Antiques*, June 1947, p. 355). Chairs similar to these have been found throughout New England. While some could have been made in New Hampshire, Connecticut, and Rhode Island, they could as easily have been sent out from Boston, much in the earlier "Boston chair" tradition. The pre-eminence of Boston as a major influence on New England's arts did not begin to wane until the time of the Revolution.

The side chair at the far left (75) is very similar to six owned by president Edward Holyoke of Harvard, now at the Garvan Collection, Yale University Art Gallery (Comstock, no. 157). The rounded "compass Seat' became popular in Queen Anne chairs, especially those made in the Middle Colonies, and this seat was often covered in leather originally.

Stools were also rather popular according to early records, but they are rarely encountered today. Like chairs, they were made in sets. As early as 1691, a Roxbury, Massachusetts inventory listed "4 Stools wth needle work covers" (Cummings, p. 55). The Queen Anne example above (76) does not have stretchers and is similar to a maple example from Connecticut (*Antiques*, September 1971, p. 343).

Chairs with "stuft Back and Seats" are listed in a 1746 Boston auction notice (Dow, p. 111). The earliest chairs of this sort had a very high cresting similar to those on easy chair 69, page 40 (see Downs, no. 96). These chairs all have rather low seats and were later called slipper chairs. As the style developed, the backs continued to be high (Downs, nos. 95, 98), but the cresting vanished. The example above (77) has a slightly lower back, however, indicating it was made later in the Queen Anne style. The use of mahogany as a primary wood corroborates this. The very full, high disc under the pads on the front feet also is a sign of this later date, and it also indicates the chair's Boston-Salem area origin (see page 41). This chair has been published as a Newport slipper chair, but none of the Newport pieces in the famous 1953 and 1965 Rhode Island furniture exhibitions have this feature.

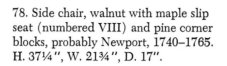

78. Side chair, walnut with maple slip seat (numbered VIII) and pine corner blocks, probably Newport, 1740–1765. H. 37¼", W. 21¾", D. 17".

79. Side chair, walnut with maple slip seat (numbered VI) and pine corner blocks, Newport type, 1740–1770. Williams family, Deerfield. H. 40¼", W. 20¾", D. 17".

On these pages are the three most highly developed Queen Anne side chairs at Deerfield. The two above, with carved shells on the top rails and the front knees together with pendant husks, are representative of the Newport type. Figure 78 has an unusual short, straight neck on the vase-shaped splat, as well as sharply turned rings on the central stretcher, both features not normally found on Newport examples. The chamfered rear legs, balloon-shaped seat, and stocky front legs are typically Newport (see Joseph K. Ott, "Some Rhode Island Furniture," *Antiques,* May 1975, p. 940, fig. 4).

Figure 79 was owned by the Williams family of Deerfield, probably by Doctor Thomas Williams (1718–1775) originally and then his son Ephraim (1760–1835). It was then owned by Ephraim's son John, born in 1817, who became president of Trinity College in Hartford, as well as presiding Episcopal bishop first of Connecticut and then of the United States. It is similar to a chair found in Hartford (Lyon, no. 72); and one wonders if, when compared to Newport chairs, the higher, narrower back and lack of sophistication in the carving of the claw feet might not point toward a Connecticut origin. Similar chairs are at the Metropolitan Museum of Art and the Wadsworth Atheneum (Kirk, *Chairs,* no. 171).

80. H. 38¼", W. 20¾", D. 18½".

One of the highest style chairs in the Deerfield collection, this urbane example in the New York style was made between 1740 and 1760. The carving of the shells and top rail, as well as the bow-shaped shoe which seats the splat, are executed with great skill. The staunch "English look" of the chair relates to other variants made in New York (Kirk, *Chairs*, nos. 129–131 and Comstock, no. 159). One of a pair, this chair was owned in the Bromfield-Weld families of Boston. Margaret Fayerweather (1732–1761) married Henry Bromfield, a prominent merchant of Boston who also lived in London, in 1749. According to family tradition, she wrought the needlework seats, which have polychrome flowers on a mustard ground (*Antiques*, June 1964, p. 631 and June 1967, inside front cover). The chairs are made of walnut, with pine corner blocks and maple slip seats. One of the seats is numbered VI, the other with two inverted V's. A similar chair was owned in the family of Governor Joseph Yates of Albany (*Antiques*, December 1957, inside front cover). Two chairs of this set are at the Brooklyn Museum, and two are at the Museum of Fine Arts, Boston (see *Paul Revere's Boston: 1735–1818,* Boston, Museum of Fine Arts, 1975, p. 89, no. 104).

81. Side chair, walnut and white pine, Boston-Salem area, 1760–1790. One of a set of six. H. 37″, W. 21¼″, D. 15⅝″.

The chairs on these pages are all transitional, with elements in them ranging from William and Mary to Chippendale. The side chair (81) at the upper left is entirely Queen Anne in inspiration, with the exception of the eared top rail of the Chippendale style. The feet are another later feature, the high, platformed discs under the pads indicating a date well after mid-century (see Randall, no. 153). With the exception of the splat, this chair is very similar to number 95 on page 54. A chair similar to 81 was owned by Elbridge Gerry of Marblehead (see Esther Singleton, *The Furniture of Our Forefathers*, New York, I, 1901, 276).

The chair at the lower left (82), while not as sophisticated as the one above it, has a pierced splat as its latest feature. This same, rather ungainly splat is seen on English Chippendale chairs (*Antiques*, October 1969, p. 528), but in this case the Connecticut maker has added a heart-shaped opening at the top. At least two other types of splats—one solid and one pierced—have been found on these distinctive three-stretchered chairs made in the Norwich area (see Kirk, *Connecticut*, nos. 232, 233). This chair was owned by the Skinner family of East Hampton, Connecticut, a town between Middletown and Colchester.

"Maple fram'd chairs with straw Bottoms" were advertised in Boston in 1759 (Dow, p. 118). The two side chairs at the top of the opposite page continue the styles of straw or "flag bottom'd" chairs. The example at the left (83) combines William and Mary turnings, a Queen Anne splat and pad feet, and a Chippendale top rail most effectively. The outline of the upper part of the splat is unusual and appears on another side chair with Spanish feet with a Salem-Beverly, Massachusetts history. The chair at the upper right (85) has Spanish feet, and its upper and lower side stretchers are turned differently. It is identical to a set of side chairs owned by the Saltonstall family of Essex County, Massachusetts (*Antiques*, June 1965, p. 673). It was originally painted red, and on the back of the top rail a small area of old paint has the initials "MP" painted in white.

The roundabout chair (84) combines a single pad foot with an earlier turned base and a later pierced splat. Its turnings lack the definition of those on the chair above (83). While transitional chairs can be exercises in scholarly amusement for the student of American furniture, they can also be successful productions in their own right. Thus, while this roundabout chair has a whimsical combination of elements, it also has a good, if unpretentious, feeling as a corner chair.

The side chair at the lower right (86) is an early manifestation of the Chippendale style. The base has cabriole legs and the earlier type of turned front pad feet, with the rear legs quite square in section and ending in a squared-off pad (see Randall, no. 148 for a more elaborate chair of the type). Related chairs have histories in the Hingham, Massachusetts, area, as well as west of Boston. The seat of this chair is only 14¾ inches above the floor, indicating its possible use as a slipper chair. The pierced splat and carved top rail with pronounced ears are definite Chippendale characteristics, and they are exaggerated by the low seat of the chair.

82. Side chair, cherry and pine, probably Norwich, Connecticut area, 1760–1795. One of a pair. H. 40½″, W. 20″, D. 17″.

83. Side chair, maple, probably
Essex County, Massachusetts,
1760–1790. Repainted black.
H. 40″, W. 14″, D. 14½″.

85. Side chair, maple, eastern
Massachusetts, 1760–1790.
Originally painted red, now black.
H. 40¼″, W. 13¼″, D. 14¼″.

84. Roundabout chair, maple
mahoganized, eastern
Massachusetts, 1760–1790.
H. 30¾″, W. 15″, D. (diag.) 21″.

86. Side chair, mahogany (maple
seat frame), eastern Massachusetts,
1760–1785. H. 36″, W. 19½″,
D. 13½″.

87. Side chair, mahogany with pine corner blocks, Salem, 1765–1780. One of six. H. 37″, W. 20¾″, D. 16½″.

88. Side chair, mahogany, Salem or Marblehead area, 1765–1785. One of a pair. H. 38″, W. 21¾″, D. 16″.

The publication of Thomas Chippendale's *The Gentleman and Cabinet-Maker's Director* in 1754 in London made fashionable furniture designs easily available to both customers and craftsmen. The work was re-issued in 1755, and by 1762 a greatly enlarged third edition appeared. This was used by craftsmen in the Colonies; and in the 1760s the new style became popular in the major cabinetmaking centers, although the older styles continued to be made. Chairs made in this new style had intricately pierced splats, bow-shaped top rails, and either cabriole legs with claw feet or square legs fluted or plain. Mahogany had become the fashionable wood, and it lent itself perfectly to carved decoration that was inspired by rococo, Gothic, and chinoiserie designs that were part of the vocabulary of the style. Upholstery extended over the seat rails of chairs, and brass nails became an integral part of the chairs' designs.

The popularity of Chippendale's work influenced others from the 1760s on. One was Robert Manwaring's *The Cabinet and Chair-Maker's Real Friend and Companion*, which appeared, with its cozy title in London in 1765. A copy of this book has long been at the Essex Institute in Salem and was presumably owned by a local craftsman. The back of the chair

(above left, 87) is based on a Manwaring design for "Parlour Chairs" (plate 9, left), with the carved decoration shown in the design virtually eliminated (see Fales, *Essex*, no. 55). As Manwaring said in his preface, "Should the ornamented Parts be left out, there will still remain Grandeur and Magnificence behind, and the Design will appear open and genteel." The chair is identical to one at Winterthur inscribed on the front rail, "Bottum'd June 1773 by WVE Salem." Similar chairs with fully carved backs exist (see Kirk, *Chairs*, no. 114), and this Manwaring type could have been made also in Boston.

Regional characteristics can be as tantalizing as they are helpful, but the three chairs on these pages show one eastern Massachusetts tendency—the raked side claws of the feet. Instead of coming down straight, the side claws angle off to the rear. The chair above (88) and the one at the right (89) make use of the same splat, one that exists in English prototypes (see *Antiques*, March 1929, p. 213). The treatment of the bases of the chairs differs markedly, the stretchers of 89 being a relief to the heavy knees of 88. Other chairs with similar backs are still owned in Salem and Marblehead families. One set has pad feet of the early type (Nutting, II, no. 2168).

89. Side chair, mahogany with pine corner blocks, Boston-Salem area, 1765–1790. Carved top rail, knees, and claw feet. Note the continued use of stretchers and the unusual turnings on the central member of the base. Covered in blue damask.
H. 37¾″, W. 21½″, D. 16¼″.

90. Easy chair, mahogany with
maple frame, Boston area,
1755–1790. Covered in eighteenth-
century embroidered silk.
H. 47⅝", W. 33", D. 21".

While "crowfoot" chairs are listed in Boston in 1737 and "Eagles foot" chairs
in 1750 (Lyon, pp. 161, 163), it was not until well after the middle of the
century that the new claw foot became popular. This foot was used interchange-
ably with the earlier pad foot, and the easy chair above (90) was probably made
at the same time as the Queen Anne example on page 40. Since the turned pad
foot was less expensive than the carved claw foot, this could explain the continued love of the former in New England. The combination of economy with
established precedent always appeals!

The varieties of upholstery materials were endless. Huge quantities of silks,
cottons, woolens, and linens were imported to Boston and other major ports.
The range of imported fabrics from 1710–1765 can be seen in Dow, pages 154–
172. Domestic coverings, such as needlepoint and leather, were also used. In the
Colonies, crewelwork was used generally for bed hangings. This broad range
can be seen in a 1765 advertisement of John Simpkins of Boston (Dow, p. 172).
Imports included "Crimson, green and yellow Harrateens, Chaneys, Linceys,
Trimmings of all Sorts, Quilts, Counterpins, Coverlids and Bed-ticks, Buckram,
Looking Glasses &c . . . all sorts of Curtains, Feathers, Easy Chairs, Cushions,
or any sort of Upholsterers' Work done in the best Manner, at the lowest Rates."

91. Side chair, mahogany with pine corner blocks, Philadelphia school, possibly Maryland, 1765–1790. One of a set of four. H. 39″, W. 21″, D. 16″. Gift of George A. Cluett, Jr.

92. Side chair, mahogany with maple rails and pine corner blocks, Boston-Salem area, 1765–1795. Both chairs are upholstered in old damasks. H. 38″, W. 21½″, D. 16″.

While the designs of Chippendale and Manwaring had some direct influence on chairs made in the Colonies, it was the large number of chairs imported here that probably influenced Colonial design most. Little attention has been paid to English furniture owned in the Colonies (see Milo M. Naeve, "English Furniture in Colonial America," *Antiques*, April 1971, pp. 551–555). Examples still exist, frequently lurking in distant corners of historical societies; and the Public Record Office in London possesses accounts of the furniture (and other decorative arts) shipped to the Colonies between 1697 and 1780 (see R. W. Symonds, "The English Export Trade in Furniture to Colonial America, Part II," *Antiques*, October 1935, pp. 156–159). Exports of furniture increased dramatically from 1760–1767, compared to the 1740–1747 period.

The design sources of the two chairs above presumably came from actual imports, since they are not found in design books. The chair at the left (91) has a most unusual trellislike splat which appears on a double-backed English settee (*Antiques*, December 1960, p. 516). Identical backs are found on two chairs said to be of Irish origin (F. Lewis Hinckley, *A Directory of Antique Furniture*, New York 1953, nos. 722 and 786). The similarities of this chair to the Irish

example are very great. Details suggest Philadelphia as the chair's birthplace, but the higher back, exaggerated ears, use of the intricate splat, and the fact that the side rails are not mortised through the rear legs in the normal Philadelphia manner, point to a possible Maryland origin.

The chair at the right (92) has a pierced baluster splat that was the most popular type used on New England Chippendale chairs. It was also used extensively elsewhere, but the chairmakers in the Boston-Charlestown-Salem area of eastern Massachusetts had an especial affinity for this back. While modern terminology is not always helpful in the decorative arts, it can be descriptive; and the term "owl eye" splat has been used to denote this particular type. English prototypes of this splat are known (one very similar to this chair is shown in Kirk, *Chairs*, no. 105).

Due to its carving and quality, this chair has been considered the work of Benjamin Frothingham of Charlestown. Frothingham has suffered a fate similar to William Savery of Philadelphia in being the first (not necessarily the best) cabinetmaker of an area whose works were rediscovered. Attributions have followed based on hope more than reason. The chair remains an eloquent example of its type.

The four chairs and couch on these two pages show variants of the pierced baluster splat that was the favorite of eastern New England. While not the most handsome of Chippendale style splats, this type was a good, serviceable one—and one that could be cut out and finished quite easily. The side chairs were made within a thirty-mile area and their similarities far outweigh their differences. They all have chamfered rear legs above the stretchers, and the carving on their backs ranges from sparse (96), to the two volutes in the splat (94, 95), and to a well-carved shell at the center of the top rail (93). Figure 93 has a flattened blub on its central stretcher, and the raked-back side claws can be clearly seen on the feet of 94. Figure 95 makes use of the later type of pad foot on an elevated disc (see fig. 81, page 48).

All of these chairs had triangular corner blocks of white pine, both glued and nailed to the seat rails. This technique is characteristic of eastern Massachusetts chairs and is one of the easiest—and least expensive—lasting methods of chair frame construction.

The couch (97) is heavily constructed, perhaps from necessity (or perhaps from suspicion), and the legs and splat have a hefty feeling. It is made of cherry, a wood especially favored in Connecticut and also used occasionally by other New England craftsmen. In 1763, "Cherry-tree" chairs were listed in a Boston auction (Dow, p. 121).

94. Side chair, mahogany (secondary woods not visible), eastern Massachusetts, 1765–1795. Upholstered in green damask. H. 37¾", W. 21½", D. 17½".

93. Side chair, mahogany (secondary woods not visible), eastern Massachusetts, 1765–1795. H. 38", W. 21", D. 16". Gift of Vincent D. Andrus.

95. Side chair, mahogany with white pine triangular corner blocks and slip seat frame, eastern Massachusetts, 1765–1795. H. 38", W. 19½", D. 14½". Lucius D. Potter Memorial.

96. Side chair, mahogany and white pine, probably Essex County, Massachusetts, 1765–1780. One of a set owned by the Saltonstall family of Haverhill, Massachusetts. According to an old inscription, the flame stitch seats were started by Anna White (1752–1841) at the age of fourteen. She married Dr. Nathaniel Saltonstall November 21, 1780. H. 36″, W. 21¼″, D. 16″.

97. Couch, cherry with maple struts, probably eastern Connecticut, 1780–1800. Squab of yellow bourette. Traditionally owned by Brigadier General Ebenezer Huntington (1754–1834) of Norwich, Connecticut, and later by the Wolcott family of Massachusetts. H. 37″, W. 24″, L. 71″.

99 (right). The most sophisticated eighteenth-century house on the Street, the Old Manse was built for Joseph Barnard between 1768 and 1772. He was from a Salem family with Deerfield antecedents, and the house shows strong Essex County influences throughout. It is now owned by Deerfield Academy.

98 (below). Side chair, cherry, attributed to Eliphalet Chapin, East Windsor, Connecticut, 1780–1785. One of three. Owned originally by Joseph Barnard (1717–1785) of Deerfield, and then by his son Samuel who moved to Montgomery, Vermont, in 1795. Numbered III, V, VI on seat frames and seats. H. 39″, W. 21½″, D. 16″.

One of the most famous names in Connecticut cabinetmaking is that of Eliphalet Chapin (1741–1807) of East Windsor. Most of the examples attributed to him are based on circumstantial evidence, and not even the basic facts of his life are yet known (see Emily M. Davis, "Elephelet Chapin," *Antiques*, April 1939, pp. 172–175). He grew up in Enfield, Connecticut, and lived most of his working days in East Windsor. However, there is a gap in his records between 1767 and 1769 and a probability that he worked in Philadelphia during this time (see Kirk, *Chairs*, p. 187). The side chair at the left (98) is very similar to one at Yale that is the Rosetta Stone of Chapin attributions—one of a dozen made by Chapin for Alexander King of Windsor Hill in 1781. The bill for these was seen by Irving Lyon when he owned the King chair (see Kirk, *Chairs*, no. 193). The chair at the left has a slightly different shell on the top rail and its volutes are carved, but in every other particular it is identical with the King chair. The three at Deerfield have a good history, having been owned originally by Joseph Barnard, who built the elegant house above. Barnard died in 1785, thus providing an end-date for these chairs. They have a Philadelphia look—with heavy ears, stump rear legs, rounded corner blocks, and the tenons of the side seat rails mortised through the rear legs—all features characteristic of Philadelphia craftsmanship. The use of cherry as a primary wood and white pine for the corner blocks and seat frames, however, is indicative of New England manufacture. The seats are upholstered in yellow damask, and the chairs resemble an armchair owned originally by the Rev. John Marsh of Wethersfield, Connecticut (see *Antiques*, October 1973, p. 516).

Joseph Barnard had married Thankful Sheldon in 1740. After his uncle Samuel died in 1762, Joseph inherited a considerable estate and built the Manse on high land north of the Common. He brought timbers from Salem by teams and employed a joiner, Jonas Locke, originally from the Concord, Massachusetts area to build it. He had purchased furniture from local cabinetmakers such as Benjamin Munn, Jr. of Deerfield and James Couch of Northampton between 1747 and 1760. He also made purchases in eastern Massachusetts, buying twenty-three pieces of furniture for his daughter Sarah from Nathaniel Ruggles of Roxbury in 1773 (Barnard papers, P.V.M.A.). After his death in 1785, his inventory listed many fine possessions, such as three looking glasses, a "Fancy Looking Glass," a "mahogany Screen and Stand," cane-back and leather chairs, an easy chair, and two "Sconce Glasses." (See "The Willard House," P.V.M.A. *Proceedings*, II, 268–294; and John J. Synder, Jr., "The Original Furnishing of the Manse: An Interpretive Study," unpublished Heritage Foundation paper, Deerfield, 1967). The house serves as an elegant reminder that Deerfield had been settled by people from the Massachusetts Bay Colony, and that throughout the eighteenth and nineteenth centuries, the town felt these strong influences from the east. At the same time, southerly breezes blew up the Connecticut Valley, as his chairs show.

The addition of a diamond onto the splat of the chair opposite (98), with a few necessary changes to the proportion, result in the splat on the chair on this page (100). This splat was used in both Massachusetts (Kirk, *Chairs*, no. 112) and New York (Downs, no. 149); but here, as in the chair on the previous page, the "feel" of Philadelphia is combined with the woods of New England, all pointing to a possible attribution to Eliphalet Chapin as the maker. One of a pair, this chair is made of cherry, with rounded corner blocks of white pine. Instead of having a slip seat, the upholstery extends over the entire seat frame. Both treatments are seen on these "Chapin" chairs. The squareness of the ball-and-claw feet is another notable feature of this chair.

In addition to the pair at Deerfield, a matching side chair and armchair from the same set are in the Barbour Collection at the Connecticut Historical Society (see Kirk, *Chairs*, nos. 197, 198), and others are privately owned. The set was owned originally by the Reverend John Marsh of Wethersfield, a brigade chaplain during the Revolution, who had married Ann Grant of East Windsor in 1775. The chairs could have been made at this time, since her father, Ebenezer Grant, was a prosperous merchant who had dealings with Chapin from 1769 to 1771. The chairs remained in Wethersfield until the last Marsh heir at the Parsonage died in 1880. Then, together with a handsome Boston blockfront desk and bookcase (now at Deerfield, see page 239) and a center table, they were inherited by Marsh's granddaughter, Mrs. Richard Henry Dana, Jr., of Cambridge, Massachusetts and brought there. Her husband was the author of *Two Years Before The Mast*, written earlier in 1840.

100. H. 38⅜", W. 22", D. 15½".

101. Side chair, cherry with pine corner blocks, probably made by Eliphalet Chapin, East Windsor, Connecticut, 1770–1785. H. 38″, W. 19¼″, D. 15″.

102. Side chair, cherry and pine, Connecticut Valley, 1790–1810. Both chairs are upholstered in yellow damask. H. 38½″, W. 19½″, D. 15″.

One of the handsomest Chapin-type splats can be seen on the chair above (101), which was found in Hartford. It combines a diamond, a prominent X-member, and a Gothic quatrefoil with a crisp lightness that results in a most successful statement of American Chippendale. The details of construction are identical to the two preceding side chairs, and Eliphalet Chapin was its probable maker. Similar side chairs at Deerfield (not illustrated) have upholstery extending completely over their seat frames. A similar armchair with a slip seat is in the Barbour Collection (Kirk, *Chairs*, no. 199).

Another armchair, with a slightly different shell on the top rail, was part of the wedding furniture of Anna Barnard of Northampton, Massachusetts, who married Joseph H. Clarke in 1772 (see Elizabeth Whitmore, "The Wedding Furniture of Anna Barnard," *Antiques*, November 1926, pp. 369–371, fig. 1). The tradition that it was made by her father, Abner Barnard, is not supported by proof of his being a cabinetmaker. A second family candidate is Julius Barnard, who was a cabinetmaker in Northampton between 1792 and 1802, after training or working in

New York. However, this was almost a generation after the wedding had taken place.

This back is also found on chairs with square Chippendale legs (Downs, no. 158). Another variant —and a good lesson in attribution—can be seen in the side chair at the right (102). The splat is the same shape as that on 101, and there is an obvious relationship between the chairs, but there the similarity ends. The back stiles of 102 are much lighter, the legs are the square tapered legs of the Federal period, the shell on the top rail is less ably executed, and the proportions of the entire chair lack the staunchness of the cabriole example. It just misses, and with a tipsy, backward lean to its back, it certainly could not be considered the work of Eliphalet Chapin. Whether it could have been made by his second cousin, Aaron Chapin (1753–1835), who worked with Eliphalet from 1774 to 1783, or by Aaron's son Laertes (1778–1847) is purely conjectural. In spite of its shortcomings, it is a lovable failure. It shows that even in a watered down, later version, a strong individual style could persist in the Connecticut Valley.

103. The original part of the Wells-Thorn house was built by Ebenezer Wells about 1717 (see page 19), and in 1751 he built the main part of the house fronting on the Street (see page 265). This is the north parlor of that addition, showing changes made about 1801 by Hezekiah Wright Strong, an Amherst lawyer who owned the house for seven years. He added the Federal style overmantel and chimney breast to the room. (See Joseph Peter Spang III, "The Wells-Thorn House in Deerfield, Massachusetts," *Antiques,* May 1966, pp. 730–733.) The room is furnished with both Chippendale and Federal furniture. At the left is the desk and bookcase owned by Governor Caleb Strong of Northampton, a relative of the lawyer (page 241), two of the Barnard family chairs probably by Eliphalet Chapin (page 56), and a large round Chippendale tea table (page 155). Beyond the fireplace is an easy chair associated with Aaron Chapin (page 68). An embroidered picture over the fireplace is in a frame made by Nathan Ruggles (page 281). The large looking glass with an eagle on top is American (page 277), while the sofa is English. The firescreen at the right of the fireplace is shown on page 163.

104 (left). Side chair, mahogany with maple seat rails, probably Massachusetts, 1770–1795. H. 38″, W. 21″, D. 21¼″.

105 (below). Roundabout chair, mahogany with maple and pine, eastern Massachusetts, 1770–1795. H. 33″, W. 16½″, D. (diag.) 23″. Gift of Elizabeth Fuller.

The square Chippendale leg gradually superseded the carved cabriole leg in New England and was widely used from the 1770s on. It was easier and cheaper to manufacture, and it was often decorated with a single bead on the outer edge (104), although it could be molded (108)—or occasionally even carved on some of the most sophisticated Philadelphia and Boston chairs and tables. Rectangular stretchers normally accompanied the square leg, as turned stretchers were usually used with the cabriole leg or with the block-and-turned leg with Spanish foot.

The two chairs above use a delicately pierced splat that was favored in the Boston area. Based on an English prototype (see Kirk, *Chairs,* no. 124), this splat is also found on highly carved cabriole chairs (Kirk, *Chairs,* no. 125) and on square-legged chairs with the same highly carved backs (Essex Institute *Historical Collections,* April 1961, fig. 9). The chair above (104) is a simplified version, but the carved

ears and the chamfered rear legs provide mild touches of grandeur.

The roundabout chair (105) was owned in the Williams family of Deerfield. It lost a portion of a splat through some unknown accident, and the apparent solution for its repair was to reduce the other splat by the same amount! The use of this splat in a low-backed chair can be seen in an English writing chair (Percy Macquoid, *A History of English Furniture: The Age of Mahogany,* London, 1906, reprinted New York, 1972, fig. 122). Shortening the splat necessitated some changes to the upper two openings. The chamfering on the inner parts of the side legs relieves the blockiness of the legs effectively. The woods of this roundabout chair show how many species were used together. The primary wood is mahogany, and the seat rails are made of both mahogany and maple. A diagonal strut added to the frame near the front leg is made of white pine.

106. The two armchairs on this page make use of the favorite "owl eye" splat of eastern New England (see pages 53–55). This armchair is made of maple and was originally painted red, the black and gold coach painting having been added in the 1800s. The strips around the edges of the rush seat appear to be original. This is a late feature, and the chair was probably made about 1800 in Massachusetts. H. 39½", W. 23", D. 17½". Gift of John B. Morris, Jr.

107. This armchair has the lightness, decoration, and grace of a city production. It was found in Plymouth, Massachusetts, and is similar to an armchair found in New Hampshire (Antiques, September 1935, p. 97, fig. 8). Made in eastern Massachusetts between 1775 and 1795, this chair has a narrow width which accentuates its upward thrust. It is made of maple and birch and was originally mahoganized. The carving of its arms, splat, and top rail, together with its molded stiles and front legs, result in a quality not usually found in splint or rush-seated chairs. H. 41", W. 19", D. 17¼".

108. Side chair, cherry, probably
Massachusetts (Connecticut Valley),
1780–1810. H. 36″, W. 16″, D. 14¼.

110. Side chair, maple, mahoganized,
Massachusetts, 1780–1810.
H. 38″, W. 14½″, D. 14½″.

These chairs have associations with Deerfield. The two above have "owl eye" splats, and 108 is unusual for a rush-seated chair in that it is made of cherry instead of maple or birch. It also has turned side and rear stretchers, instead of the usual rectangular ones found with square legs. Its front molded legs are very stylish. It came to Deerfield through a dealer in Bernardston, Massachusetts—just north of Deerfield—who found most of his things in the immediate area.

The chairs in figures 109 and 110 have mahoganized finishes, made by a two-tone technique of painting black over red to imitate the grain of the finer wood. The chair at the left (109), with its slip seat, is a simpler "city" type, probably from eastern Massachusetts. It was bought at the sale of "Squire" John Williams' belongings after his death in Deerfield in 1816. He was a well-known local merchant, politician, outspoken Tory, and the first registrar of deeds for the north district of Hampshire County in 1787 (Sheldon, *History*, II, 382). This chair (109) and the one above (110) were both owned later by Miss C. Alice Baker and were part of her bequest, with the Frary house, to P.V.M.A. They were turned over together with the house to Historic Deerfield, Inc. in 1969.

109. Side chair, birch, mahoganized,
probably eastern Massachusetts, 1780–1810.
H. 38″, W. 20¾″, D. 16¾″.

Miss C. Alice Baker was an antiquarian who became George Sheldon's right arm in the Pocumtuck Valley Memorial Association. She did a great deal of historical writing, and she purchased the Frary house on the Street in 1890, thus saving this important structure (see Chamberlain and Flynt, pp. 126–134). While many of Miss Baker's possessions were acquired locally, she brought some to Deerfield from eastern Massachusetts. She owned the chair below at the left (111), which was originally painted black. It has a very narrow seat and an upright primness.

The chair at the left (112) was owned in the Williams family of Deerfield. Its seat was altered later, as were the outer rails.

The chair below (113) was painted black originally, and according to family history, was one of a set made by a Mr. North in North Bennington, Vermont, for the wedding of Elizabeth Denio (1767–1836) of Greenfield to Stebbins Walbridge of Bennington on October 18, 1796 (Sheldon, *History*, II, 140). The splat is a simplified version of a type favored in eastern Massachusetts (see page 51), with a heart added in the center. A similar chair was traditionally made by Joseph Hosmer of Concord, Massachusetts (*Antiques*, April 1958, p. 357, fig. 2); and another was owned originally in eastern Connecticut (Myers and Mayhew, no. 84).

112. Side chair, mahogany with maple seat rails, Massachusetts, 1780–1810. H. 38¼", W. 20", D. 15".

111. Side chair, maple, probably eastern Massachusetts, 1780–1810. H. 40", W. 15", D. 15¼".

113. Side chair, maple, probably North Bennington, Vermont, 1796. H. 39", W. 19½", D. 15½". Gift of Mrs. Ernest T. A. Walbridge.

114. Side chair, cherry, probably
Norwich, Connecticut, 1780–1800.
One of a pair. H. 38⅝″, W. 20″, D. 13″.

116. Side chair, mahogany and maple,
Rhode Island, 1770–1795.
H. 37½″, W. 20″, D. 14¾″.

With the exception of the "Chapin" types, there are not too many other pierced Chippendale splats that were made in Connecticut. The chair above (114) is identical to a pair from the Jabez Huntington house in Norwich (see *American Furniture from Israel Sack Collection*, II, Washington, 1969, 375). These are all of cherry, but a mahogany example is said to exist also (Kirk, *Chairs*, no. 201).

The side chair at the above right (116) was made in Newport or Providence (see Joseph K. Ott, *The John Brown House Loan Exhibition of Rhode Island Furniture*, Providence, 1965, no. 12). It is based on an English chair (see Kirk, *Chairs*, no. 181) rather than a design source. The stop fluting of the legs combines with crosshatching, punch work and gouged decoration on the back and top rail to produce a stylish Rhode Island expression of Chippendale.

The armchair at the right (115) has an unusual splat, like one on a mahogany chair, stamped "Hart" on its seat rail (*Antiques*, January 1954, p. 56, fig. 13). This chair is heavier in feeling, perhaps due to its being made of cherry instead of mahogany. Hart was possibly the maker, but he has not yet been identified. The scrolls at the base of the arm supports are a feature of the Newburyport area (see 123, page 67). This armchair is the chair Henry Flynt selected for use in his portrait by David Ewart shown on page 5.

115. Armchair, cherry and white pine,
probably Newburyport, Massachusetts,
1780–1800. H. 38″, W. 20½″, D. 17¾″.

117. Side chair, maple,
upper Connecticut Valley, 1790–1825.
H. 36½″, W. 15½″, D. 15¼″.

119. Side chair, mahogany,
eastern Massachusetts, 1780–1795.
H. 36½″, W. 21¾″, D. 17¼″.

118. Side chair, mahogany with maple and beech,
Newburyport, Massachusetts, 1785–1827.
H. 37¾″, W. 22¼″, D. 18¾″.

In England, the ladder-back was revived about 1750 and began to appear in Chippendale style chairs, although it never appeared in design books (Edwards, p. 148). From the 1780s on, this back was made in America, usually appearing with the square Chippendale leg, although a few cabriole examples have been found (119, above, like Nutting, II, no. 2253). They seem to emanate from Essex County, Massachusetts, which could firmly explain any anachronism!

The chair at the left (118) is a sophisticated ladder-back, with a saddle seat and carved back. It would be tempting to date the chair between 1780 and 1805. However, written on a paper label on the seat frame is "Isaac Short, Newburyport, Mass." Isaac (1803–1847) was one of four cabinetmaking sons of Joseph Short (1771–1819), the well-known cabinetmaker of Newburyport (see Martha Gandy Fales, "The Shorts, New-buryport Cabinetmakers," Essex Institute *Historical Collections*, July 1966, pp. 224–240). Whether Isaac, who left Newburyport temporarily by 1827, or some other family member made this chair is not known. The use of beech in the seat frame is unusual, but possible, in Massachusetts. Diagonal maple braces join the seat rails in the English manner.

The small side chair at the upper left (117) is of a type that is found in the Connecticut Valley of Vermont, New Hampshire, and Massachusetts. One was owned in the Barnard family of Northampton (*Antiques,* November 1926, p. 369), and this one was owned by Miss C. Alice Baker in the Frary house in Deerfield.

120. Side chair or back stool, cherry,
Massachusetts, 1780–1810. Upholstered in
French cotton, c. 1800.
H. 38¼″, W. 21¼″, D. 17½″.

121. Side chair or back stool, mahogany
and maple, Massachusetts, 1780–1810.
H. 37½″, W. 22″, D. 18″.
Gift of Mrs. John Hedrick.

The square Chippendale leg was especially suited to upholstered chairs and
sofas. The back stool at the left (120) is identical to another in the Deerfield
collection (not illustrated) that was owned in the Trumbull and Cogswell
families of Worcester, Massachusetts. Both are made of cherry and have boldly
channeled legs. A third cherry chair in the collection, with arms added, is quite
similar to 120 also, and it has a history of ownership in the Crafts family of
Whately, Massachusetts, a town in the Connecticut Valley just south of Deerfield.

The back stool at the right (121) does not have such well molded front legs,
but the "kick" to its rear legs, the shaping of its back, and its scooped seat all
add to its distinction. It was owned in the family of Joseph Barnard, who built
the Manse between 1768 and 1772 (see pages 56 and 57). Probably his son
Samuel (1746–1819) was its original owner. He was forced by reduced circum-
stances to Montgomery, Vermont in 1795. The chair went with him, was later
owned by his son Charles (1781–1869) who rebuilt the family's fortunes in
Boston, and was then taken by the next generation to Virginia, where it was
owned by descendants until being given to Historic Deerfield, Inc., in 1973.

122 (below). This armchair has a late, thin square-legged base, without the rear stretcher that usually connects the back legs. It has a slip seat and retains a great amount of its original mahoganized finish. The thinness of its members, its narrowness, and its height, together with the flare of its upper back, result in a highly spirited and individual rural statement. It was found in Hopkinton, New Hampshire, and was probably made in that area between 1790 and 1815. Its woods are maple and birch. H. 47¾", W. 21½", D. 16½".

123 (above). This trim lolling chair is made of maple and was probably mahoganized originally. The carved scrolls at the juncture of the arm supports and seat rail are like those on a similar chair thought to be the work of Joseph Short of Newburyport (*Antiques*, April 1945, p. 222, fig. 2). Since no firm reason for attribution is given, and since this feature can be found on other chairs made in the area (see fig. 115, page 64), it is safer to think of these scrolled arm supports as a regional rather than a personal characteristic, and that this chair was made in the Newburyport area between 1785 and 1810. The later term Martha Washington is used for this type of chair, but it seems far less descriptive than its original designation, a lolling chair. It is upholstered in an eighteenth-century French silk brocade, with ivory ground and polychrome flowers. H. 42", W. 24", D. 18½".

124. Easy chair, cherry (secondary woods not visible), probably by Aaron Chapin, Hartford, Connecticut, 1806. Upholstered in gold damask. H. 46½″, W. 30″, D. 24″.

A basic change in the construction of easy chairs had occurred by the time George Hepplewhite's *Cabinet-Maker and Upholsterer's Guide* was published in London in 1788. Instead of the arms added onto the wings, as had been done in Queen Anne and Chippendale easy chairs, the wings were now grafted onto a chair built basically as an armchair (see 126, and see Morrison H. Heckscher, "Form and Frame: New Thoughts on the American Easy Chair," *Antiques*, December 1971, pp. 886–893).

The commodious chair above (124) is constructed in this new manner, although it retains the square Chippendale leg. The arms now roll horizontally, rather than vertically as they tended to do on earlier New England easy chairs (see pages 40 and 52).

When this chair was stripped down for reupholstering, an advertisement of Aaron Chapin (1753–1838) dated "December 20" was found glued to the outside of one of the wings. The chair was made for the wedding of Hepzibah Loomis of East Windsor in 1806, and she was an in-law of Chapin, whose wife was Mary King Loomis. A newspaper advertisement is a most unusual method of documentation. Chapin had worked with his second cousin, Eliphalet, in East Windsor from 1774 until 1783, when he moved to Hartford (see pages 56–58). His career in Hartford continued until his death in 1853, his son Laertes

forming a partnership with his father in 1807 that lasted into the 1840s (see Penrose R. Hoopes, "Aaron Chapin, Hartford Cabinetmaker," *Antiques*, September 1933, pp. 97–98). Only a few documented pieces of Aaron Chapin's work exist. A handsome early Federal eight-legged inlaid sideboard is at the Wadsworth Atheneum (*Antiques*, December 1928, p. 522, fig. 9). It was made in 1804, and two cherry bookcases made in 1807 and 1811 are at the Connecticut Historical Society (illustrated in the Hoopes article, above). Among the pieces made by him and listed in the advertisement are "Card and Pembroke Tables; dining and breakfast Tables; bason Stands; candle Stands; Sofa's easy Chairs . . ."

The sofa, as we know it today, developed from the settle in the eighteenth century (Edwards, pp. 442, 456), and the earliest American examples were made during the mid-1700s in Philadelphia (Downs, no. 269). Sofas never were plentiful until the nineteenth century, but they became more popular in New England after 1780. Figure 125 is a small example of a type made in Massachusetts and Rhode Island from the 1780s to at least 1812 (see Downs, no. 276). The sofa has square legs, while the easy chair (126 and 126a, shown both clothed and bare) has the square tapered leg of the Federal period. Their styles may differ, but both types were made at the same time.

125. Sofa, mahogany and maple, eastern New England, 1780–1810.
Upholstered in yellow damask. H. 36¾″, W. 54″, D. 21″.

126 and 126a. Child's easy chair, mahogany, maple and pine, Massachusetts,
1790–1810. Upholstered in pale green bourette. H. 37½″, W. 21″, D. 16″.

128 Easy chair, mahogany and maple, probably Massachusetts (Connecticut Valley), 1800–1820. Hoop inlay on front legs. H. 47″, W. 29″, D. 22″. Gift of Mrs. D. W. Hartigan.

127 Easy chair, maple and white pine, New Hampshire, 1800–1840. Original upholstery foundation of ticking and linen. H. 48¾″, W. 25½″, D. 20″.

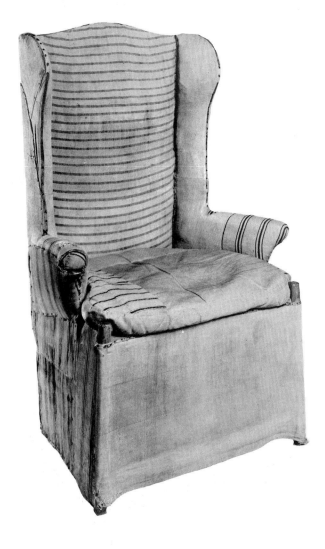

One of the strengths of the Flynts' collecting was that they were as interested in the lowly, mundane objects that represented everyday life as they were in the finest pieces of highest quality. The rather disheveled derelict at the left (127) is not only an example of a rural adaptation of an urban form, but it is also a document in its intimate glimpse of what really happened under upholstery in the early nineteenth century. Instead of muslin for an under cover, it seems anything was used in this case. Old ticking was combined with linen scraps, with leather edgings tacked on, and all this would have disappeared from view when the chair was finally covered and clothed in period respectability.

The easy chair above (128) is more urbane. With its front tapered legs and lack of stretchers, it is representative of the Federal period. Very simple hoop inlay is on the front legs, and this treatment was often used throughout New England on Federal pieces. The chair belonged to Dr. Stephen West Williams (1790–1855), the last of the Doctors Williams to care for the people of Deerfield (see page 24). It went west when Dr. Williams moved to Laona, Illinois, in 1850 and subsequently went all the way to California before being returned to Deerfield by a descendant (see Sheldon, *History*, II, 384).

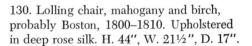

129. Lolling chair, mahogany (secondary woods not visible), Massachusetts, 1795–1805. Upholstered in green moreen. One of a pair. H. 43¼″, W. 26″, D. 19½″.

130. Lolling chair, mahogany and birch, probably Boston, 1800–1810. Upholstered in deep rose silk. H. 44″, W. 21½″, D. 17″.

Lolling chairs were rather generous chairs with upholstered backs and seats, their wooden bases and arms exposed. As early as 1758, "a lolling chair frame" was advertised in a Boston sale (Dow, p. 118), but it was not until the end of the century that these chairs, now known as Martha Washingtons, became popular and plentiful. The one above (129) is a classic eastern New England type, with molded arm supports and front tapered legs, the channeling done in a manner similar to that on upholstered pieces with square legs (see 125). While a serpentine top rail is used on this chair, straight ones were also popular (130).

The chair at the upper right (130) is a highly sophisticated lolling chair, with its flared "hollow back," its molded arm supports continuing right into the front legs, and its jauntily canted rear legs. It is a Boston chair, slightly smaller than a very similiar example at Winterthur, and also reminiscent of another chair labeled by Lemuel Churchill of Boston (Montgomery, nos. 116, 117).

The chair at the right (131) has exposed wooden seat rails and a slip seat which once held a chamber utensil. It is reminiscent of a cherry easy chair at Winterthur (Montgomery, no. 121). This chair was owned in the Higginson-Fuller-Williams families of Deerfield.

131. Lolling chair, mahogany (maple and pine), mid to upper Connecticut Valley, 1795–1815. H. 43¾″, W. 22½″, D. 20″.

132. Side chair, mahogany with birch and pine, probably Boston area, 1795–1805. (Compare with Montgomery, no. 33 and Warren, no. 140.) H. 37″, W. 21″, D. 18″.

The classic revival of the eighteenth century came slowly to America. While a few isolated sprouts budded forth in architecture and silver in the 1770s, it was not until two decades later that the new look had been widely accepted in New England in all the decorative arts. In furniture, the English design books of George Hepplewhite (*The Cabinet-Maker and Upholsterer's Guide, 1788*) and Thomas Sheraton (*The Cabinet-Maker and Upholsterer's Drawing Book, 1793*) did much to popularize the new movement, which had been spearheaded by Robert Adam. These design books transmitted the new vocabulary of decoration which included swags, tablets, paterae, and urns. They also included new forms, such as sideboards and commodes; and, most importantly, they included the new shapes and designs for existing forms. On chairs, shield-shaped backs framing delicate splats were trademarks of Hepplewhite's influence, as were square, tapered legs. Balance and delicacy were featured. Mahogany remained the wood supreme, but delicate inlays or stringing replaced the sometimes boisterous carving of the Chippendale style. Sheraton revived the square back and preferred the turned, reeded leg. The influences of both Hepplewhite and Sheraton merged in America at the same time and coincided with the birth of the new country itself. Actual English examples were still imported, but the designs of Hepplewhite and Sheraton were wider reaching here than had been those of Chippendale, which were used mostly in Philadelphia. The newer design books were owned throughout the young country, and chairs made in Salem could resemble those made in New York more closely than they ever had a generation earlier. Styles became national, although many local preferences and eccentricities remained. In the Federal period, the new styles were a complete break with the past; and, coupled with advances in technology which looked ahead to the industrial revolution, they produced a fascinating and successful novelty, which, in true New England tradition, became accepted slowly. Architecture sets the pace for the decorative arts, and the first expressions of the new style in Boston were to be found in houses Charles Bulfinch designed for Thomas Russell and Joseph Barrell in 1791 and 1792. In 1793, Samuel McIntire built Salem's first "classical" house for Nathan Read. The John Peirce mansion in Portsmouth was built in 1799. With these "firsts" in coastal towns, it was not until the nineteenth century that the new styles had penetrated all of New England.

Little "classical" furniture was made in the Boston area before 1790 (see Montgomery, no. 176), most of it having been constructed after 1795. The side chair on the opposite page is an elegant expression of the new style. The shield-shaped back has a carved basket of fruit and trailing oak leaves on its top rail. The splats are carved, with inlays of paterae and a fan at the base. The moldings of the legs and use of stretchers are carry-overs from chairs of the preceding decade. This particular back does not appear in Hepplewhite and is likely based on an English chair. It was a popular design (with variations) in both Boston and Salem, where it reached its highest expression at the hands of Samuel McIntire in chairs made for the Derby and Waters families (Montgomery, nos. 15 and 19).

High quality painted furniture became very popular again in the Federal period. In 1796, and 1801, members of the Derby family ordered sets of elegantly painted chairs from Philadelphia (Fales, *Painted*, nos. 156, 161). The simpler chair at the right (133) is one of a set found in Salem. Painted a brownish red, with gilt, red, and gray decoration, it is made of maple and American beech, beech being an unusual wood for Salem. Without suitable documentation, the decoration has been linked with Robert Cowan (1762–1846), an ornamental painter who worked in Salem around 1800.

133. Side chair, maple and beech, possibly Salem, 1800–1805. One of six, which vary slightly. H. 34¾", W. 19½", D. 17".

134. Side chair, cherry and pine, attributed to Kneeland and Adams, Hartford, 1792–1795. One of a pair. H. 38½″, W. 19½″, D. 16½″.

135. Armchair, cherry and birch, probably Hartford area, 1790–1805. Originally mahoganized. H. 41¾″, W. 18½″, D. 17¼″.

The stylistic progression of the four chairs on these pages shows that the new "classical" style edged into Connecticut, as elsewhere, haltingly rather than entering with a roar. Figure 134 is for all practical purposes a Chippendale chair, with the exception of the carved urn in the splat. The top rail of 135 is bowed and the urn uncarved, but it, too, is basically Chippendale. The two chairs on the next page, however, have shield-shaped backs and square, tapered legs, thus qualifying as examples of the new style–although with some hesitation and uncertainty.

The chair above (134) is well executed and identical (except for the treatment of the top rail) to a set of "6 Parlor Chairs" made by Kneeland and Adams of Hartford for Mrs. Dickerson in 1793 (see *Antiques*, April 1967, p. 404). This chair, with its slip seat and many Chippendale features, could date early in the

Kneeland and Adams partnership, which lasted from 1792 to 1795. The Dickerson chairs were made in 1793; and in 1796, after the partnership had dissolved, Lemuel Adams made twenty-two elegant shield-back armchairs based on a design of Hepplewhite for the State House at Hartford (see *Bulletin*, the Connecticut Historical Society, October 1967, pp. 99–102). Two looking glasses and two chests labeled by Kneeland and Adams all attest to their high quality of workmanship. This side chair and its mate were part of a set made for the Watsons, who built the Watson-Bancroft house in East Windsor Hill, Connecticut, in 1785.

Obviously related to the side chair, although less urbane, is the armchair above (135). This type of splat was also used in Rhode Island and southeastern Massachusetts, but it was in the Hartford area that it was particularly favored. The uncarved back of the arm-

136. Side chair, cherry (inlaid), Connecticut, 1795–1805. H. 39¼″, W. 22″, D. 18″.

137. Side chair, mahogany (inlaid), probably Connecticut, 1795–1805. One of a set of four. H. 37″, W. 20″, D. 17″.

chair, heavier than that of the side chair, is obviously handled with less dexterity and deftness. The splat has an inverted heart at its base, however, and the chair has a good, solid stance in the best rural tradition.

In Hartford, Samuel Kneeland advertised "Parlour Chairs Chamber ditto, Sofas, Easy Chairs, Elbow ditto, and Chairs of various other kinds" as early as 1786. He and Lemuel Adams were accomplished cabinetmakers, and in 1796, after the Kneeland and Adams partnership had dissolved, Adams stated that he employed "the best workmen from New-York and Boston" (*Bulletin,* the Connecticut Historical Society October 1967, pp. 101, 138). Hartford had solidified its position as the style leader of the towns in the Connecticut Valley and had brought the new classical style to furniture by 1796. The side chair at the left

above (136) makes extensive use of inlaid decoration. The back, splats and front legs all have line inlay, or "stringing" as it was called. The inlaid fan on the back and "icicle" inlay at the top of the legs, with four dependent, graduated diamonds below, have been burned to produce a shaded contrast. The back is quite plain, and interesting in its use of an even number of splats, rather than the odd number usually found with this back. A nearly identical chair has been linked with the work of Lemuel Adams (*Antiques,* January 1956, p. 68) on the basis of the inlays, but those on this chair seem more tentative than do those on the Adams State House chairs.

The chair above (137) is made of mahogany and is very similar to one at Winterthur that has even more swirl to its inlaid fan and patera (see Montgomery, no. 49). Its spirit outweighs its perfection.

138. Side chair, mahogany, New York type, 1795–1805. One of a pair. H. 38¼", W. 19¾", D. 15¾".

140. Side chair, mahogany, probably New York, 1795–1805. One of a set of six. H. 39", W. 20½", D. 18".

139. Side chair, mahogany (ash and maple), New York, 1795–1800. One of a pair. H. 39", W. 21½", D. 17½".

The chairs on these two pages are not native New England types, although similar examples did become naturalized there during the Federal period. The two at the left, with carved plumes and drapery folds in their backs, are of a type favored in New York. Figure 139 is a very suave chair, its carving executed with finesse, and its outflaring front legs distinctive. It has been conjectured that an identical chair might be the early work of Duncan Phyfe (*Antiques,* December 1929, p. 499). Two medial braces run fore-and-aft under the seat frame, in a manner often used in the New York area. These chairs traditionally were owned in a Springfield, Massachusetts family. Salem versions of this type of chair are also known (Montgomery, no. 22, and Randall, no. 159). Figure 138 is a slightly simpler variant of this type of chair.

The chair above (140) has a back similar to a New York type chair owned in the Eupaphroditus Champion mansion, built in East Haddam, Connecticut, about 1795 (see Edwin J. Hipkiss, *Eighteenth Century American Arts,* Boston, 1941, no. 95; also Warren, no. 145). The side rails are mortised through the back legs in Philadelphia fashion, but in the New York 1796 price book of cabinetmakers' charges, this "extra" was listed (Montgomery, p. 103).

141. Side chair, mahogany, New York, c. 1800. One of two. H. 36¼", W. 20", D. 17¼".

142. Side chair, mahogany, New York, c. 1800. One of two. H. 35", W. 20¾", D. 18".

143. Side chair, mahogany, Philadelphia or Baltimore, 1795–1805. H. 36½", W. 20", D. 16".

The chair above (141) is a New York production, based on Plate 36, No. 1 of Thomas Sheraton's *The Cabinet-Maker and Upholsterer's Drawing Book*, London, 1793. The reeded, tapered legs ending in spade feet were used often in New York. The two chairs at Deerfield of this type practically match, but one has two fore-and-aft seat braces, while the other has only one placed under the middle of the seat.

Accompanying the two chairs above were two similar chairs, with different backs (142). These have the single seat brace and are based on an English prototype rather than a design source (see *Antiques,* October 1942, p. 191, fig. 6).

The heart-back chair at the right (143) is elaborately carved and was found in eastern Massachusetts. Robert Fulton owned New York chairs of this type (Comstock, no. 431), as did the William H. Jones family of New Haven (Lyon, p. 186, fig. 89). A set of four similar chairs, with stretcher bases, have a history of ownership by George Washington (Frances Clary Morse, *Furniture of the Olden Time*, New York, 1940, 3rd ed., p. 205, fig. 189). Philadelphia and Baltimore examples are known (Montgomery, nos 101–102), but the carved bowknot on the top rail and the "thumbnail" elements below point toward Baltimore as the spot of this chair's manufacture.

144. Sofa, mahogany with birch inlay, northern Essex County, Massachusetts, or coastal New Hampshire, 1800–1815. Upholstery modern. H. 34¼″, W. 78″, D. 22″. Gift of Mrs. Joseph N. White.

145. Sofa, mahogany with maple inlay, cherry and ash, Massachusetts (Connecticut Valley), 1800–1815. Tan and brown striped velvet upholstery. H. 36″, W. 80″, D. 24½″. Lucius D. Potter Memorial.

Sofas had been luxuries in the eighteenth century, and while they became more popular in the Federal period, it was not until after 1825 that they could be considered plentiful. They were used in halls and chambers, as well as in parlors (see Montgomery, p. 291). The sofa at the left (144) is related to a group of handsome Sheraton sofas made between Boston and Portsmouth. Some of these have a strip of veneer running across the top rail (Montgomery, nos. 271–273). This one does not, but it has birch veneers behind and below the arm supports, tapered reeding on its front turned legs, and an unusual tongue where the wooden arm cappings join the front legs. This feature and the bulbs at the feet point to an origin east of the Boston-Salem area.

Figure 145 has excellent lines, with its serpentine top rail and delicate turnings. While the front legs are not reeded, there are inlays at the junction of the legs and seat, and stringing is used on the tops of the arms and behind them. This seven-legged sofa was owned by Mr. and Mrs. Lucius D. Potter in their home in Greenfield and probably was a family heirloom. Rowena Russell Potter, a Sheldon descendant, left all the pieces she and her husband had owned or collected to Historic Deerfield, Inc. as a memorial to her late husband.

The sofa below (146) is a most stylish later Sheraton example from the Boston-Salem area. The scrolled arms with fluted urns beneath, the extra rolled shoulders at the rear of the arms, and the reeded mahogany top rail and arm cappings all add to its feeling of elegance. The rolled shoulders seem to be a presage of Grecian influences. The three front legs are reeded, but the rear three are merely turned to conform to the front legs. Casters had come into use by the Federal period, and they can be found on sofas, chairs, tables, and even case pieces occasionally.

146. Sofa, mahogany, maple, eastern Massachusetts, 1805–1820. Upholstered in figured green bourette. H. 37½", W. 77", D. 29".

147. Side chair, maple and birch, Connecticut or New York, 1805–1820. Black ground, with gold and red decoration. One of a pair. H. 35½″, W. 14⅛″, D. 14¼″.

148. Side chair, maple, probably eastern Massachusetts, 1805-1820. Black ground, with gold and white decoration. One of a pair. H. 36″, W. 14½″, D. 14¾″.

Both Hepplewhite and Sheraton had encouraged the painting of furniture, and in the Federal period many stylish chairs, settees, and tables were decorated. New York became the style leader of the United States, and decorated or fancy chairs were advertised there as early as 1797. They were made everywhere by the nineteenth century, and even their rush seats were painted (see Montgomery, pp. 445–470; and Fales, *Painted,* pp. 132–147).

Fancy chairs were inexpensive and extensively exported from the larger coastal cities. Their decoration made use of the vocabulary of the classic revival. On the two chairs above may be seen urns, shells, and an eagle on 147, and paterae and drapery folds on 148. While 147 was found in Massachusetts, it is identical to one at Winterthur made in southern New England or New York (see Montgomery, nos. 487, 488). A rising sun peers over the center of the front stretchers on this chair. The chair at the right above (148) is similar to an armchair found in Plymouth County in Massachusetts (Nutting, II, no. 2449).

On the opposite page, the side chair and armchair at the top (149, 150) are painted a greenish-oyster ground, and the decoration consists of delicate bowknots with stylized leaves. The thumb-back tops of the

rear posts are similar to those used on Windsors and stenciled chairs (see pages 92 and 93). This set of fancy chairs was traditionally owned by Caleb Strong of Northampton. Born there in 1744, he was active in politics during the Revolutionary War period, was a United States Senator from 1789 to 1797, and was Governor of Massachusetts from 1800 to 1807 and again during the War of 1812 from 1812 to 1816 (see John S. Barry, *The History of Massachusetts,* III, Boston, 1857, 346 *et. seq.*). His cousin, Hezekiah Wright Strong, was a later owner of the Wells-Thorn house in Deerfield (see page 59).

The two chairs at the bottom of the opposite page (151, 152) are delightful country cousins combining features of both fancy chairs and Windsors. The leafy swags on their top rails, together with the shaping and decoration of the stiles, is a bit shaky! On the under side of the pine seats are the initials "JB" in chalk, signifying perhaps an unknown maker or painter. They were owned by the Hoyt family of Deerfield originally, and later by Miss C. Alice Baker. As early as 1808, Allen Holcomb was advertising "Fancy, Dining, Sewing & Common Chairs in the newest Fashion" in the *Greenfield Gazette.* This set shows how their popularity continued in the nineteenth century.

149 and 150. Side chair and armchair, maple and birch, probably Massachusetts, 1810–1820. Green ground, with decoration in gold, brown, and black. Two of a set of two armchairs and four side chairs. Side chair, H. 36″, W. 14″, D. 15¼″; armchair, H. 35½″, W. 15″, D. 15⅝″.

151 and 152. Rocker and side chair, maple and pine, Deerfield-Greenfield area, 1815–1835. Ochre ground, with decoration in black, green, and red. Two of a set of five side chairs and a rocker. Rocker, H. 28⅜″, W. 15¼″, D. 14¼″; side chair, H. 32¼″, W. 15½″, D. 13¼″.

153. Photograph of George Sheldon taken about 1910 by the Misses Allen. Although born in the Sheldon-Hawks house (see page 39), George Sheldon moved in 1898 to the Joseph Stebbins house and is seen here in the parlor surrounded by family chairs.

In his later life, George Sheldon (1818–1916) lived in the Joseph Stebbins house. He is shown above, in a photograph taken by Mary and Frances Allen (see *Historic Deerfield Quarterly*, October 1974, pp. 3–5); and he reposes in the roundabout chair shown on page 39, figure 66. A family banister back and later Windsor rocker also surround the hearth. In his later years, George Sheldon enjoyed his reputation as the historian of Deerfield and posed frequently for pictures taken by the Allen sisters (see Chamberlain and Flynt, p. 49). He was a successful farmer and served in the state legislature and senate. In the last half of his long life, his interest turned to Deerfield history. He founded the Pocumtuck Valley Memorial Association in 1870 and served as its president for forty-six years. He wrote articles and catalogues, and his major work, *The History of Deerfield* (1895/6), is one of the best chronicles of the golden age of local history. After he died, a friend said, "What he did is permanent, and not only of lasting but of gaining worth as the people draw further away from the heroic era whose chief recorder he was" (P.V.M.A. *Proceedings*, VI, 363).

The Windsor rocker (154) descended in Sheldon's family and started off with a high back and no rockers. Many of these chairs were "improved" in the later 1800s, comfort winning out over authenticity.

154 (above). Windsor armchair, maple and pine, 1800–1810. Repainted dark green; rockers added, back cut down. Sheldon family. H. 24″, W. 20″, D. 13⅜″.

155 (right). The Joseph Stebbins house is a large gambrel roofed house on the west side of the Street built about 1772. Owned by Deerfield Academy.

Windsors and Hitchcocks

156. Bench, hickory, maple, and pine, New England, 1770–1800. Originally painted red; now black. H. 29¼", W. 81", D. 22½".

No form of furniture combined lightness and durability, portability and beauty, and simplicity and comfort better than the American Windsor chair. Inspired by English examples, the form developed in Philadelphia during the Queen Anne period and spread to New York and New England by the time of the Revolution. Many woods were used in Windsors. Generally, the seats were made of softwoods like pine, the legs of hard woods such as maple, and the spindle and bows were fashioned from a wood like hickory which could be turned or bent. They were always painted originally, with green, black, and red the most popular eighteenth century colors.

The Deerfield collections are rich in New England Windsors of the eighteenth and early nineteenth centuries. Their heyday there occurred from about 1780 to 1830. The bench above is of the low-back type that harks back to the earliest Windsor chairs produced in Philadelphia. The absence of taper from the lower part of the baluster front legs is unusual (see Randall, no. 194); and while the bench has an earlier appearance, it was probably made rather late in the eighteenth century. The settee below (157) is an elongated sack-back armchair (see page 88). **This type of rounded back came into use in New England in the 1780s.** The slight swell to the spindles below the rail was a feature often favored in eastern Connecticut Windsors.

157. Settee, hickory, maple, and pine, Connecticut, 1780–1800. Repainted red. H. 35½", W. 76½", D. 20¼".

158. High-back armchair, hickory, ash, pine, and maple, Rhode Island type, 1775–1790. Refinished; traces of old green and red paint. H. 43¼″, W. 19¼″, D. 15″. P.V.M.A. Source unknown.

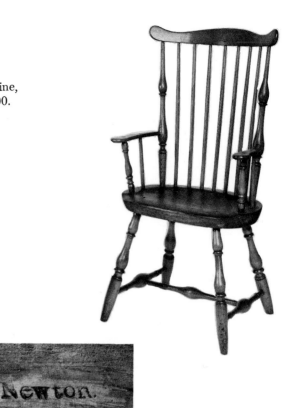

160, 160a. Fan-back armchair, hickory, pine and maple, New England, c. 1800. Refinished; originally painted red. One of a pair; one branded "R. Newton." H. 37¾″, W. 19″, D. 14¼″. Lucius D. Potter Memorial.

159. High-back armchair, hickory, pine and maple, Rhode Island type, 1785–1800. Repainted medium green. H. 39¼″, W. 14¾″, D. 15¾″.

The earliest types of Windsors were usually armchairs and were called "high back'd," "low back'd," and "sack back" (see Nancy A. Goyne, "American Windsor Chairs: a Style Survey," *Antiques*, April 1969, 538–543; and Fales, *Painted*, pp. 84–91 and 240–249). These high-back examples were made in New England. Rhode Island Windsors with early baluster-turned legs invariably taper inward sharply near the foot (158, 159). Figure 158 (left, above) has fine balance, excellent turnings, and a generous seat, while 159 (left) is less well coordinated in its prim stance, with unusual turnings under the arms. Both chairs have ring turnings on their central stretchers. The feel of 160 is much on the chunky side, and it was probably made in inland Connecticut or Massachusetts. Windsors can be stamped or branded by their makers or owners. The "R. Newton" mark appears to be a maker's brand, but Newton has not yet been pinned down as to locale and date.

On the next page is a high-back, writing arm Windsor by Connecticut's most accomplished maker, Colonel Ebenezer Tracy (1744–1803) of Lisbon (see Ada R. Chase, "Ebenezer Tracy, Connecticut Chairmaker," *Antiques*, December 1936, pp. 266–269). A similar, stubbier writing arm example is at Yale (Myers and Mayhew, no. 74).

161. One of the finest American Windsors known, this high-back armchair with writing arm was made by Ebenezer Tracy of Lisbon, Connecticut, between 1765 and 1790. Made of oak, hickory, maple, and pine, it was painted red originally (now black). It was owned by the Rev. Theophilus Packard (1769–1855), who was pastor of the Congregational Church at Shelburne, near Deerfield, from 1799–1855. He was buried in South Deerfield. H. 45¼″, W. 27″, D. 18¾″. P.V.M.A., bequest of Francis J. Kellogg.

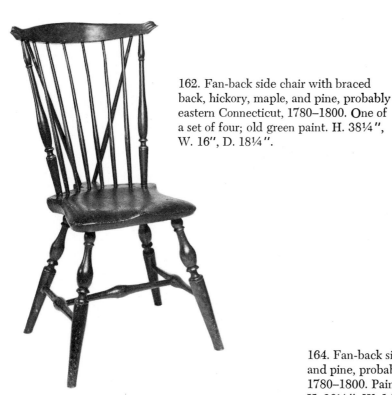

162. Fan-back side chair with braced back, hickory, maple, and pine, probably eastern Connecticut, 1780–1800. One of a set of four; old green paint. H. 38¼", W. 16", D. 18¼".

164. Fan-back side chair, hickory, maple, and pine, probably eastern Connecticut, 1780–1800. Painted black originally. H. 36½", W. 14", D. 15½".

163. Fan-back side chair, hickory, maple, and pine, eastern Connecticut, 1780–1800. Stamped "AS" on seat back (163a). Painted green. H. 35½", W. 14¼", D. 15¼".

163a.

165. Side chair, maple and hickory, Connecticut, 1800–1825. Painted black originally; rush seat replaced. H. 38¾", W. 15", D. 14".

166.

167.

168.

166a.

166, 168. Pair of fan-back side chairs, hickory, maple, and pine, made by Ansel Goodrich, Northampton, Massachusetts, 1795–1803. Originally painted red; now black. H. 37¾", W. 16⅝", D. 16¼".

167. Bow-back side chair, hickory, maple and pine, made by Ansel Goodrich, Northampton, Massachusetts, 1795–1803. Old green paint. H. 37¾", W. 16½", D. 16¼".

167a.

The three fan-back side chairs on the opposite page (162–164) were probably all made in New London County, Connecticut. Rhode Island influences can be seen in the sharply tapering front feet of 164. The bold turnings, bulging spindles, and braces of 162 result in a most satisfying chair. Unusual carved ears on its top rail are executed with more certainty than the carving on 163 and 164. The stamped "AS" on the back of the seat of 163 is enclosed by a deckled edge resembling silversmiths' marks of the late eighteenth century; and while it cannot be definitely assigned to a maker, one wonders if it might be a later production of Abel Spicer (1736–1784) of Groton, Connecticut (see Myers and Mayhew, p. 125).

Fan-back Windsors developed from the high-back and were popular in New England from the 1780s to the early nineteenth century. A most interesting maverick can be seen at the bottom right of the opposite page (figure 165). It combines elements of porch and fancy furniture with Windsor influences

and is similar to a chair with a Hartford County, Connecticut, history (see *George Dudley Seymour's Furniture Collection in the Connecticut Historical Society*, Hartford, 1958, p. 84; or Kirk, *Connecticut*, no. 248). Windsor chairs are occasionally labeled, and the three above were made by a local Northampton maker, Ansel Goodrich (c. 1773–1803; see Florence Thompson Howe, "The Brief Career of Ansel Goodrich," *Antiques*, July 1930, pp. 38–39). The chairs have weaker, more flaccid turnings than do earlier Windsors; and while the tops and seats vary between the two types of chairs, the legs and stretchers are the same. Goodrich was one of a group of Federal furniture craftsmen working in Northampton. After his untimely death in 1803, a full inventory listed his shop stock, tools, and personal possessions. Green, black, and white paints were included, as were 12 fan-back chairs primed, 14 not painted, and 56 partly finished; 120 chair seats, 150 bows and 400 spindles also give evidence of Goodrich's industry.

169. Sack-back armchair, hickory, maple, and pine, probably Massachusetts, 1790–1805. Painted dark green; branded "J. H. Woodbury." H. 37½", W. 19", D. 13¼". P.V.M.A., gift of Jason B. Woodbury.

170. Continuous-bow armchair, hickory, maple, and pine, probably Connecticut Valley, 1795–1810. Painted red. H. 34½", W. 18⅜", D. 14". P.V.M.A., gift of Elsie Catlin.

171. Continuous-bow armchair, hickory, maple, and pine, Deerfield area, 1800–1815. Painted blue/gray originally; now black. From Louise Billings estate, Deerfield. H. 39", W. 19⅜", D. 14⅝".

When green Windsor chairs—"Round-Top" and "fan-back Garden-chairs . . . painted equally as well as those made at Philadelphia"—were advertised in Boston in 1786, it was fifty years after they were first mentioned in Philadelphia records (Lyon, pp. 176–181). Between 1786 and 1788, Windsors were also advertised as made locally in Hartford, New Haven, New London, and Providence. Their manufacture spread to more rural areas in the 1790s. Near Deerfield, they were made by Lewis S. Sage in Northampton in 1793, by William Shipman in Hadley in 1794, and by Daniel Clay of Greenfield in 1796. Remaining extremely popular until the fancy chair won universal acceptance in the nineteenth century, Windsors were used in the best rooms in Federal houses. When the prominent Boston merchant Joseph Barrell furnished his new mansion in 1795, he ordered eighteen "light blue grey" bow-back Windsor chairs for his dining room and hall (Fales, *Painted*, p. 90).

Green was the most used color for Windsors in the eighteenth century. A manuscript of an unidentified apprentice cabinetmaker in 1801 lists a recipe for this process (*Bulletin*, the Connecticut Historical Society, January 1943, p. 12):

to paint green on Windsor chairs take your verdigrease and grinde it with the linseed oil and A small matter of white lead as to give a Boddy grinde this as thick as you can with the oil and

when ground put it in your Paint pot and Stur in as much common Chair varnish as to thin it Down proper for your Brush.

The sack-back armchair at the left above (169) is painted dark green and bears the owner's brand of a member of the Woodbury family of Sunderland, Massachusetts, a town across the Connecticut River from South Deerfield. Its arms are well shaped, and its bow is round in cross section. Bows could be molded before they were steamed also (nos. 170, 171). Figure 170 was probably made not far from Deerfield, and it was given to Miss C. Alice Baker by the French nuns of the Ursuline convent in Quebec when Miss Baker was doing research there on early Deerfielders who had been taken as prisoners to Canada by the Indians. An inscription on the chair states that it was owned by Archbishop Joseph-Octave Plessis of Canada, who was the grandson of Mary Catlin, one of the girl captives taken north from Deerfield after the infamous 1704 massacre. She was given by the Indians to nuns and, like some other prisoners, eventually chose to live in Canada. The chair was an exchange of later generations. Figure 171 was owned in the Deerfield area, and its limpid, bamboo-turned base is indicative of later Windsors of the nineteenth century. The bending of the bow to form both the back and arms of these last two chairs (170, 171) was a feature used by makers in New York and New England.

172. Bow-back side chair, hickory, maple and pine, Deerfield area (Connecticut Valley of Massachusetts), 1800–1810. Painted brown and yellow over older black and gold. Stebbins-Sheldon families. H. 36½″, W. 15¾″, D. 15⅜″.

173. Sack-back armchair with upholstered seat, hickory, maple and pine, Massachusetts or Connecticut, 1790–1805. Repainted dark green with gilt stripes over original medium green. Seat upholstered in 19th century black leather. One of a pair. H. 35″, W. 20½″, D. 16¼″.

174. Bow-back side chair, hickory, maple and pine, probably eastern Massachusetts, 1790–1805. Mahoganized in old brown paint. Nine spindles in back. One of a set of four. H. 37″, W. 15½″, D. 15½″.

The bow-back side chair above (172) was owned by Caroline Stebbins Sheldon (1789–1865). In 1810 she married Seth Sheldon (1787–1860), a farmer and selectman of Deerfield. They were the parents of the historian George Sheldon. The later brown and yellow decoration appears on other Windsors owned in the family (see page 90). The chair is a good, forthright bow-back. The other one (174, above right) is an excellent example of this type, with nine spindles in its back and very well defined bamboo turnings on its legs and stretchers. The temporary, collarlike flatten-

ing of its legs just below the stretchers can be seen on Boston area chairs.

"Stuff-seat" Windsors were advertised in Boston in 1786 (Lyon, p. 179); and while the leather on 173 is Victorian, it was probably put on at the same time the chair was redecorated with gold striping in the coach painting manner. Windsor furniture was not confined to chairs and settees. Tables and stands were made, and below can be seen a high, backless stool and a small cricket, both with bamboo turnings of the early nineteenth century.

175. High stool, maple and pine, found in northern New Jersey, 1800–1810. Refinished; traces of old reddish-brown paint. H. 22⅝″, W. 16″, D. 10½″.

176. Small stool, maple and pine, New England, 1800–1820. Repainted black. H. 6½″, W. 15⅝″, D. 13¾″.

177. Rod-back side chair, maple and whitewood, probably Connecticut Valley (Massachusetts), 1805–1810. Black and dark red with gold stripings. Stebbins-Sheldon families. H. 34¼″, W. 15¾″, D. 15½″.

178. Rod-back (or "birdcage") side chair, maple and pine, probably Connecticut Valley (Massachusetts), 1805–1810. Black and gold over old green. Stebbins-Sheldon families. H. 34¾″, W. 16½″, D. 15⅝″. P.V.M.A., gift of George Sheldon.

179. Rod-back side chair, maple and whitewood, probably Connecticut Valley (Massachusetts), 1805–1810. Black and dark red, with yellow stripings over gold. Stebbins-Sheldon families. H. 32½″, W. 16″, D. 15½″.

In the nineteenth century, the rod-back Windsor became popular. Easily made and with many variants, this type of chair went hand in hand with the fancy chair. These later Windsors could be painted in a combination of colors, and their turnings were often accented by colored or gilt stripings. "Birdcage" tops (178), straight tops with the stiles extending above (180), and solid top rails that stepped down (182) were used in these later chairs.

The three above were owned in the Stebbins and Sheldon families. The chair at the right (179) is inscribed "Caroline (Stebbins) Sheldon m⁽ᵈ⁾ 1810," so there is a possibility these were her wedding chairs (see page 89). Earlier, Daniel Clay of Greenfield billed Epaphrus Sheldon for a Pembroke table (see page 124), and the bill included fancy chairs. Since Clay clearly differentiated between fancy and Windsor chairs in his advertisements, these are not the ones listed.

The Spooner and Fitts chair (opposite) is the first Windsor recorded by this firm and has a most delicious swoop to its back. The cradle (184), with its convertible top, seems to be a jaunty precursor of a Model A roadster.

180. Settee, ash, maple and pine, probably Connecticut 1815–1835. Refinished; originally painted blue/green. H. 34″, W. 80″, D. 18⅝″.

181, 181a. "Birdcage" side chair, maple and pine, stamped by Spooner & Fitts, Athol, Massachusetts, 1805–1815. Refinished; probably mahoganized originally. The partnership of Alden Spooner and George Fitts also stamped a Hepplewhite chest (*Antiques*, October 1952, p. 263). Spooner stamped a sofa (*Antiques*, June 1971, p. 791) and inscribed and dated (1807) a Hepplewhite chest (*Antiques*, February 1971, p. 216). H. 31½", W. 15½", D. 15".

182. "Step-down" armchair, hickory, maple, and pine, probably Connecticut Valley (Massachusetts), 1805–1820. Repainted dark green. Later inscription: "F. W. Stowe, So. Deerfield." Owned later by Miss C. Alice Baker. H. 35½", W. 19¾", D. 15¼".

183. Child's side chair, hickory, maple and pine, probably Deerfield area, 1805–1825. Refinished; painted black earlier. Owned by Allen family, Deerfield. H. 24", W. 11½", D. 12".

184. Rocking cradle, maple and pine, probably Massachusetts, 1805–1825. Traces of original red stain remain. H. 33", W. 36½", D. 14".

185 (left). Comb-back rocker, maple and pine, Connecticut Valley, 1820–1835. Original decoration. Allen family, Deerfield. H. 41″, W. 17¾″, D. 16¾″.

186. (right). Comb-back rocker, hickory, maple and pine, New England, 1815–1830. Repainted black. H. 41″, W. 17¾″, D. 16¾″.

The two rockers above are later Windsors, with an extra comb added. The one at the left is a thumb-back chair, while the one at the right is of the step-down type. Figure 185 has much of its original decoration left; it is painted with green stripes, and floral scrolls and borders on a gray ground. It was owned by the Allen family of Deerfield. Both chairs, incidentally, have the same measurements. The rocking settee (below) has stenciled decoration on a rosewood-grained ground. The removable retainer, when in position as below, enabled an infant to sleep on the settee, while its mother or attendant could sit at the other end and provide rocking power. The turnings of this settee relate to those on Boston rockers (see figure 191), while others are found that are kith and kin of arrow-back Windsors (see Fales, *Painted*, p. 244, no. 419).

187. Rocking settee, maple and pine, New England, 1820–1835. Rosewood graining, bronze stenciling, yellow striping. H. 27½″, W. 47⅝″, D. 14½″.

189. Side chair, maple and pine, Massachusetts, c. 1830. Painted with yellow ground, decoration in plum and green. One of a set of six. H. 34″, W. 12½″, D. 14″.

188. Hitchcock-type side chair, maple and cane, Connecticut, 1830–1835. Black, with bronze stenciled decoration. One of a set of six. H. 34⅜″, W. 17⅞″, D. 15¼″.

190. Side chair, maple and rush, probably Connecticut, 1830–1835. Black with stenciled bronze decoration not original. One of a set of six. H. 32½″, W. 16¼″, D. 15⅝″.

The introduction of stencils, accompanied by less expensive methods of gilding, revolutionized the decoration of furniture after 1815. Bronze powders are substituted for gold leaf, and then even the bronze could be imitated at far less cost (see Fales, *Painted,* p. 159). These developments occurred in New York, but it was not long until they were used everywhere. In Connecticut, as one might expect, the ultimate occurred. Lambert Hitchcock (1795–1852) combined elements of fancy chairs with interchangeable parts and stenciled decoration to create a new type of low-cost chair named modestly for himself and produced in a town (now Riverton) named Hitchcocksville (see John Tarrant Kenney, *The Hitchcock Chair,* New York: Clarkson N. Potter, Inc., 1971). Hitchcock chairs were made in different patterns, could have rush, cane, or plank seats, and were shipped knocked-down to the South and Midwest for final assembly. Figure 188 (above, left) is not signed but is a Hitchcock type,

with a pillow top, slat back, and an unusual crown stretcher. The popularity of these chairs was very great, and other chairmakers made them in New England, New York, and Ohio (see Fales, *Painted,* p. 188).

Figure 190 (above right) relates to Hitchcock chairs but was probably made by another firm. It combines a thumb-back with graduated slats. This chair was repainted and restenciled in 1944. While it is tempting to redo old chairs whose decoration has become worn or damaged, the result, no matter how well done, can be only an echo of the original.

The chair in the center (189) is typical of large groups of plank-seat chairs with painted decoration that were made in New England in the 1820s and 1830s. This one is quite similar to one made by Nathan Haskell at the Newburyport (Massachusetts) Chair Factory in the late 1820s (Fales, *Essex,* no. 29). Grapes, plums and even seashells were favored motifs on these chairs.

191. Boston rocker, maple and pine, probably Massachusetts, 1825–1840. Rosewood graining, with gold stenciling and stripings in green and yellow. H. 43″, W. 20″, D. 20½″. P.V.M.A., Peabody bequest, gift of Miss Laura A. Martin.

192. Rocker, hickory, maple, and pine, probably Connecticut Valley, 1795–1840. Painted black. Rockers and top rail added later. H. 42¼″, W. 19¾″, D. 15¼″. P.V.M.A., source unknown.

The Boston rocker, which developed from the more slender Salem-type rocking chair in the 1820s, was to the rocking chair what Hitchcocks were to Windsors. With their comfort, stenciled decoration, and low cost, Boston rockers became very popular and were made by chairmakers well beyond the Boston area (see Fales, *Painted*, p. 246). Hitchcock, Alford & Co. made and signed examples of this type. Figure 191 has the crown top, rolled seat, and generous proportions typical of Boston rockers. It was owned by Nathaniel and Rebecca (Peabody) Martin of Bridgton, Maine and presented with over four hundred family objects to the Pocumtuck Valley Memorial Association by one of their daughters.

An altered Windsor armchair at the right recalls the Windsor owned by George Sheldon on page 82. In the case of 192, however, the upper spindles were retained when the rockers were added. The top rail must have been broken, so it was replaced with a scrolled top of the type that was used on chairs in the second quarter of the nineteenth century. These changes bring to mind a comment of George Sheldon in the catalogue of the Pocumtuck Valley Memorial Association: "Many articles may seem trivial in themselves, but as a part of the whole broad scheme of the projectors the most humble belong here as much as the most notable" (P.V.M.A. *Catalogue*, p. 3).

193, 194. One of the most handsome sets of American stenciled chairs is at
Deerfield. Consisting of an armchair and six side chairs, they were made
between 1820 and 1835 and combine elements of Hitchcock-type chairs (the
pillow top, cornucopia back, and busily turned arm supports) and earlier fancy
chairs (the horseshoe-shaped seat and more simply turned legs). These maple
chairs are painted yellow with olive stripings and scrolls, and the stenciled
decoration is executed in both bronze gilt and silver gilt. The measurements
of the armchair are H. 34¼″, W. 16″, D. 12¾″; and of the side chair are
H. 34½″, W. 14⅝″, D. 12⅝″.

Settles

195. Made of so-called hard pine in Southern Connecticut or the Middle
Colonies between 1725 and 1775, this settle was painted red. A similar example
found in South Jersey is shown in *Antiques*, May 1944, p. 255, fig. 12.
Another similar one is shown in Russell Hawes Kettell, *The Pine Furniture of
Early New England*, New York, 1929, no. 68. "1 long wainscot settle"
is listed in a 1706 Philadelphia inventory (see Luke Vincent Lockwood,
Colonial Furniture in America, II, New York, 1926, 129). H. 58″, W. 72″,
D. 16½″.

196. This settle was made of white pine in New England toward the end of the
eighteenth century. It is painted blue-gray, and its seat is hinged to provide
a storage area underneath. H. 50¼″, W. 78½″, D. 14½″.

Settles were used in seventeenth-century New England homes, usually in kitchens or great halls. Their use continued until after the Revolution, and their purpose was never better stated than by George Sheldon in reporting that members at the 1891 Pocumtuck Valley Memorial Association annual meeting sat "on the settles whose backs no longer need to be so high to protect against searching blasts that used to creep into the old-time houses they once ornamented" (P.V.M.A. *Proceedings,* III, 43).

Obviously highly architectural in character, settles often closely followed the paneling (195) or vertical sheathing (198) of the room in which they stood. The arms of early examples (195, 198) approximated the front mushroom finials of chairs. Added stability was provided to 198 by means of a diagonal brace under the right-hand side of the seat.

197. Settle, white pine, New England, 1780–1810. Painted blue/gray over old red. H. 50¼″, W. 34½″, D. 17½″.

198. Curved settle, pine with a band of ash at the top, New England, 1720–1780. Traces of old black paint. H. 64″, W. 67″, D. 17″.

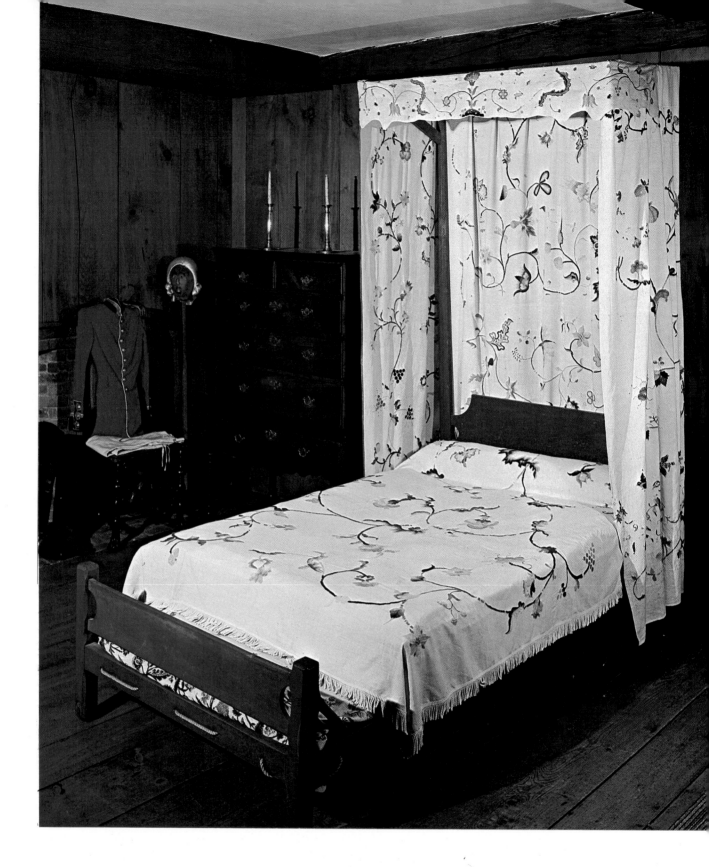

199, 200. In the Ashley house, the south bedroom has two bedsteads. The folding one (199) was made of birch and pine in the Connecticut Valley between 1740 and 1800. Painted red, it has unusual trestle feet (H. 90½", W. 50", D. 75¼"). In 1796, the house joiners and cabinetmakers of Hampshire County (in which Deerfield was located) charged four dollars for a bedstead "to turn against the wall" in a price list issued at Hatfield (see page 286). The small maple trundle bedstead on rollers was the gift of Charles F. Montgomery. The crewel work bed set was wrought by a member of the Ashley family, and the chest-on-frame is also an Ashley heirloom. Parson Ashley, an ardent Tory, would have cringed at the uniform taken from a British officer by a Whig nephew at an action near Boston. The wig stand is shown on page 163.

Bedsteads and Cradles

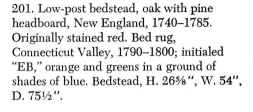

201. Low-post bedstead, oak with pine headboard, New England, 1740–1785. Originally stained red. Bed rug, Connecticut Valley, 1790–1800; initialed "EB," orange and greens in a ground of shades of blue. Bedstead, H. 26⅝", W. 54", D. 75½".

202. Low-post bedstead, maple with pine headboard, Connecticut Valley, 1750–1810. Red and black mahoganized graining. Yellow coverlet, and green coverlet with pink edge (at foot) both glazed, quilted linsey-woolsey, c. 1800. Bedstead, H. 36¾", W. 52", D. 76". Gift of Vincent D. Andrus.

The most valuable pieces of furnishings in an inventory of the Colonial period were always the beds. The bedstead was the wooden frame, while the bed itself was the feather (or stuffed) bedding. The estate of Thomas Hawley of Roxbury, Massachusetts, in 1676, lists in the parlor "one. standing bedsteed with. a ffeather. bed 2. ffeather boulsters, 2. ffeather pillows, curtains and vallants, blankets & coverlit thereto belonging" (Cummings, p. 14). In the inventory of Benjamin Barrit of Deerfield (1690), his "Bedsted and Bedding" at £2/6 almost equalled the rest of his household goods. In 1784, the inventory of Ebenezer Wells listed seven beds and bedsteads. To each of his daughters he left a bedstead, a trundle bed, and equipage such as a calico quilt, a striped blanket, a bolster and pillows (Hampshire County Probate Records).

New England bedsteads made before the Queen Anne period have rarely survived. The octagonal posts and deeply scalloped headboard of the bed above (201) are earlier features, as are the trestle feet of the folding, or "turn up," bedstead (199). Low-post bedsteads with turned legs (202) were made throughout the eighteenth and well into the nineteenth century (see Greenlaw, no. 21). They frequently seem to be earlier in appearance than in actuality and are almost always plain painted or grained.

The bed rug on 201 is made of wool, with a running stitch and cut pile (see William L. Warren, *Bed Ruggs/1722–1833*, Hartford, Wadsworth Atheneum, 1972, p. 48, no. 23).

On these two pages are three examples of so-called pencil-post bedsteads. Combining grace and utility, they were popular in both rural and urban areas from the Revolution into the 1800s. Figures 204 and 205 (below) were owned by Miss C. Alice Baker and both have local histories. The high-post bedstead was the wedding bed of Miss Baker's great uncle, Dennis Stebbins (1778–1842), who married Lois Hawks in 1800. They had eleven children. The double scalloping of the headboard is unusual. The trundle bed came to Miss Baker from the Bryant family of South Deerfield, with the tradition that it formerly held three of the Bryant children with their Newfoundland dog!

203. Doll's bedstead, pine, New England, 1790–1820. Painted blue, with red stain underneath. Crewel work coverlet English, 18th century. H. 22¼", W. 11", D. 19¾". Gift of Spinning Wheel Shop.

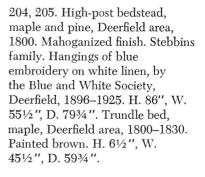

204, 205. High-post bedstead, maple and pine, Deerfield area, 1800. Mahoganized finish. Stebbins family. Hangings of blue embroidery on white linen, by the Blue and White Society, Deerfield, 1896–1925. H. 86", W. 55½", D. 79¾". Trundle bed, maple, Deerfield area, 1800–1830. Painted brown. H. 6½", W. 45½", D. 59¾".

206, 207. The high-post bedstead is typical of the delicate pencil-post examples made in New England between 1780 and 1820 (see Greenlaw, nos. 14, 15 and 18). Made of maple with a pine headboard, it is painted red. The polychrome embroidered hangings and coverlet were traditionally made about 1750 by Esther Meacham Strong (1725–1793) of Coventry, Connecticut. She was a granddaughter of Parson John Williams of Deerfield, author of *The Redeemed Captive* (see Sheldon, *History*, II, 377; inscription on coverlet in Ann Pollard Rowe, "Crewel Embroidered Bed Hangings in Old and New England," *Bulletin*, Museum of Fine Arts, Boston, LXXI (1973), 161, n. 91). H. 75″, W. 53¾″, D. 77¾″. The red trundle bedstead is also made of maple and pine, as are the early tables on the wall. The small chest on the table at the left is shown on page 178.

208. H. 83½″, W. 57″, D. 80″.

American Chippendale bedsteads with claw feet are very rare, and those with the added feature of removable carved wooden kneecaps (which hide the bolts) are practically unheard of. This bedstead combines claw feet with swept-back side claws, rich carving, and stop-fluting on the posts in a most stylish manner; yet its place of manufacture is unknown. Since it was altered at one time, the headboard, rails, and tester are not original, and only the mahogany posts survive intact. Other beds of this type are shown in Luke Vincent Lockwood, *Colonial Furniture in America,* New York, II, 1926, 256; Nutting, I, no. 1497; and *Antiques,* March 1941, p. 128. The importance of this bedstead to Deerfield is evident, since another similar example at the Lindens (near Washington) was found in Deerfield (see *Antiques,* February 1938, p. 78). The bed hangings are of eighteenth-century English polychrome crewel work.

209. H. 93½", W. 58", D. 79¾".

Found in Connecticut and owned by the Wyllys and Talcott families, this maple bedstead is mahoganized in red and brown, with traces of gilding in the flutes of the front posts. While the front legs are square, the overall thinness of the posts and the shaping of the headboard indicate that it was made about 1800. The pine headboard has been raised up about a foot from its original position, undoubtedly to make it more visible when a box spring was added at a later date. The red and white French copperplate toile bedhangings and coverlet were made in the late eighteenth century. Toiles and especially English chintzes of all sorts were used throughout the country in the Federal period. In 1803, R. E. Newcomb advertised in the Greenfield *Gazette* "*Copper Plate*—1 suit Copper Plate bed furniture; curtains of 5 windows made in the newest fashion with Cords & Tassels."

210 (left). Bed post from field bed, probably eastern Massachusetts, 1800–1810. Maple, originally mahoganized. H. 66".

211 (above, left). Detail of bed post, probably New York area, 1795–1805. Mahogany front posts, square birch rear posts.

212 (above, center). Detail of bed post, probably carved by Joseph True, Salem, 1811–1815. Mahogany. Lucius D. Potter Memorial.

213 (above, right). Detail of bed post, New England, 1810–1825. Birch, mahoganized. Gift of the Honorable William Vanderbilt.

Painted beds and matching sets of furniture were popular after 1800. The columbine bed (215, 215a) has very delicate turnings and decoration. The columbines on the front posts are red, and the leaves are shaded in green and gold. Grapes and acorns of dark blue and tans twine up the posts. Borders in two shades of gray, with gilt and black striping, complete the decoration, which is ably executed on a white ground. The coverlet is an Italian brocade of the eighteenth century, with metallic threads.

The post at the right (214) is from a later field bed, its turnings heavier and less well articulated than those on the columbine bed. This later bed was owned by the Williams family (see page 24), probably by Dr. Stephen West Williams, who married Harriet Goodhue of Newcastle, New Hampshire, in 1818. Originally, a matching white and gold dressing table and a set of chairs accompanied this bed (entire bed, illustrated in Chamberlain and Flynt, p. 162).

Field (or camp) beds were defined by Thomas Sheraton in *The Cabinet Dictionary* (London, 1803, pp. 123, 124) as portable beds that could be easily set up or taken apart. They usually had arched folding testers, and they could be used in homes as well. Many lighter bedsteads can be called field beds. The post at the left, with its turned foot and leg, urn-shaped member with flattened leaf carving, and reeded swelling upper post, is from a bed of the Sheraton style which has a Deerfield area history. The three details of posts (left) show the development and gradual thickening of the posts during the Federal period. Figure 211 is similar to, but more delicate than, 210; the bed was owned in the Gould family of Salisbury, Connecticut. The post in the center (212) has carved wheat sheaves and leafage identical to a bed post carved by the Salem carver, Joseph True (Fales, *Essex*, no. 68). The carving on 213 (right) is well executed and is a delicate example of later Federal period pineapple carving.

Bedposts could be made of many woods. When a fine wood like mahogany was used, New England cabinetmakers usually employed this more expensive wood for the front posts only, the rear posts being of birch or maple stained to resemble the finer wood.

215a.

214. Bed post, from field bed, Massachusetts, 1815–1830. Maple; painted off-white ground, with decoration in green, gold, red, brown, and black. H. 61″, W. 57¼″, D. 18″.

215. Bed, New England, 1800–1815. Cherry and birch; painted white ground, with decoration in blue, tan, and red, with shadings in green and gold. H. 81½″, W. 54″, D. 73¾″.

216. Painted blue-green, this substantial bed was made only of pine in New England between 1820 and 1845. Featuring a footboard as well as a scalloped headboard, it retains its old molded cornice. The turnings indicate a rural survival of the Sheraton influence at a rather late date. The trapunto bedspread is from the Covington family near Salisbury, Maryland, and is dated 1809. The hangings are of Chinese silk. H. 80″, W. 50″, D. 78″.

The field bed (below) is capped by two sparkling urns. It is in the Hall Tavern, a building moved by the Flynts from East Charlemont, a town between Greenfield and Williamstown on the Mohawk Trail, to Deerfield. The wool bedspread was made by Lucretia Street Hall, the wife of Joel Hall, the innkeeper, in 1837 for her niece Harriet's marriage. According to family tradition, Mrs. Hall also made bedspreads for each of her daughters (P.V. M.A. *Proceedings*, VII, 527–528).

The folding cot at the right (218) is an unusual form, as is the bed rest (219), which was found south of Boston. The angle of the back is adjustable, and the curved base permits it to be placed over a pillow. An upholstered Queen Anne bed rest is at the Marblehead Historical Society, and a pretzel-back example is at the Henry Ford Museum. Bed steps were often used, and those at the right were purchased in Deerfield at the Susan Hawks auction at the Sheldon-Hawks house in the late 1940s.

218. Field or camp bed, maple, beech, and pine, New England, 1800–1835. Painted red. H. 35½", W. 38", D. 76".

219. Bed rest, cherry, probably southeastern Massachusetts, 1795–1810. H. 24", W. 26", D. 22".

220. Bed steps, pine, Deerfield, 1800–1840. Originally red. H. 14", W. 16", D. 14½". Gift of Martha K. Humphrey.

217. Folding bed, maple and pine, Connecticut Valley (Massachusetts), 1800–1825. Stained red. Wool bedspread with black ground, polychrome decoration, green fringe. H. 40¾", W. 52¼", D. 76½"

Cradles were necessary accessories in many Colonial and Federal homes. The earliest ones were made of oak or wicker; and in the eighteenth century, fine woods like walnut or mahogany could be used, or the cradles could be painted. Figure 221 is a typical post-Revolutionary period cradle, with scalloped foot, hooded head, cutouts along the sides for portability, and generous rockers. It is dovetailed, and pine is used for its bottom and for strips joining the five-sectioned hood. Its rockers have been repaired. Several similar cradles with local Deerfield histories are at Memorial Hall.

Figure 222 was owned by the Williams family of Deerfield, possibly by Dr. Stephen West Williams, whose children were born between 1819 and 1825. With its acorn finials and sabre legs combined with later turnings, it was made in the Empire style and is nailed together.

The simplest of the three cradles at the right (223) is painted with black sponged decoration on an orange ground. It was made about 1833 by Wyman H. Stebbins (1807–1837), a Deerfield carpenter, for his daughter Frances.

221 (above). Hooded cradle, mahogany and pine, Massachusetts, 1780–1815. H. 25″, W. 19¼″, D. 40″.

222 (above, right). Swinging cradle, maple and pine, Massachusetts, 1810–1825. Red. H. 37″, W. 12″, D. 34½″.

223 (right). Cradle, pine, Deerfield, c. 1833. Black and orange. Made by Wyman H. Stebbins. H. 23½″, W. 12¾″, D. 35½″. P.V.M.A., gift of Mrs. Laura W. Wilkinson.

224. The first house that was rescued, restored, and furnished by the Flynts was the Ashley House at the north end of the Street. Built between 1726 and 1733, the gambrel-roofed house was bought by the Reverend Jonathan Ashley (1712–1780) in 1733. A man of strong opinion, Ashley was a Tory and was permitted to remain in Deerfield during the Revolution. The kitchen of his house is shown on the next page.

II. TABLES AND STANDS

225. Table, H. 28¼", W. 45½", D. 46¼".

In the kitchen of the Ashley house stands the Queen Anne curled maple table that was brought by Dorothy Williams of Hatfield to her marriage to Jonathan Ashley in 1736. Originally grained, the table features bold cabriole legs with pad feet, scalloped aprons at the ends, and an unusual drawer. No inventory exists for Parson Ashley's estate, but that of his son Jonathan, Jr. in 1787 lists "1 Square leaf Curl Maple Table" at £ ½ (see John Snyder, Jr., "The Original Furnishings of the Manse," unpublished Heritage Foundation paper, 1967). The table is on loan to Historic Deerfield, Inc. from Williams College. The local cupboard in the background is shown on page 252.

Tables and stands were made in more varying types and for more differing uses than any other form in furniture. In this study, they are divided by type into various categories, with stands appearing at the end. Since dressing tables (or lowboys) are more properly case pieces often relating directly to high chests, they are included with the latter and appear with them on pages 206 through 222.

Dining, Drop-leaf, and Miscellaneous Tables

226. Table, pine, Middlesex County, Massachusetts, 1700–1750. Painted gray. H. 27¼″, W. 65″, D. 27½″.

227. Table, pine and "hard" pine, Connecticut or Massachusetts, 1795–1825. Red paint originally. H. 29⅝″, W. 90″, D. 25″.

228. Large Shaker table, cherry, birch, and pine, New England, 1840–1885. Painted red. H. 26½″, W. 141½″, D. 35½″.

The earliest dining tables in the Colonies were boards that were supported by a trestle base. They related to table boards which had been in use in England since medieval times, and their manufacture lingered in New England throughout the eighteenth century. The trestle table on the opposite page (226) is made entirely of pine and was found in Sherborn, Massachusetts, a charming rural town in Middlesex County west of Boston near Framingham. While its form is of the seventeenth century, the thinness of the top and overall design indicate it was made later, carrying on an earlier style.

The inventory of Samuel Childs of Deerfield, taken after his death in 1808, listed "1 cross leg table." Sawbuck tables, as they were called later, had X-bases of rectangular members joined by long boards. In 227, a storage shelf is formed under the top by these boards. Easily constructed, cross-legged tables were made throughout the eighteenth and nineteenth centuries. Figure 227 is held together by cut nails and was not made until after 1800. It has a large, one-piece top of white pine and was found in the Boston area.

Some of the most handsome of the large trestle tables in American furniture were made in Shaker enclaves in New York and New England after 1800. One of these is in the Hall Tavern at Deerfield (above). Its base appears to be slightly arthritic, but it is well chamfered and supports a top which is almost twelve feet in length. The pine settle in the background is shown on page 96.

229. Table with drawer, maple base, white pine top and drawer, New England, 1710–1735. Painted red. H. 25¼″, W. 42″, D. 25″.

230. Table with drawer, maple base, top, and drawer front; pine drawer linings, New England, 1780–1800. Originally painted black. H. 27½″, W. 41″, D. 27½″, P.V.M.A., gift of John B. Morris, Jr.

The term tavern table, a nineteenth-century designation, has been given to all early stretcher-base, easily movable low tables. In early inventories, they were referred to merely as tables or tables with drawers. Figure 229 at the left is a good example of an early eighteenth-century table with drawer. With excellent varied turnings on the base, it has a wide overhang to its top, which is finished at both ends with cleats to hide the end grain of the wood. The drawer is lipped, and it has a wooden pull, which was invariably used on early tables (see 230 and 231). Tables of this type were used throughout the early home, and occasionally one is found with a well scrubbed top that indicates it was used in a kitchen for the preparation of food. Other drawerless examples of turned tables are shown on pages 141–143.

The table at the left below (230) is a later example of this type, with an unusual top of maple rather than pine. Its grooved legs are reminiscent of chairs and beds that have been found in the Connecticut Valley area of New Hampshire.

The large table with drawer at the top of the opposite page (231) is a handsome example, with excellent proportions. Rectangular stretchers are used on these larger tables, since they provide more needed strength than would turned members. A similar large table is shown in Wallace Nutting, *Furniture of the Pilgrim Century*, Framingham, Massachusetts, 1924, no. 697. Some restoration has been done to two of the turned feet—a fate which commonly befalls these early tables.

Below is another large stretcher-base table (232) of later date and of lesser style which was probably used in a kitchen at the end of the eighteenth century.

231. With a base of maple and birch and a top and drawer of white pine, this large table with drawer was probably made in the Connecticut Valley between 1710 and 1740. It was painted red originally, and two of its feet have been restored. Large tables of this type are rare in New England furniture, and while some have histories of use in early churches, they could also be used in homes. On the inside of the frame, the conjoined initials TB are carved upside down. H. 28", W. 68½", D. 27¾".

232. This table is made entirely of pine and is repainted red. Many simple tables of this type were made throughout New England between 1785 and 1820. The wear on the soft wood stretchers is evident. This table does not have a drawer. H. 27", W. 60", D. 34¼".

As early as 1644, a chair table was listed in a Watertown, Massachusetts inventory. Not only are these tables ideal space-saving convertibles which could be used for a seat as well as a table; but, when in use as tables, they invariably have an overhang which permits the sitters to near the table without obstruction and the knee-knocking obstacles that are present in many tables—early and late. Figure 233 (left) has watered-down turnings of the seventeenth-century type and its original two-tone paint. It was owned in the Abercrombie family of Pelham, Massachusetts, and Deerfield, and was probably made in the eighteenth century. New Hampshire is a happy hunting ground for chair tables of the late 1700s, and 234 was found there. The trestle feet of 235 and 236 recall those on great tables of the seventeenth century (see 226, page 110). Chair and hutch (or box) tables were made in New England as late as the Victorian era, although they often seem deceivingly earlier.

233 (above). Chair table, maple base with pine top, probably Massachusetts, 1695–1740. Painted red with black on turnings. H. 28½", Diam. (top) 35½".

234 (below). Chair table, maple base with pine top, New Hampshire, 1780–1810. Painted red. H. 28", W. 43¾", D. 59¾".

235 (right). Chair table, all maple, probably Connecticut Valley, 1750–1800. Painted red. H. 27⅛", Diam. (top) 44"–45".

236. In the kitchen of the Frary house is a pine table with its original red paint. It was made as a true hutch table (not merely as a chair table), with a storage area under a hinged lid, probably in southwestern Connecticut in the eighteenth century (H. 27½", top 17" x 41½"). In the background, the cupboard is repainted red over white, and the green slatback side chair is an early nineteenth century example. The banister-back armchair is shown on page 31, figure 43. Over the mantel is a small gray hanging wall box that was owned in the Old Indian house by the Hoyt family.

237. Drop-leaf gateleg table, walnut and white pine, probably Boston, 1695–1720. Drawer in other end runs full width of table. Owned by Bowdoin family. H. 28¾″, top 60¼″ x 50⅜″.

Tables that could be taken apart or folded were used in the seventeenth century. By the end of the 1600s, drop-leaf tables had come into use (Randall, nos. 71, 72), and these became the standard dining table of the eighteenth century. With six or eight legs usually, the gateleg table was popular in the first half of the century. The legs were fashioned with vase-and-ring turnings like those on early chair legs, and a swinging gate on each side supported the leaves. Maple was the most used wood in gatelegs, and drawers often occur in the ends. Figure 238 (right) shows a fine contrast between a plain, oval top and varied turned legs. The table above (237) is unusually large and is made of walnut, a wood that was used rarely in New England in the late seventeenth century. The turnings are extremely bold, and a drawer runs the entire width of the frame. The table was owned by James Bowdoin III (1752–1811), momentary ambassador to Spain under Jefferson and founder of Bowdoin College in Maine. It could have been owned in Boston by his father, James II (1726–1790) or even his grandfather James (1676–1747).

238. Drop-leaf gateleg table, curled maple and maple, New England, 1710–1740. Originally painted red. H. 25¾″, top 43″ x 37½″.

116

239. Drop-leaf gateleg table, maple and pine, Essex County, Massachusetts, or coastal New Hampshire, 1710–1740. Painted black originally. Carved Spanish feet. H. 28″, top 41½″ x 50″.

240. Drop-leaf gateleg table, cherry and pine, Deerfield area, 1720–1765. Old mahoganized finish. Drawer at each end. H. 27½″, top 53¾″ x 46½″.

With their commodious tops and sparkling interplay of turnings in their bases, gateleg tables can be extremely exciting, balanced pieces of furniture. The table above (239) has excellent turnings and is one of a small group of tables with the added distinction of having carved Spanish feet. While rarity and quality do not necessarily have to go hand in hand, they meld successfully in this case.

On gateleg tables, the joints between the tops and leaves invariably were of the tongue-and-groove type, with the ruled joint appearing on Queen Anne tables. All the gateleg tables on these two pages have the earlier type of joint.

The table at the left (240) has a local history of ownership in Deerfield. With a drawer at each end, the table retains its old dark finish. While we think of cherry today as a handsome, medium colored wood, it was invariably darkened with a stain or painted finish in the eighteenth century. The later turnings are less well defined and softer than those on the other tables shown here.

241. Butterfly table, all maple, probably eastern Massachusetts, 1710–1740. Originally painted black. H. 24″, Diam. (top opened) 39″.

Butterfly tables combine early stretcher bases and drop leaves, with the shaped leaf supports or wings giving them their name—obviously of recent vintage. They are usually rather small, and their stretchers usually rectangular. It was once thought that these tables all came from Connecticut, but other examples from New England are known. A table with cranelike supports at Winterthur was found in southern New Hampshire (Nutting, I, no. 900), as was another with fully developed wings (Randall, no. 76). The table above has turnings reminiscent of an example owned originally in West Newbury, Massachusetts (*Antiques*, October 1968, p. 526).

The best butterfly tables have a canted splay to their legs (241, 243). They may have a drawer, and tongue-and-groove type leaf joints are usually found. However, 242 has the later type ruled joint. It was painted red originally, then green, and finally reddish brown. Figure 243 (below) is a fine table, with a good splay and wide overhang. It is similar to one from Litchfield, Connecticut (*Antiques*, February 1965, p. 166).

242. Butterfly table, maple and pine, New England, 1720–1750. Repainted red-brown. H. 25″, top 41½″ x 41″.

243. Butterfly table with drawer, cherry, maple, and pine, Connecticut, 1710–1740. Painted red, H. 26″, top 36″ x 44¼″.

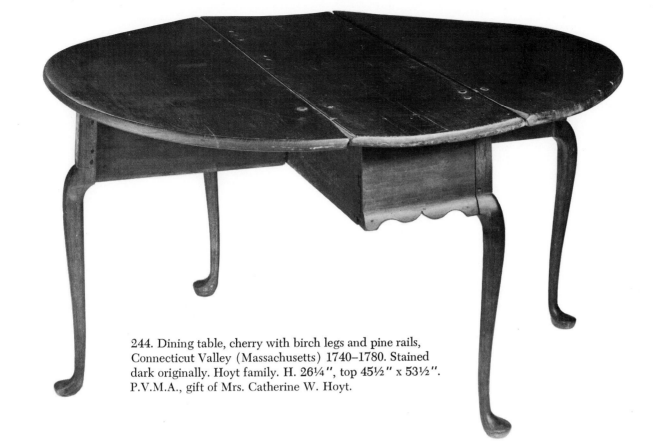

244. Dining table, cherry with birch legs and pine rails, Connecticut Valley (Massachusetts) 1740–1780. Stained dark originally. Hoyt family. H. 26¼″, top 45½″ x 53½″. P.V.M.A., gift of Mrs. Catherine W. Hoyt.

Queen Anne dining tables, with cabriole legs and rectangular or oval tops, are as handsome to look at as they are comfortable to sit at. While they were made throughout New England, the three on this page have Deerfield histories and were all probably made in that area. Early inventories and listings are often vague in describing specific types of furniture, and drop-leaf tables were often referred to merely by size —"4 foot table," "4½ foot table," etc. These sizes were approximate, and these three tables would have been referred to as "4-foot tables." The table above has oval leaves and was owned in the Old Indian House in Deerfield by the Hoyt family (see page 32). It is dated 1760 in the Memorial Hall records (P.V.M.A. *Catalogue*, p. 160, no. 5). The convex scalloped aprons on it and on 245 (below left) provide a counterpoint of motion to the cabriole legs. Figure 245 was owned by the Childs family and probably made in the Deerfield-Hatfield area. Its feet have faint ribs similar to those on a tea table (312, page 149) and dressing table (445, page 219). The table below (246) is a simpler version, with straight, turned tapering legs.

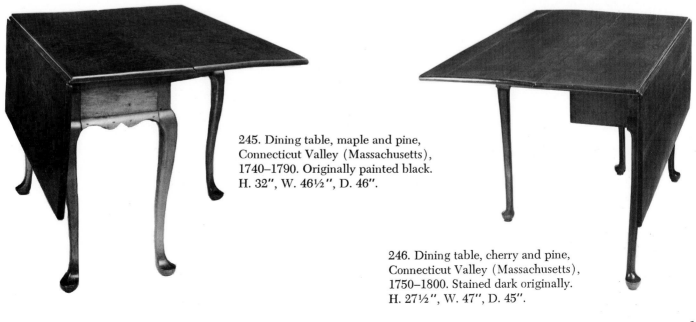

245. Dining table, maple and pine, Connecticut Valley (Massachusetts), 1740–1790. Originally painted black. H. 32″, W. 46½″, D. 46″.

246. Dining table, cherry and pine, Connecticut Valley (Massachusetts), 1750–1800. Stained dark originally. H. 27½″, W. 47″, D. 45″.

247. Breakfast table, walnut with birch and pine, southeastern Massachusetts or Rhode Island, 1730–1760. H. 24″, top 30″ x 32⅜″.

249. Breakfast table, mahogany and pine, eastern Massachusetts, 1730–1770. H. 25½″, top 29″ x 26″.

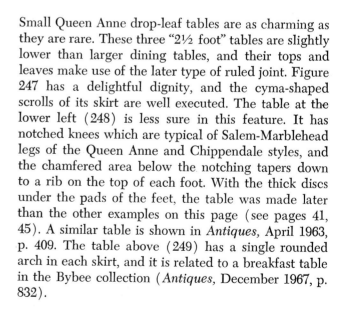

248. Breakfast table, walnut and pine, Essex County, Massachusetts, 1750–1790. H. 26½″, top 31″ x 32½″.

Small Queen Anne drop-leaf tables are as charming as they are rare. These three "2½ foot" tables are slightly lower than larger dining tables, and their tops and leaves make use of the later type of ruled joint. Figure 247 has a delightful dignity, and the cyma-shaped scrolls of its skirt are well executed. The table at the lower left (248) is less sure in this feature. It has notched knees which are typical of Salem-Marblehead legs of the Queen Anne and Chippendale styles, and the chamfered area below the notching tapers down to a rib on the top of each foot. With the thick discs under the pads of the feet, the table was made later than the other examples on this page (see pages 41, 45). A similar table is shown in *Antiques,* April 1963, p. 409. The table above (249) has a single rounded arch in each skirt, and it is related to a breakfast table in the Bybee collection (*Antiques,* December 1967, p. 832).

250. Dining table, walnut and loblolly pine (or pine of the Taeda group) with oak rails, probably Maryland, 1750–1785. H. 28¼″, W. 56¼″, top (opened) 55″.

Large drop-leaf Queen Anne tables are not frequently encountered, and the twelve-sided example above is most unusual. The legs have the heavier feel of furniture made toward the South, and the arched skirt and flanking vertical moldings are similar to those on an oval table at Winterthur considered to be from Virginia (Downs, no. 317). The carved shells on the knees, however, relate more to Maryland work (see William Voss Elder III, *Maryland Queen Anne and Chippendale Furniture of the Eighteenth Century*, Baltimore Museum of Art, 1968, pp. 67–69). This table has details in common with two Maryland tables, one having an octagonal top (Elder, pp. 39–41).

Made to fit in a corner and having a small drawer in the back, the triangular "handkerchief" table at the right has a sliding center leg which supports its top. It is a rare form in American furniture and was owned by the Higginson family of Boston and Deerfield.

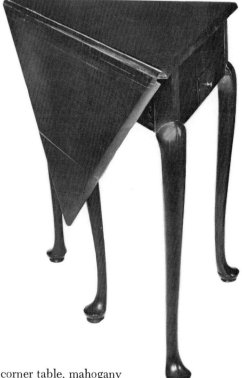

251. Drop-leaf corner table, mahogany and white pine, Boston-Salem area, 1750–1780. H. 27¾″, top 25½″ x 25½″.

252. Dining table, cherry,
mahogany, and pine,
Massachusetts, 1760–1790.
Refinished, mahoganized originally.
H. 27¼″, top 42″ x 40″.
Lucius D. Potter Memorial.

253. Drop-leaf table, mahogany
and pine with whitewood drawer
linings, Massachusetts or Rhode
Island, 1760–1790. Concealed
drawer in one end. H. 27½″,
W. 33″, D. 32½″. Lucius D.
Potter Memorial.

With swept-back talons on its claw feet and a well shaped skirt, the dining table above is made of cherry, an unusual wood for an eastern Massachusetts table. However, in 1772, Nathaniel Ruggles, a Roxbury, Massachusetts cabinetmaker, charged Joseph Barnard of Deerfield £2/18/8 for "a Mehogany Table" and £1/8/0 for "1 Cherry Tree Table" (P.V.M.A. mss.).

The table at the right with a single leaf is a rare form in American furniture. A very similar table has been considered made in Newport (*Antiques*, August 1956, p. 95), but locating this one is not easy. The form is a Boston one, and a table at Winterthur with swept-back talons on its claw feet resembles this one quite closely (Downs, no. 310). This table has cutout corners on the top and whitewood drawer linings, non-Boston features. Its legs and feet appear Newport-like (see Ralph E. Carpenter, Jr., *The Arts and Crafts of Newport Rhode Island 1640–1820*, Newport, 1954, p. 93, no. 65). To compound the matter further, this table has a chalk inscription with "Cabot" on it, and that name should refer to only one city.

254 (above). Pembroke table, mahogany and white pine, Essex County, Massachusetts, 1785–1805. H. 28″, top 35½″ x 31½″.

256 . Table with drawer, cherry and tulip, Connecticut, 1790–1810. Mahoganized. H. 27½″, top 23½″ x 23¾″.

255 (above). Pembroke table, mahogany, oak, and whitewood, probably New London County, Connecticut, 1790–1810. H. 29″, top 29″ x 36″.

Pembroke tables were first mentioned in this country in Philadelphia in 1771 (Downs, no. 312, text). Their leaf supports were wooden brackets hinged to the side frames.

Figure 254 is a typical "quiet" Pembroke table from Massachusetts. Its handsome pierced stretchers relate to late ladder-back Chippendale chairs (see 118, page 65). The serpentine shaping of the top was used by Elijah and Jacob Sanderson of Salem on a Pembroke table (see Montgomery, no. 322). Another table privately owned, nearly identical to this except for slightly tapered legs, was made of cherry and found in Lawrence, Massachusetts.

Figure 255 (left) has heart-shaped piercings in its stretchers, oak rails and wings, and whitewood drawer linings. It is similar to a cherry table from New London (Myers and Mayhew, no. 93) and another with a Norwich, Connecticut, history. A third example is considered to be New York (*Antiques*, January 1966, p. 101). The drawer brass, apparently left over from several generations, is original to the table!

Above (256) is a Pembroke-inspired side table, with pierced stretchers and wavy top.

257a

257. Pembroke table with drawer, cherry and basswood, made by Daniel Clay, Greenfield, Massachusetts, 1805, for Epaphras Sheldon of Deerfield. H. 27¾″, W. 34″, D. 18⅞″. The table cost $5.00 and is the first item listed in the bill (257a, P.V.M.A.)

The best known cabinetmaker of the Deerfield area is Daniel Clay (1770–1848). Born in New London, Connecticut, he was trained there or in Middletown or Windham before coming to Greenfield in 1792. He worked in Greenfield as a cabinetmaker and chairmaker for almost forty years. After business failures, he moved to New York in 1831 and became a druggist. His working dates, 1792–1831, embraced all the styles in vogue during the Federal period, and he advertised a general line of cabinetwares in mahogany and cherry, as well as Windsor chairs, fancy chairs (after 1808), and "common cottage chairs" in 1826. His first advertisement was in the *Greenfield Gazette* in 1794, and his earliest label was also dated in the same year (see page 266. An earlier table can be seen on page 133).

These two Pembroke tables with delicately pierced stretchers are nearly identical though their brasses differ. They are made of cherry and were originally stained dark. Clay's later label, used after 1800, appears below (see *Antiques*, June 1966, pp. 840–841).

For references to Clay, see Peter Rippe, "Greenfield Area Cabinetmakers, 1790–1830," unpublished master's thesis, University of Delaware, 1962; and Julia D. Sophronia Snow, "Daniel Clay, Cabinetmaker of Greenfield," *Antiques*, April 1934, 138–139.

258a

258. Pembroke table with drawer, cherry with white pine and basswood, labeled twice by Daniel Clay, Greenfield Massachusetts, 1800–1810. H. 27¾″, W. 34″, D. 18½″. Gift of Charles E. Brainard. One of the labels is at left (258a). His earlier label appears on the Stevens family clock at Deerfield (see page 266). A third table, practically identical to the two shown here, was owned in the Childs and Arms families of Deerfield (see Jairus B. Barnes and Moselle Taylor Meals, *American Furniture in the Western Reserve 1680–1830*, The Western Reserve Historical Society, Cleveland, 1972, p. 101, no. 108).

259. The large mahogany dining table in the Asa Stebbins house dining room was owned by the Buck family of Hartford, Connecticut, and is a good example of the two and three sectioned tables that were made for Federal period dining rooms. Probably made in Hartford County about 1800, it has oak and pine as secondary woods. The half-round ends have two extra legs that swing out to take two extension leaves. Only one is used in the table as shown. H. 29″, top as shown 62″ x 47⅝″. A detail of the inlay at the top of the leg is at the right (259a). The Simon Willard clock appears on page 262 and the Seymour sideboard on page 246.

259a

260. Simpler than the dining table shown on the preceding page, this cherry table has white pine as its secondary wood and was owned in the Allen family of Deerfield. Made in the Connecticut Valley of Massachusetts, it was stained dark originally. The two sections could have been used as pier tables against walls when the table was not set up. c. 1805. H. 29⅜″, top 90″ x 47½″.

261. Made of white pine with chamfered maple legs, this table retains much of its old blue paint. It was made in New England between 1790 and 1815. Long, lower tables of this type have been called harvest tables in recent times. The gentle curving of the long skirt and the rounded leaves lighten the mass of the table. H. 27¼″, W. 38¼″, D. 81¾″. Gift of Mr. S. W. Peloubet.

262. This elegant Sheraton dining table was made in central or western Massachusetts between 1805 and 1820. Found in Brook-field, Massachusetts, it is made of mahogany and mahogany veneers, with cherry wings and pine underbracing. The bulbous reeded legs have unusual fluted collars near their feet, and the edge of the top is reeded. H. 28½″, W. 37″, D. 86″.

263. Table, tile and maple with pine, probably Norwich, Connecticut, 1735–1770. Painted black. Owned in Leffingwell family. H. 27⅜″, W. 22¼″, D. 17½″.

Queen Anne tables with marble or tile tops are very rare in American furniture. Their practicality is obvious, and the floral wisps on the tiles of the table above seem more suited to the debasements of everyday usage than do the biblical scenes on tile-top tables at the Ford Museum and at Winterthur (Comstock, no. 226; and Downs, no. 350). Figure 263 is smaller than the other two, and it was owned by a descendant of Phillip Leffingwell of the famed Leffingwell Inn in Norwich, Conecticut. A shelf was added later below the top, but this was carefully removed and the table restored to its present state under the watchful eyes of Joseph Downs, the great furniture historian. It

never had any corner brackets at the juncture of its legs and apron. The tapered discs under the pad feet are reminiscent of those found occasionally on Rhode Island Queen Anne feet.

The marble top table below (264) is unusual in that the frame is made entirely of walnut, with no secondary woods at all. The underside of the marble is rough cut, and the molded corners of the top are similar to those on tables now owned in Salem and Marblehead. While a marble table was listed as early as 1665, most are mentioned in Boston inventories from 1740 to 1759, in various rooms of houses (Lyon, pp. 206, 207).

264. Side table, marble and walnut, probably eastern Massachusetts, 1725–1760. Finials on skirt added later. H. 28¼″, W. 37¾″, D. 23″.

265. Side table, marble, mahogany, inlaid with pine and tulipwood, probably Newport, Rhode Island, 1790–1805. H. 29", W. 28", D. 19½".

The side table above (265) is a most unusual Rhode Island form. With a marble top and slides at both ends, it has rather staunch legs—the better to hold the marble—with tapering feet that are often associated with Boston or Salem work. Line inlays are used on the legs and drawer front; and so-called book inlay, or "Inlaid Flutes in Friezes" (Montgomery, p. 324), are used at the top of the legs, with segmented "icicle" inlay, popular in Rhode Island and Connecticut, underneath. The table was owned in the Geivell family

of Newport.

Below are two work tables. Figure 266 is a puzzle. The stringing on the skirt is wide, and while squared cuffs were occasionally used on Rhode Island legs, this form is not usual in New England. Figure 267 is a type of Sheraton work table with splashy birch veneers and scalloped shelves made from Boston to Portsmouth (see Montgomery, no. 393). The bulbous feet on this example are of a type often seen in Salem cabinetmaking in the early nineteenth century.

266 (left). Work table, mahogany and white pine, probably American, 1795–1805. Hinged top; lined inside with blue and white paper. H. 27", W. 24¼", D. 17".

267 (right). Work table, mahogany, birch and white pine, Salem area, 1800–1810. H. 30½", W. 15¾", D. 15¼".

Card and Gaming Tables

268. Card table with drawer,
mahogany and white pine,
Marblehead or Salem,
1750–1785. Top covered with
old green baize. H. 27½",
W. 30", D. 15".

Recreation and diversion have always been a necessity to man, and playing cards had been introduced to England before the fifteenth century. It was not until the very late 1600s that card tables were introduced there (see Edwards, pp. 518–521); and, in the Colonies, it was not until the 1700s that tables made especially for cards and other games became fashionable. The card table above is made in the Queen Anne style, with squared corners on the top made to hold candlesticks. The slight notching on the knees, barely visible in the photograph, reflects its Essex County heritage. The tops of card tables were normally kept closed, except when the table was in use. The blocked shaping of the top and skirt is similar to that on a larger labeled card table at Winterthur made by Benjamin Frothingham of Charlestown (Downs, no. 349).

269. Card table with concealed
drawer, Cuban mahogany and
whitewood, New York, 1765–1785.
H. 27¾″, W. 33½″, D. 16⅜″.
Lucius D. Potter Memorial.

Two sturdy foils to the New England card
tables in the Deerfield collection are these
two claw-foot examples from New York and
Philadelphia. The New Yorker (269) has
the robust quality so often found in furniture of that area. It has a fifth leg which,
when open, reveals a small drawer in the
frame (see *Antiques*, August 1955, p. 107).
The gadrooning on the apron and the
"squared" quality of the claw feet are other
New York characteristics, although it
should be noted that this table is in fact
one of the simpler New York claw-foot card
tables (see Morrison H. Heckscher, "The
New York Serpentine Card Table," *Antiques*, May 1973, pp. 974–983). It is made
of dark Cuban mahogany of considerable
heft.

Both tables have rounded corners for
holding candlesticks. The inside of the top
of 269 is uncovered, while that of 270 is
lined with green baize and has depressions
for gaming wagers, with circles outlined at
the corners for candlesticks. This, too, is a
simpler statement of Philadelphia Chippendale gaming tables, but one which has perfect balance. Its brasses are original.

270. Gaming table with drawer,
mahogany with tulip and pine,
Philadelphia area, 1760–1780.
H. 29⅝″, W. 32⅞″, D. 16⅛″.

271. H. 27½″, W. 34½″, D. 18½″.

271a.

Similar to a card table at Winterthur (Downs, no. 348), this card table is typical of the best Chippendale work in Newport in the 1760s. The serpentine shaping of the apron and top, the flattened leafy scroll carving on the knees, and the use of claw feet in front and pad feet in back are all characteristics of the work of the Townsend and Goddard craftsmen. The front claw feet have undercut—or open—talons that are occasionally seen in Newport work, and the table has many affinities to the great tea table made in 1763 by John Goddard for Jabez Bowen (Downs, no. 373). The top is plain, with no depressions cut out for money pockets or candlesticks. Made of mahogany, the secondary woods include maple and white pine. A detail of the carving on a knee appears at the left (271a). The table was formerly in the collection of Mr. and Mrs. Norvin H. Green of Tuxedo Park, New York (see Parke-Bernet Galleries, Inc., Catalogue 1202, December 1950, no. 504).

272. Card table, mahogany and pine, Newport, Rhode Island, 1780–1790. H. 28⅝″, W. 24⅜″, D. 12¾″.

273. Card table, cherry and white pine, probably Rhode Island, 1785–1805. H. 28″, W. 31¾″, D. 14½″.

274. Card table, mahogany and pine, probably Rhode Island, 1780–1795. H. 28″, W. 33½″, D. 15″.

The square molded-leg card tables on these pages are all in the late Chippendale style. Figure 272 is notable for its extremely small size. Both the front and bottom of the skirt are serpentine; and the shaping of the top, together with the chipped beads on the skirt and edge of the top, are similar to other Newport card tables (see Greenlaw, nos. 140, 141). The card table below (274) has another Newport feature, stop-fluting on the bold legs, but the table has a heavier feel in the shaping of the top, the pierced corner brackets and in overall execution, so that it could have been made by a less tutored craftsman of the Newport school in Rhode Island or even eastern Connecticut. A tea table with many similar details but with the finesse of the best Newport work is shown in Downs, no. 371. The table at the right above (273) is a highly successful, simpler translation in cherry of the other two card tables. While it is always most tempting to think of cherry tables as Connecticut work, this table was found in Bristol, Rhode Island. It recalls a very fine card table made by the little-known cabinetmaker David Poignard of Boston about 1787 (Comstock, no. 364).

Combining strength with bold crispness, the card table at the right (275) is an impressive statement of Connecticut cabinet-making. The bold gadrooning at the bottom of the skirt moors the upper section to the legs with great force, while the intricately carved brackets at the top of the front legs add a delightful and needed aimlessness that breaks up the severity of the strong horoizontal and vertical lines of the table.

The card table below (276) lacks the force of the one above. Nevertheless, it is a good, straightforward table, with a gad-rooned skirt and more conventionally grooved legs. Both tables have the inner edges of their legs chamfered. When the rear leg of 276 is swung out, a drawer is revealed in the frame, with a bit of the frame cut out to clear the brass knob on the drawer. On the underside of the drawer is the signature of Daniel Clay in ink. Since Clay's earliest label is dated 1794 and appears on a Chippendale chest of drawers (see pages 196, 197 and 266), this card table could have been made before his label was printed. The handwriting of the signature is substantiated by other known Clay autographs.

Both tables, like 273 on the opposite page, have been refinished and would have been stained dark to resemble mahogany originally. An unidentified apprentice cabinetmaker's recipe book of 1801 details the means, using red lead and stone yellow ground in water, "to gain the Colour of Cherry wood the appearance of mahogany" (*Bulletin*, the Connecticut Historical Society, January 1943, p. 13).

275. Card table with drawer, cherry and pine, Connecticut, 1785–1810. H. 29½″, W. 36″, D. 17″. Gift of Mr. and Mrs. Ralph E. Carpenter, Jr.

276a. Signature on underside of "secret" drawer of the card table.

276. Card table with secret drawer, cherry, pine, and basswood, made by Daniel Clay, Greenfield, Massachusetts, probably 1792–1794. H. 27¾″, W. 36″, D. 16½″.

277. Circular card table, mahogany and white pine, made by Amzi Chapin, Hartford, c. 1790. On the tops of both rear swing legs appears his impressed mark . H. 28⅝″, W. 37″, D. 18½″.

The collections at Deerfield are especially rich in New England card tables of the early Federal period. The table at the left (277) has a gadrooned skirt, but its molded legs taper slightly and its top is circular. It is marked by Amzi Chapin. He was a younger brother of Aaron Chapin and was born in Springfield, Massachusetts, in 1768. He most likely apprenticed to Aaron, who was working in Hartford by 1783. Amzi then moved west, marrying Hannah Power in Westmoreland, Pennsylvania, in 1800; and he died in Northfield, Ohio, in 1835 (information from Thompson R. Harlow, the Connecticut Historical Society). This table was made for the Loomis family of Bloomfield, Connecticut. A tripod table also exists with Amzi Chapin's mark, which is an unusual furniture stamp, closely resembling a silversmith's touch of the Federal period.

In 1792, the cabinetmakers of Hartford listed four types of card tables in their price list (Lyon, p. 269):

—For a circular Card Table, with carv'd molding, 3 feet long £2 5 0
—Ditto square and plain without drawers 19 0
—Ditto with fluted legs and carved molding 1 16 0
—Ditto with drawer in front 1 19 0

The card table at the left below (278) has distinctive dart inlay on its top edge, with inlaid paterae at the tops of its legs, which have an additional taper at their feet seen often in Boston and Salem work. Benjamin A. Hewitt, in a pioneer study of documented Federal card tables, has compared this table to three documented card tables made by Jacob Forster (1764–1838), a cabinetmaker of Charlestown, Massachusetts. The result is that of nine characteristics that differentiate his work from that of other cabinetmakers, this table has eight and may properly be attributed to him.

On the next page are two card tables with Deerfield histories. Figure 279 was owned by Miss C. Alice Baker in the Frary house and was acquired in Conway, Massachusetts, just west of Deerfield. Figure 280 was owned by the Stebbins family of Deerfield, and its rather bumpkinesque construction is like that of some tables from the Springfield, Massachusetts area of the Connecticut Valley.

278. Circular card table, mahogany with birch, tulip, and white pine, attributed to Jacob Forster, Charlestown, Massachusetts, 1790–1805. H. 29¾″, W. 35⅜″, D. 17½″.

279. Square card table, cherry and white pine, probably Connecticut Valley (Massachusetts), 1790–1810. Found in Conway by C. Alice Baker. H. 29½″, W. 35½″, D. 17¼″.

280. Circular card table, mahogany and pine, possibly Springfield, Massachusetts, 1790–1810. Crude construction. Owned in Stebbins family. H. 28½″, W. 36¼″, D. 18″.

281. The first—and one of the finest—brick dwelling houses in the area was built by Asa Stebbins on the Street between 1799 and 1810. It now contains Historic Deerfield's best Federal furniture. Part of the dining room is shown on page 125 and one of the parlors on page 258. (See J. Peter Spang III, "Brick Architecture in Deerfield, Massachusetts, 1797–1825," *Antiques*, October 1974, pp. 628–633.)

282 . Square card table
with elliptic or bowed front, maple
with birdseye maple and mahogany
veneers and white pine, New
Hampshire, 1795–1815. H. 28½",
W. 36", D. 17¼".

Federal furniture made north and east of
Boston frequently featured startling contrasts between areas of dark and light
woods. The card table above (282) is made
of maple, with compartmented veneers of
rich birdseye maple enframed with borders
of mahogany veneers. Its gently bowed
front was a shape often used in the Granite
State (see Richard H. Randall, Jr., *The
Decorative Arts of New Hampshire, 1725–
1825*, Manchester, The Currier Gallery of
Art, 1964, nos. 53, 55, 60).

At the left is a classic example of a
Salem Federal card table. Stringing, veneers, and inlaid banding on the edges combine a glorious conservative fashion that
typifies the best in Salem furniture. The
slight inward taper of the feet is another
feature of the area. The shape of the top is
often referred to in Salem documents as
"sash-cornered" (see Mabel M. Swan, *Samuel McIntire, Carver and the Sandersons,
Early Salem Cabinetmakers*, Salem, Essex
Institute, 1934, pp. 21, 23, etc.).

283 . Sash-cornered square
card table, mahogany with
mahogany veneers and white pine,
Salem area, 1795–1805. H. 29",
W. 34½", D. 17¼".

284. Circular card table, mahogany, maple and pine, Rhode Island or eastern Massachusetts, 1795–1810. 284a. Details of crossed vine inlay, H. 28″, W. 35½″, D. 17⅜″.

The two circular card tables on this page provide exercises in cautious attribution. The card table at the top (284) is decorated with inlays of a star, ovals, and crossed vines. The vines are similar to those on a server attributed to Thomas Howard, Jr. (1774–1833) of Rhode Island (see Eleanore Bradford Monahon, "Thomas Howard Jr., Providence Cabinetmaker," *Antiques*, June 1965, pp. 702–704). However, one vine does not make too clinging an attribution. The other inlays do not appear in Howard's documented work. He advertised "sash-cornered and eliptic" card tables in the *Providence Gazette* in 1804.

The other table (285) is unusual in that it has script initials (presumably of its unknown owner) inlaid on the apron. It has inward tapering feet and came from the Wheelwright house in Cohasset, Massachusetts. The meandering vine inlay is similar to that used occasionally by Jacob Forster of Charlestown, Massachusetts (see page 134 and Montgomery, no. 287).

285 (below). Circular card table, mahogany and white pine, Boston area, 1790–1805. Initials "WT" in script on apron. H. 28½″, W. 34½″, D. 17½″.

286. H. 28½″, W. 37¾″, D. 18″.

One of the earliest examples of Boston cabinetwork in the Sheraton style is the card table above, made by Adams and Todd in Boston in 1798 or 1799. Samuel Adams and William Todd formed a partnership in 1798 that lasted only briefly, with Todd dying in 1800 (see Richard H. Randall, Jr., "Works of Boston Cabinetmakers, 1795–1825," *Antiques*, April 1962, pp. 412–413). A fragmentary label of the firm is under the top. Made of mahogany with veneers of figured birch and mahogany banding, the table has white pine as secondary wood. The half-lunette inlays on the front and top edges are characteristic of Boston stringing of the period, and the reeding of the legs is accomplished with proficiency and delicacy.

According to early cabinetmakers' price books, the three tables on these pages would have been termed square card tables with half-serpentine ends, serpentine fronts, and ovolo corners (Montgomery, nos. 311–313). The names of John and Thomas Seymour have been associated with the splashy veneers on the front of 287, with two rectangular panels of maple framing a central oval panel of light maple bordered with mahogany, the half-lunette inlay along the edge of the top and apron, the Boston-type feet, and the overall quality of the table. However tempting an attribution to them might be, it must be remembered that other fine craftsmen like Adams and Todd and Elisha Tucker were working in the same idiom in Boston, and that prudence would only condone the placing of this fine table to the town, rather than to the doorstep of a particular craftsman.

Figure 288 (below) bears the stamp of an unknown craftsman, T. Green. The stamp is similar to those used on Windsor chairs, and it appears to be that of a maker rather than an owner. The table has compartmented veneers on its front, but they are not as fancy as those on the other two tables shown here, and the legs have banded turnings rather than reeding. Similar legs appear on a card table at Sturbridge, possibly made by John Wilder of Keene, New Hampshire (*Antiques,* March 1971, p. 348); and four turned bands are also on the legs of a sideboard made by Anson T. Fairchild of Northampton, Massachusetts (*Antiques,* May 1959, p. 461). The inspiration of the table is definitely from eastern Massachusetts, although the thickness of its construction indicates a rural origin for it. Another rural card table inspired by Boston styles was made in 1815 by Samuel S. Noyes of East Sudbury, Massachusetts (Montgomery, no. 310).

287. Card table, mahogany with maple and mahogany veneers and white pine, Boston, 1800–1810. H. 30″, W. 37″, D. 17¾″.

288. Card table, mahogany with birch and mahogany veneers and white pine, probably rural Massachusetts or southern New Hampshire, 1805–1815. Maker's stamp "T. GREEN" (288a). H. 28¾″, W. 35″, D. 17½″.

288a.

139

289. Card table, mahogany with birch veneer and pine, eastern Massachusetts, 1805–1815. One of a pair. H. 29¼", W. 38", D. 18¼".

These three card tables cover a wide gamut of style and quality. The example at the top (289) relates to the high-style Sheraton tables made in Boston, but the handling of the veneers is less sure, as are the simple types of stringing and the straight (rather than bulbous) taper of the reeded legs. The wood enframing the center oval on the apron is unidentified. There are a pair of these tables at Deerfield, and card tables were often made and used as pairs in the Federal period.

The table in the center (290) is a mild disaster, with rather uninspired ovolo corners, ungainly straight, reeded legs, and a drawer that has been remade, with inappropriate brasses. Not every piece of furniture has to be a great one, and this homey table was found by Miss C. Alice Baker in Conway, just west of Deerfield.

The rope-legged card table at the bottom (291) is a sophisticated example for its period. It has the staunch solidity of late Sheraton pieces that stayed in vogue in New England during the heyday of the Empire style. The exaggerated quality of the feet and the rope carving of the legs support a heavy upper section with blocked serpentining on the front, half serpentine sides, and ovolo corners. This table is one of three tables ordered for the newly completed meeting house of the First Church of Deerfield from Boston in 1825. The church records do not reveal the name of the cabinetmaker. The casters at the bottoms of the legs are original to the table.

290. Card table with drawer, cherry and white pine, possibly Conway, Massachusetts, 1810–1835. Brasses replaced, drawer remade. H. 28¾", W. 36", D. 17".

291. Card table, mahogany and mahogany veneer with white pine, Boston, 1825. H. 28½", W. 36", D.17⅝". The First Church of Deerfield.

Tavern and Tea Tables

The term tavern table has been applied to all early, stretcher-base tables that are easily portable and lower than dining tables. They can have a drawer (see page 112), and their tops can be rectangular or oval. The best examples (see 294) have bold turnings, a splay to their legs, cutout skirts with bold curves and reverse curves, and an oval top that contrasts with the usual rectangular stretchers below. While tables of this type have been found in Connecticut, this one is similar to a New Hampshire example (*Antiques*, November 1924, p. 239, no. 2), and the turned legs seem to be earlier versions of those on a table made by Thomas Kidd of Exeter in 1743 (*Antiques*, January 1957, p. 41).

Figure 292 has less definition in its turned legs and has a straight skirt. The trestle-base table at the right (293) is well designed and executed, and early tables of this type have been found in Massachusetts and the Connecticut Valley (see *Antiques*, November 1961, p. 401 for one owned in Greenfield).

293. Table, maple, probably Connecticut Valley, 1700–1740. Black and red paint indicates original graining. H. 28¾", W. 27½", D. 20¼".

292. Table, maple and pine, probably Connecticut, 1720–1780. Originally painted red; painted black later. H. 24¾", W. 29½", D. 19⅜".

294. Table, maple and pine, probably New Hampshire, 1710–1750. Painted black. Splayed legs, deeply scalloped skirt. H. 24½", W. 28¾", D. 19¾".

295. H. 25⅝″, W. 31¾″, D. 26½″.

Rarity and quality do not always coexist in the decorative arts. However, in the realm of the tavern table, the rare Spanish foot table has always been considered the most desirable type for good reason. The motion of the turnings and the cutouts is held and nicely controlled by splayed legs ending in massive carved Spanish feet. In the Deerfield example, even the stretchers, usually plain, have a boldly molded top edge. The base of this table is made of maple, and the pine top is a later replacement. The base has its old Spanish brown paint. These tables were made between 1710 and 1750 in Essex County, Massachusetts, and neighboring Rockingham County, New Hampshire. A similar table, even with a later rectangular top, possibly from Ipswich, Massachusetts, is in the Bayou Bend Collection (Comstock, no. 132 and Warren, no. 23). One from Marblehead is at the Shelburne Museum (*Antiques,* July 1954, p. 7); and an example from the Portsmouth area is at the Old Gaol Museum in York, Maine (Fales, *Painted,* no. 38). The Deerfield table is shown in Wallace Nutting, *Furniture of the Pilgrim Century,* Framingham, Massachusetts, 1924, number 786.

296. Table, maple base and white pine top, New England, 1720–1750. Traces of black stain or paint remain. H. 24″, W. 27″, D. 17½″.

The table above invites comparison to a similar example at the Museum of Fine Arts in Boston (Randall, no. 75). Both tables have molded edges on their rectangular tops and the lower edges of their frames. The turnings of both are rather similar, and they have a transverse support running acros the frame under the center of the top. The Boston table has a maple top, while the Deerfield example has a pine top. Both tables are well executed and have the sophistication of the Queen Anne period.

The table below has a long history of ownership in Isleboro, Maine, a small town on Long Island in Penobscot Bay. Its octagonal top is equally handsome and unusual. While the table has an early look to it at first glance, the turnings of the legs are slightly elongated and of a later period, although the feet are original and definitely of the nineteenth century. It is a successful continuation of an earlier type and is painted a good red of the early 1800s. Under the top is a wooden double hook that was used to hold twine while knitting nets for fish nets and lobster pot heads. With such a piscatorial heritage, the term tavern table would evidently be improper in this case!

297. Table, maple base, oak rails, white pine top, probably Maine, 1810–1835. Painted red. H. 26½″, top 26″ x 25¼″.

298. Table, maple and pine, Connecticut or Rhode Island, 1730–1800. Graining later. H. 25⅝″, W. 37¾″, D. 26½″.

When the cabriole leg was introduced to New England furniture in the second quarter of the eighteenth century, it was often translated into a straight, tapering turned leg with a pad foot that was easier to make. The foot could be either off-set or made in the same turning as the leg itself. These straight legs with so-called button feet were used with rectangular and oval tops that were later survivals of stretcher-base tavern tables. In turn, these newer types could be made in a more elegant manner, with molded tops, as tea tables.

"Button-foot" tables were made throughout New England from the 1730s to the early nineteenth century. Figure 298 has rather thick pad feet, and the quarter ovals at the juncture of the skirt and legs reflect the shape of the top (a similar table is shown in Greenlaw, no. 122). It was repainted in the 1820s with wild, decorative graining in ochre and brown. Figure 299 was also repainted in the nineteenth-century coach-painting tradition, with black paint and gold stripings on the legs. It has a rectangular top with lobed corners, and its feet have flatter pads than 298.

Figure 300 is an exuberant table, with true button feet, made with the legs in a single turning operation. The serpentining of the top and skirts is notable, and the table has a marvelous wiggly quality of motion. It relates to the fine scalloped-top chests made in the Deerfield area (see pages 186–188; a similar table is shown in *Antiques*, December 1932, inside front cover). The table has a good bit of its old brownish-red paint remaining. This color was known as both Spanish brown and Indian red in the eighteenth century, both terms denoting the area from which the earths came that made up the pigments.

299. Table, all maple, probably Connecticut, 1730–1800. Repainted black with gold stripings. H. 25¾″, W. 33″, D. 25½″.

300. Table, maple and pine, Connecticut Valley, 1750–1790. Originally painted Spanish brown. H. 27¼″, W. 33″, D. 21″.

301. Table, all maple, probably Newport area, 1740–1790. Painted black originally. H. 26¼″, W. 35″, D. 26½″.

The tables on this page are called "porringer top" tables in honor of their bold, rounded corners. They were used for various occasional purposes and were made in the Newport area, although related tables are occasionally found in eastern Connecticut or southeastern Massachusetts. This type of table appears in Newport portraits by Samuel King and Gilbert Stuart (see *Antiques,* November 1969, p. 728; and Downs, 301n).

While the tables on this page have straight skirts that are shaped at the junctions of the legs, other porringer tables have scrolled aprons (Downs, no. 301); and a larger maple side table has deep scalloping combined with four cabriole legs ending in long, pointed slipper feet (Downs, no. 352). While refinished, these three tables have traces of their original paints.

Figure 301 has the broad overhang and bold top that characterize these tables. Its feet taper inward to small discs at the base. Similar tables are at Williamsburg (Greenlaw, no. 125), and one made of walnut is at Winterthur (Downs, no. 302).

The table in the center (302) differs from the other two in that it has a molded dish top. This was made by cutting and planing away most of the two boards that form the top, the molded edge almost giving the impression that it was applied. With this molded edge, the table could be considered a tea table. The construction of this table is heavier than the other two, and its feet are bolder. It could have been made in rural Rhode Island or even in eastern Connecticut. Curled maple is used for the top, as it is on 303. The latter is the ultimate of this type of table, with an overhang to the top and corners that as nearly defies gravity as much as it does good taste.

302. Table, all maple, Rhode Island or Connecticut, 1740–1790. Painted red originally. H. 26½″, W. 33″, D. 26¾″.

303. Table, all maple, probably Newport area, 1740–1790. Painted Spanish brown originally. H. 26½″, W. 33¼″, D. 23¾″.

304. Table, all maple, Connecticut Shore, 1730–1790. Stained red. From the Lay Tavern, Westbrook, Connecticut. H. 26½″, W. 33½″, D. 27½″.

305. Tea table, all maple, eastern New England, 1730–1780. Repainted black over original black paint. H. 26½″, W. 30″, D. 22″.

Deerfield has an excellent group of New England Queen Anne style tea tables. Figure 304 (above, left) is in the tavern table tradition, with cabriole legs in place of a stretcher base. The table was used in the Lay Tavern in Westbrook for five generations. Next to it is a handsome rectangular tea table (305). The molded top, which can be either applied or cut from the solid, and which retained the precious tea vessels, is a necessity for a tea table. Deceivingly simple and glorious, this table has well-turned, hocked pad feet

and a plain molded apron. It is the sort of table that could have been japanned originally.

Below are two different tables. Figure 306 has wonderfully exaggerated Spanish feet and is like many tables made in Bermuda (see Bryden B. Hyde, *Bermuda's Antique Furniture and Silver*, Bermuda National Trust, 1971, pp. 91, 99). Bermuda furniture occasionally was brought to New England in the 1700s: a cedar wainscot armchair and dovetailed chest exist with Massachusetts histories.

306. Tea table, base cedar, Bermuda, 1720–1760, top northern white cedar (replaced in nineteenth century). Dark stain. H. 27″, W. 32¾″, D. 20⅝″.

307. Tea table, maple with pine top, Connecticut, 1750–1800. Refinished, originally painted black. Top molding replaced. H. 27⅛″, W. 30¾″, D. 24″.

146

On the opposite page, 307 is a maverick, with flatly arched skirts, scrolls at the sides of the knees, and molded slipper feet. The latter occurring on a table with a Connecticut history is very unusual.

The table at the right (308) is a crisp statement of northern New England Queen Anne, made in a small size with a highly delicate poise. Birch was often used in coastal New Hampshire, and this tea table is similar to a larger one owned by Love Wingate Gookin of North Hampton, New Hampshire (*Antiques,* July 1964, p. 57, no. 5). Figure 309 (below) is a very suave Massachusetts tea table with a tray top and delicate cabriole legs that flow into the wavy skirt. It is similar to another tea table with a drawer (*Antiques,* December 1970, inside front cover) and to one owned by Nathaniel Hawthorne (*Antiques,* November 1930, p. 446).

308. Tea table, birch, maple, and pine, New Hampshire, 1730–1785. Probably mahoganized originally. H. 27″, W. 21¼″, D. 18″.

309. Tea table, maple with cherry skirt, eastern Massachusetts, 1730–1780. Painted black. H. 25¾″, W. 28¼″, D. 21¼″.

310 (right). Tea table, walnut, possibly Hartford County, Connecticut, 1730–1790. H. 28½″, W. 29¾″, D. 18¾″.

311 (below). Tea table, cherry with pine blocks, Connecticut or southeastern Massachusetts, 1730–1790. H. 25⅛″, W. 24″, D. 18″.

The tea tables on these two pages are from Connecticut or the Connecticut Valley. The table below (311) is a highly satisfying example, with a tray top, a good transition from the tops of the legs to the scalloped apron, and cabriole legs with robust pad feet.

Figure 310 (above) has a heavy top molding and delicate cabriole legs and feet. The scalloping on the apron resembles that on a tea table owned in Wethersfield, Connecticut (Luke Vincent Lockwood, *Colonial Furniture in America*, New York, II, 1926, 206, no. 730). This table is made of walnut, an unusual primary wood in Connecticut furniture. An even heavier top molding may be seen on 312 at the right. It almost overpowers the delicate legs which terminate in tiny, raised pads. The feet have a rib on them like those on a drop-leaf table at Deerfield (245, page 119). This same small disc is also found on 313, which has more deftly carved cabriole legs and a less top-heavy feeling. The bold scalloping of the apron adds to the table's stance.

The fine tea table below (314) has excellent balance. The heaviness of the top is relieved by delightfully minute scalloping on the convex apron. It was owned by the Williams and Billings families of Deerfield and was retrieved by the Flynts after it and several other fine pieces with local histories (including the "bird" desk-and-bookcase on pages 242 and 243) were spirited away from a private Deerfield home in 1955.

312. Tea table, cherry, Connecticut Valley (Massachusetts), 1740–1800. H. 29¼″, W. 25″, D. 21″. Lucius D. Potter Memorial.

313. Tea table, cherry top and apron, maple legs, Connecticut Valley, 1740–1800. Originally painted black. H. 26″, W. 27¼″, D. 20¼″.

314. Tea table, cherry, Connecticut Valley, 1740–1800. Owned in Williams and Billings families of Hatfield and Deerfield. One leg restored. Originally mahoganized. H. 26″, W. 26″, D. 16″.

149

315. Tea table, mahogany and white pine, Boston, 1740–1770. Ex coll. Mr. and Mrs. Reginald M. Lewis. H. 27½″, W. 30″, D. 19⅜″.

One of a half-dozen Boston turret-top tea tables known, this table combines rarity and quality most harmoniously. It is a tour de force of the cabinetmaker's ability, with great precision needed for the execution of the top and the scalloped half-round bays. This table has 12 bays, as does a table at Winterthur which also has rococo carving on its knees (Downs, no. 370). The other four have 14 rounded bays, with one at the Boston Museum of Fine Arts having carved knees (Edwin J. Hipkiss, *Eighteenth-Century American Arts*, Boston, 1941, no. 60); while the other three are uncarved, except for the feet (see Randall, no. 81; Comstock, no. 393; and *Antiques*, March 1957, p. 258, no. 17). They all relate to a type of Boston Queen Anne card table with rounded corners (Randall, no. 79; and *Antiques*, March 1968 and April 1974, inside front cover) and to a lobed-top mahogany kettle stand at Deerfield (see page 160). This table was found near Duxbury, Massachusetts, on the coast south of Boston. It is interesting to note that the construction details and even the measurements are identical to the Winterthur table.

In the inventory of Peter Minot of Boston taken in 1757, there is listed "a Mohogony Turn up Table" (Downs, no. 385). This term seems the best for pillar and tripod-base tables with tops that tilt up for easier storage along a wall when not in use. While these could be called tea tables, it should be noted that all the examples shown as such in Edwards' *The Shorter Dictionary of English Furniture* (pp. 528–530) have either galleries or moldings along the edges of the tops to contain the tea or dining equipage. Chippendale does not show this type of table in his designs, but Ince and Mayhew show three tripod-base, plain top tables in *The Universal System of Household Furniture* (London, 1759–1762, plate XIII), calling them "claw tables."

Turn-up tables were made in the Colonies after the mid-1700s, and they were also made in a smaller size as candlestands. The best Chippendale style examples were made in Philadelphia, and those of New England origin tend to be fewer and plainer than the tables made to the south. The tops of these tables could be of various shapes. The two shown here have serpentine tops, which, with round tops, were the most favored in Massachusetts. Figure 316 has pointed pad feet on platforms and a tapering shaft over a flattened urn that was often used in New England. It is made of cherry, a wood used occasionally in Essex County, and the block that joins the tilting top to the pillar is made of maple in both tables. Figure 317 is made of mahogany, the usual wood for Massachusetts turn-up tables. The pillar is less well defined than that of the table above, but the legs have flattened leaf carving on their knees, and the attenuated claw feet are typical of Massachusetts. This table was bought by Miss C. Alice Baker in Gloucester, Massachusetts, early in this century for twenty-five dollars.

316. Table, cherry, Essex County, Massachusetts, 1770–1800. H. 29″, top 33″ x 31¼″.

317. Table, mahogany, Essex County, Massachusetts, 1780–1795. H. 26¾″, top 32″ x 32″.

318. Table, mahogany, with maple block, Massachusetts, 1765–1790.
H. 27″, top 34″ x 34″.

The tables on this page feature a spiral carved urn on their pillars. This feature appears on candlestands, pole screens and tables made in the Boston and Newport areas (see page 162). The Newport urns tend to be fuller and more rounded, with the spirals bolder than those carved in the Boston area. This feature was also used in England occasionally (see *Georgian Furniture*, London, Victoria & Albert Museum, 1951, no.

128). The carved claw feet on the two Massachusetts tables differ in their execution, but both have a sinewy, stretched out quality typical of the area. The two tables below are tea tables, with scooped-out dish tops. Figure 320 resembles a table at the Newport Historical Society with a bird cage supporting the top (Ralph E. Carpenter, Jr., *The Arts and Crafts of Newport Rhode Island 1640–1820*, Newport 1954, no. 78).

319. Tea table, mahogany with maple block, Massachusetts, 1770–1790.
H. 28½″, Diam. (top) 24″.

320. Tea table, mahogany with maple block, Newport, 1770–1790.
H. 26¾″, Diam. (top) 31″.

A handsome serpentine top is the chief adornment of the table at the right (321). The pillar has a tapering shaft on a flattened urn, and the feet are thick at the base. Serpentine-top turn-up tables (usually smaller than this example) have been found in both Connecticut and non-coastal Massachusetts.

In 1792, the cabinetmakers of Hartford issued a list of prices describing their wares. Both Chippendale and Federal styles mingle in the listings, and three types of tea tables are mentioned (Lyon, p. 269):

—For a small Tea Table, top 26 inches
  with a solid cap   £0 19 0
—A plain Tea or Stand Table, top 3 feet
  2 inches with box   1 13 0
—Ditto with turn'd top   1 18 0
—Candle stand   0 10 0

The first was a plain table with a fixed top, the second apparently added a "box" (a bird cage enabling the top to revolve?), while the last featured a turn-up top. The terminology also reveals that tea table and stand table were synonymous.

The lower table (322) is of the deluxe variety above. Its bird cage with shaped balusters, compressed ball at the base of the pillar, and ably carved claw feet are unmistakable Philadelphia influences on a Connecticut piece. It is tempting to summon up the name of Eliphalet Chapin as its maker. Another table attributed to him has these same characteristics expressed differently (*Antiques,* October 1964, p. 466). Connecticut tea tables of this fine quality are most unusual (see also *Antiques,* May 1974, pp. 1110, 1111).

321. Table, all cherry,
Connecticut Valley (possibly
Massachusetts), 1770–1800.
H. 28½ ", top 41" x 41".

322. Tea table, cherry,
Connecticut Valley, 1770–1800.
Ex coll. Mr. and Mrs. Ellerton M. Jetté.
H. 29¼ ", Diam. (top) 36".

323. Tea table, mahogany,
Philadelphia area, 1765–1785.
H. 28¾", Diam. (top) 36½".

On these two pages are examples of the more elaborate tea tables and candlestands of the Middle Colonies. All three have knees with carved decoration, claw feet, bird cages, and tops with scalloped edges now known as piecrust tops. In 1767, Samuel Williams, a Philadelphia joiner, advertised "mahogany and walnut tea table columns" for sale to cabinetmakers; and in 1783 he offered "tea-table ketches," the snaps used to keep the top in place (Alfred Coxe Prime, *The Arts & Crafts in Philadelphia, Maryland and South Carolina 1721–1785*, n.p., the Walpole Society, 1929, pp. 185, 186).

Figure 323 (above) is a handsome table with a staunch fluted shaft and a flattened ball near its base. The shells on the knees are simple, and the table is a modified version of a highly elaborate example in the Karolik collection (Comstock, no. 402). It could have been made in Pennsylvania or New Jersey.

Figure 324 is a fine candlestand, very close in size to an earlier Philadelphia example with less elaboration at Winterthur (Downs, no. 280).

324. Candlestand, mahogany,
Philadelphia area, 1765–1785.
H. 27", Diam. (top) 22".

325. H. 28¼", Diam. (top) 35½".

While a candlestand with some similarities to this handsome tea table has been considered to be New York work, this table has many affinities to the Philadelphia school of cabinetmaking. It is made entirely of mahogany and dates between 1755 and 1780. The top is superbly conceived and is identical to one on a slightly later table at Winterthur, as are the claw feet (Downs, nos. 378, 379). The shell carving on the knees is quite restrained, and the bulbous turnings of the pillar and birdcage resemble those on an unusual curled maple dish-top table made in Pennsylvania (Downs, no. 388).

Stands and Firescreens

A 1649 English manuscript defined a candlestand as a "little round table, set upon one pillar or poste, which in the foote branches itself out into three or four feete or toes . . . for its fast and steddy standing" (Edwards, p. 485). This description applied in the Colonies into the nineteenth century. The candlestand was a popular, versatile small piece of furniture that could be used anywhere. The earliest New England examples frequently had heavy X-bases. Figure 326 (left) has an early T-trestle base combined with an octagonal top of the early eighteenth-century type. The lightness of the base and plain turning of the shaft indicate it was made later. In *The Pine Furniture of Early New England* (no. 80), Russell Hawes Kettell advanced the theory that stands of this sort were weavers' stands.

The walnut candlestand below (327) has a fine Queen Anne base, with cabriole legs and bulbous feet. The ball at the base of the pillar and the dish top appear on other stands from the Philadelphia area (Downs, no. 280). The round bird cage is most unusual. Figure 328 is a quietly elegant New England example, with a dish top and a ridge on each of its simplified snake feet.

326. Stand, maple with pine top, New England, 1720–1800. Repainted red over old red. H. 24", top 17" x 17".

327. Candlestand, walnut, Philadelphia area, 1740–1775. H. 28¼", Diam. (top) 18¾".

328. Candlestand, cherry, Massachusetts or Connecticut, 1760–1800. H. 27", Diam. (top) 15½".

329. Candlestand with drawer, cherry with maple block, pine drawer linings, Connecticut Valley, 1750–1800. H. 25¾", Diam. (top) 18". Lucius D. Potter Memorial.

330. Candlestand with drawer, cherry with white pine drawer, Connecticut Valley, 1785–1805. Old mahoganized finish. H. 24", top 15⅞" x 16⅝".

331. Candlestand, cherry, western Massachusetts, 1805–1815. Owned by Joel and Lucretia Hall originally. H. 25½", top 16⅝" x 15⅞". Gift of Allan Healy.

332 (above). Checkerboard, pine, New England, 1800–1835. Painted blue ground, black squares, ochre stripe. H. 1", top 16½" x 16½".

333 (left). Stand wtih drawer and checkerboard top, maple and pine, southern New England, 1800–1830. Stained red, checkerboard painted in gold and black. H. 26¾", Diam. (top) 18¾".

Candlestands with double-ended drawers that were accessible from either side were popular in the upper Connecticut Valley. A bold baluster turning is featured in the pillar of 329, which also has a dish top. Now refinished, it was originally mahoganized. Figure 330 is a less successful, later version, with an urn in its pillar that indicates the stand was made in the neoclassic style.

The candlestand (and candlesticks) above (331) were owned originally by Joel Hall. He came from Connecticut to East Charlemont, Massachusetts, before 1806 and operated the Hall tavern in this small town on the Mohawk Trail between Greenfield and North Adams (see Isadore P. Taylor, "Memories of Hall Tavern," P.V.M.A. *Proceedings,* VII, 526–532). According to family tradition, this stand stood by Hall's chair and held his bible. The Hall Tavern was given to Deerfield by Mrs. John Healy and her family and was restored by the Flynts (see page 107; and Chamberlain and Flynt, pp. 99–109). A stand with a special purpose is at the left (333).

334. Candlestand, all cherry, Massachusetts or Connecticut, 1780–1805. Originally mahoganized. H. 28″, top 20″ x 19¾″.

335. Candlestand, cherry with ash, maple and mahogany inlay, central Massachusetts, 1795–1820. H. 27″, top 16¼″ x 16¼″.

336. Candlestand, all cherry, Connecticut Valley (probably Massachusetts), 1800–1825. H. 27″, top 17″ x 16½″.

Chippendale in feeling but Federal in execution, 334 (above left) has a top reminiscent of that of a serpentine Massachusetts chest (see Downs, no. 165). The hefty turning of the shaft contradicts the delicacy of the top and base.

The candlestand in the center has an old tag indicating it came from Orange, Massachusetts. Its top combines various inlays on cherry edging, and the "three-quarter" spade feet add to its pleasant feeling of rural Federal cabinetmaking. Figure 336 (right) is a spirited candlestand with exaggerated turnings having knurled decoration and a bold, scalloped top reminiscent of earlier Connecticut Valley furniture (see tea table figure 321, page 153; and the chests of drawers on pages 186–187).

Below, an octagonal-top candlestand peers out from the far corner of a room in the Sheldon-Hawks house before the Flynts' ownership.

337. A room in the Sheldon-Hawks house is shown in the early 1900s in this photograph by W. D. Griffiths of Hollywood. Miss Susan Hawks ran an antique shop in the house, and tags can be seen on some of the furniture. A representative selection of pieces from Deerfield homes is shown, including slatback chairs, chests, a tea table, a candlestand, and the early Deerfield chest shown on page 177, figure 372. P.V.M.A. photograph.

338 (left). Candlestand, all cherry with maple inlay, Connecticut Valley (possibly western New Hampshire), 1790–1815. H. 27¾″, top 20¾″ x 20″.

339 (right). Candlestand, cherry, birch cleat, Connecticut Valley, 1815–1830. Mahoganized originally. Owned by Ashley family of Deerfield. H. 29″, top 25¼″ x 16½″.

Dating from the late Federal period, two of the candlestands on this page have turn-up tops (338, 341), and the other two have fixed tops. Figure 338 was found in New Hampshire, and its sprig inlay is reminiscent of that on two card tables from southeastern New England at Deerfield (page 137). Simple stringing occurs on the incurving "spider" legs.

With a heavy, later urn in the pillar and scrolled legs sprouting from Empire influences, 339 has a double elliptic or cloverleaf top (see Montgomery, no. 387).

Figure 340 (below) has heavy turnings on its pil-lar that relate to the cannonball beds that were so popular in the 1820s and 1830s. The cornucopia-shaped legs have scrolled feet (see Montgomery, no. 376). The candlestand was found in Franklin County, one of four counties in western Massachusetts set off from Hampshire County in 1811. Franklin County included all the northern part of the Connecticut Valley in Massachusetts.

A very suave candlestand with a pineapple-carved pillar topped off by a brass collar, 341 was owned by Miss C. Alice Baker. It has an octagonal top with a molded edge that is repeated on its incurving legs.

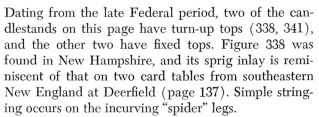

340 (left). Candlestand, cherry and maple, Franklin County, Massachusetts, 1820–1845. Apparently mahoganized originally. H. 29″, top 18¼″ x 16″.

341 (right). Candlestand, mahogany with brass collar, probably Boston area, 1810–1825. H. 28¾″, top 22⅜″ x 16¾″.

342. Kettle stand, all mahogany,
Boston, 1745–1765. H. 17½", top 9".

343. Kettle stand, cherry and
mahogany, central Massachusetts or
Connecticut Valley, 1780–1810.
H. 28", top 11" x 11".
Lucius D. Potter Memorial.

Kettle or urn stands occur more rarely in American furniture than in English. The small example at the left (342) is most important in that its trefoil top relates to the glorious turret-top tea tables that were made in Boston (see page 150). This stand was owned originally by the famous authoress/historian, Mercy Otis Warren (1728–1814) of Plymouth and Milton, Massachusetts. The daughter of Colonel James Otis and Mary Allyne Otis, and sister of the noted orator and patriot James Otis, she was married to James Warren on November 14, 1754. The kettle stand could date from this time.

Mercy Otis Warren was the original owner of a very handsome rounded-corner Queen Anne card table that relates both to this stand and the turret-top tables. It has a needlework top showing hands of cards and flowers, and this was wrought by Mercy herself. It is at Pilgrim Hall in Plymouth (see *Paul Revere's Boston: 1735–1818*, Boston, Museum of Fine Arts, 1975, nos. 94–95; Randall, nos. 79–81; and Warren, no. 57). It is interesting to note that Pilgrim Hall also has a handsome English silver rococo teakettle-on-stand, made by Benjamin Godfrey of London about 1750, that was owned by Mercy Otis Warren's brother, Samuel Allyne Otis. The Deerfield stand is accompanied by a similar copper rococo teakettle-on-stand, which traditionally had been used with this small mahogany stand. The stand itself is a robust example, with rounded pad feet having a ridge on each toe. The urn at the base of the turned pillar is an early appearance of this classical feature.

The tall stand below (343) was once advertised as being possibly of Rhode Island origin (*Antiques*, November 1958, p. 392). However, its base is cherry, and it is similar to that of a candlestand at Winterthur considered to be Connecticut (Montgomery, no. 376) and another candlestand found in the Palmer-Monson area of Massachusetts (*Antiques*, August 1952, p. 139). This urn stand has an early ovoid turning at the base of the pillar (the other two have urns); and the carved tongues on the knees and the rounded feet are more highly developed. The top, possibly a replacement, is mahogany with a scalloped gallery, and the handsome base has wooden threads enabling the top to screw onto it.

344. Corner basin stand, all mahogany, probably made by William Hook, Salem, 1805–1810. H. 40¾″, W. 22½″, D. 16″.

345. Basin stand, pine, New England, 1800–1830. Painted red originally, later white. H. 30½″, top 13¾″ square.

346. Corner basin stand, pine, Connecticut Valley (Massachusetts), 1800–1815. Probably decorated originally. H. 38⅝″, W. 22″, D. 15½″.

In *The Cabinet-Maker and Upholsterer's Guide,* Hepplewhite showed four 1785 designs for "Bason" stands, one of which was "A design for a new one" in the triangular shape for use in a corner (plate 83, left). In *The Cabinet-Maker and Upholsterer's Drawing Book,* Thomas Sheraton showed three "Corner Bason Stands" on plate 42 (1792), the center one providing general inspiration for the outer two above, both of which were owned in Deerfield by Miss C. Alice Baker.

Figure 344 (left) is an elegant basin stand, with rich mahogany veneers on the front and drawer. It is remarkably similar to a basin stand at the Museum of Fine Arts that was part of a set of five pieces made by William Hook of Salem in 1808 or 1809 as a wedding gift for his sister Hannah (Randall, no. 101). The wedding stand made use of satinwood or figured birch

veneers on the front, but the construction of both stands is identical. Mahogany drawer linings and the shaping of both the scalloping on the upper skirt and the outline of the pierced stretchers are the same on both stands.

The basin stand in the center (345) was made to be placed along a wall; and while it is simpler than the other two, the delicate uprights and scalloping of the apron under the top result in a measure of distinction, which is somewhat marred by the cloddish shelf at the base.

A Deerfield piece, the stand at the right (346) was probably owned by the Hoyt family that owned the Old Indian house. Made of pine, it would have been graced with painted decoration originally, but no traces of it remain. Later bracings have been added at the juncture of the stretchers and legs.

347. Fire screen, mahogany and white pine,
Boston, 1765–1785. H. 57″, frame 20¼″ x 16⅛″.

348. Fire screen with hinged shelf, mahogany, probably Salem, 1785–1805. H. 54″, frame 14″ x 12″.

Thomas Sheraton, in *The Cabinet Dictionary* (1803), defined a fire screen as "a piece of furniture used to shelter the face or legs from the fire." American fire screens were made from the 1750s on and are rarely found. Since they can be made up from recycled candlestand bases, they must be examined carefully. The example on the opposite page (347) was made in Boston and has the elongated "rat claw" feet typical of that area. The spiral carved urn appears on Boston candlestands, tea tables, and fire screens (see page 152; Downs, nos. 239–240; and Randall, nos. 110–111). Graceful in form, this screen has a rare carved acorn finial. The needlework picture is one of the "Fishing Lady of Boston Common" examples (see *Antiques*, July and December 1941, pp. 28–31 and 367–369). This screen was owned originally by Parson Thomas Smith of Falmouth and South Windham, Maine, and later by descendants, the Boothbay family of Gorham, Maine.

The 1785 inventory of Joseph Barnard of Deerfield listed "a mahogany Screen and Stand." The screen itself could be made out of wood or could have a picture of needlework, fabric, or wallpaper. The fire screen on this page (348) has a hinged shelf (or "flap") that could be used to hold a candlestick. The picture is embroidered work. The base of the stand has similarities to a fire screen at the Essex Institute (see Comstock, no. 545 and Montgomery, no. 203) and to a candlestand at the Museum of Fine Arts made by Jonathan Gavet of Salem (Randall, no. 106).

The wigstand (249) is intriguing. Under the wooden head is an inscription "For Elijah Williams, Esq." It was owned, according to family tradition, by Major Elijah Williams (1712–1771), an important merchant in Deerfield. While the carved head may represent the Major, the stand itself has a neutrality that defies precise dating.

349. Wig stand, pine, probably Deerfield, 1760–1840. Unfinished. H. 55″, base 10″ square.

III. CASE FURNITURE

350. Ex coll. Mrs. G. C. Bryant. H. 33",
W. 27", D. 17".

The collections at Deerfield are particularly rich in chests and case pieces made in New England. Due to their size and large surface areas, case pieces lend themselves to decoration and a resulting importance that is found in no other types of furniture. In this section, dressing tables (or lowboys) are included with high chests of drawers (pages 206–222). The chest-on-frame with drawer (above) combines rudimentary carving, heavy moldings, and applied split bosses—all early decorative features—with an early base of heavily turned legs and channeled, rectangular stretchers. Made of oak with a hard pine top and with drawer linings and applied bosses of maple, it is similar to an example at the Metropolitan Museum of Art that was made between 1675 and 1705, and which was painted black originally and found in Massachusetts (Fales, *Painted*, no. 5).

Boxes, Chests, and Chests of Drawers

351. Chest, white oak, probably Connecticut, 1640–1680.
H. 23¾", W. 54", D. 23". P.V.M.A., gift of Mrs. Catherine W. Hoyt.

The topless chest (above) is the earliest chest at Deerfield. Made of white oak, which grows on both sides of the Atlantic, it has four arched panels on the carved front which are echoes of those used in chests made in the New Haven area (see Patricia E. Kane, *Furniture of the New Haven Colony: the Seventeenth Century Style*, New Haven Colony Historical Society, 1973, pp. 16–19). The carved stiles, with lunettes at the bottom and arched flutes on the top rail, are similar to those on a chest at the Wadsworth Atheneum (Nutting, I, no. 7). While the carving is not executed with the éclat of the New Haven examples, this chest is an important, early one, owing much to English influences (Edwards, p. 190). It was owned by the Hoyt family in the Old Indian house in Deerfield, and over the years has lost its top and legs—but not its importance. The box below (352), the earliest dated piece of furniture at Deerfield, has simpler, chiseled and punched decoration. These boxes have been called bible boxes, but their use could have been purely secular. The original owners' initials "P/IS" are unidentified.

352. Box, oak with hard pine top and bottom, probably Connecticut Valley, dated 1681.
H. 7½", W. 26", D. 17".

353. Chest with drawers, oak with hard and white pine, Hartford County, Connecticut, 1685–1705. Old red and black paint. H. 40″, W. 48″, D. 21½″. P.V.M.A., gift of M. R. Kenny.

There are over forty recorded so-called sunflower chests—a later misnomer, since stylized Tudor roses and tulips are their distinguishing hallmarks. The carving on them varies, suggesting that more than one joiner could have made them. One documented chest is known, a drawerless one probably made in 1681 by Peter Blin of Wethersfield for Gershom Bulkeley (Kirk, *Connecticut*, no. 15). Other examples may also have been made in the Hartford area. Figure 353 is adorned with old red and black paint (as well as its later accession number), and has an unusual use of white pine in its lid, rather than the hard pine used in most early chests. Figure 354 retains much of its old color and, mercifully, has not been restored. It has the initials "HW" in the center panel in place of the usual roses and was owned in the Bushnell and Dolbear(e) families of Montville and Norwich, Connecticut. It resembles closely another chest at the Metropolitan Museum of Art (Frances Gruber, *The Art of Joinery*, Metropolitan Museum of Art, 1972, fig. 1).

354. Chest with drawers, oak and hard pine, Hartford County, Connecticut, 1685–1705. Traces of red and black paint. Initials HW in center panel. H. 39¾″, W. 46″, D. 21″.

355. Chest with drawers, oak with hard pine drawer bottoms and backs, Hartford County, Connecticut, 1675–1705. Lid replaced. Owned by Sarah Chester Williams (1707–1770), who was from Wethersfield. H. 40″, W. 48″, D. 20″.

More fully developed and better carved than the chests on the previous page, this chest has decoration all over its facade, obviating the need for split spindles. It relates to a chest with a Hartford history at the Connecticut Historical Society and to a "sunflower" cupboard at Yale (Patricia E. Kane, "The Joiners of Seventeenth Century Hartford County," *Bulletin,* the Connecticut Historical Society, July 1970, cover, fig. 2; also Kirk, *Connecticut,* nos. 17, 106). It was owned in the Chester family of Wethersfield and given to Sarah Chester (1707–1770) who married Col. Israel Williams of Hatfield in 1731. (His sister Dorothy married Parson Jonathan Ashley of Deerfield). Possibly this chest was owned originally by Sarah's mother Hannah Talcott (1665–1741), who married Major John Chester in 1686 at Wethersfield. Sarah brought the chest to Hatfield; and after her daughter Jerusha married William Billings, it remained in the Billings family until this century. In 1889, it was rescued from the burning Billings house. (See Judd, p. 603; and Luther, pp. 53–54, which differentiates this chest from another that was probably owned originally by Israel Williams' mother, Christian.) One of the best executed early Connecticut chests known, this chest bridges the gap between the sunflowers of Wethersfield and the more intricately decorated facades of the Hadley-type chests made to the north in the Connecticut Valley.

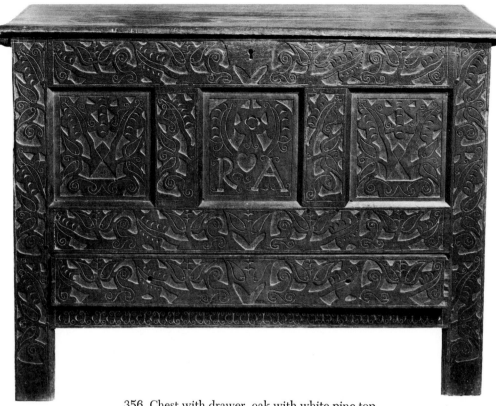

356. Chest with drawer, oak with white pine top, Hadley type, made in Hatfield, Massachusetts, 1695–1702, possibly by John Allis, for his daughter Rebecca. H. 33¾″, W. 47¼″, D. 20½″. P.V.M.A., gift of Chester G. Crafts.

With their lively carving, Hadley chests were made in the Connecticut Valley from Hartford to Deerfield from about 1680 to 1740, their heyday occurring in the early 1700s. The term Hadley chest is a generic name given to case pieces featuring the Hadley motif, a double-petaled tulip and a tilting, stylized oak leaf executed in flat carving, with doodle-like incised scrolls and granulated backgrounds frequently adding variety to the overall effect. They owed much to the early Hartford County chests (see previous page and Luther, pp. 32–37), and became more fully developed in upper valley towns like Northampton, Hadley, and especially Hatfield. They were often painted in red and black, heightening the embroidered quality of their decoration even more.

There are six carved Hadley chests and boxes at Deerfield, and four of them have good histories, which may be of great help in learning more of their makers. The "RA" chest above (Luther, no. 8) was made for Rebecca Allis of Hatfield who was born in 1683 and married Nathaniel Graves in 1702. These chests were made usually for young ladies as hope chests, although a few were made as wedding pieces. Rebecca's father, John Allis, was one of a group of carpenters in Hatfield, and the fact that his four daughters and two wives all owned carved chests makes him a worthy candidate as their maker.

John's son, Ichabod Allis, also was a carpenter, as were Samuel Belding, his son Samuel, Jr., and John Hawks, who worked in Deerfield after leaving Hatfield. Their names, with that of John Pease of Enfield, Connecticut, have been suggested as makers of these chests. However, attributing maker to chest is nebulous at best.

When family histories are not known, genealogical calisthenics have been performed occasionally to link the initials on a chest with its hoped-for original owner. Figure 357 is a case in point (see caption), but its later history is credible. Inverted hearts are in the outer panels, with a six-pointed star in the center one over the "SM" initials. Figure 358 is of interest, since it is an uncarved Hadley. Its construction, with double rows of moldings and beveled panel surrounds, relates it to the carved Hadley chests, however.

(Note: the most recent discussion on Hadley chests is Patricia E. Kane, "The Seventeenth-Century Furniture of the Connecticut Valley: The Hadley Chest Reappraised," in Ian M. G. Quimby (ed.), *Arts of the Anglo-American Community in the Seventeenth Century*, Charlottesville, the University Press of Virginia for the Henry Francis du Pont Winterthur Museum, 1975, pp. 79–122).

357. Chest with drawer, oak with oak top (replaced), probably
Hadley, Massachusetts, 1700–1735. Presumed to have been made for
Sarah Montague, born in 1717, who married John Stanley of
Killingworth, Connecticut. The chest was discovered walled up in the
chimney closet of an old house between Hadley and Amherst when it
was torn down about 1900. One of the workmen purchased it for
twenty-five cents (Luther, no. 57 and pp. 52–53). Later owned by
Tucker/Morse families. H. 34¼″, W. 46½″, D. 20¼″.

358. Chest with drawer, oak with hard pine top and drawer bottom,
uncarved Hadley type, 1695–1735. Refinished; traces remain of old
Spanish brown or Indian red. Original ownership unknown. This chest
was found in a barn loft in Wilmington, Vermont, in 1921. H. 36″,
W. 45″, D. 19½″.

359. Box, oak with pine bottom and lid, Hadley type, 1695–1725. Original black and red paint. Original owner unknown. H. 9¼″, W. 25½″, D. 16″.

Heavy is the best word to characterize the construction of Hadley chests. The framing is most substantial, and even the drawers, which usually have side runners, are hefty. Turned wooden knobs were used for pulls. For woods, oak was the basic primary wood, with lids and drawer linings of pine. Other woods were sometimes used. White pine, the basic secondary wood of northern New England furniture, was used occasionally. For the lids of the chests, another pine was used usually–a much heavier, harder pine, which in this book is called hard pine. This wood has been a bafflement to scholars for years, since it is not easily identifiable. A theory that it is larch or tamarack has been proven incorrect (*Antiques*, December 1926, pp. 466–467). When analyzed under a microscope, this pine has all the characteristics of the loblolly pine of the *taeda* group, a tree native to the southeastern United States, growing only as far north as New Jersey normally. It has been suggested that jack pine (*Pinus banksiana*) could be this wood, but it tends to be riddled with knots, which were sensibly frowned upon in early days. In *The Hadley Chest*, Luther states that this pine is *Pinus rigida,* or pitch pine, a wood

that was once common in the northeast and practically used up and consumed by early settlers (Luther, p. 64). It used to grow in great stands but is now restricted to scraggly growths mostly near the seashore. While soft when fresh cut, the wood becomes very hard as it slowly dries out.

The box above (359) is uninitialed in the central shield but has carved tulips and leaves that ally it to the Hadley type. It is similar to a box initialed "BC" at the Wadsworth Atheneum (Kirk, *Connecticut,* no. 4) which was reproduced by Wallace Nutting in the 1930s (see *Wallace Nutting Final Edition Furniture Catalogue,* Framingham, Massachusetts, 1937, p. 61, no. 901).

The "WA" chest (360; Luther, no. 9) is similar in its decoration to 357 and 361, with slightly less ornate details than 356. It was owned by the Arms family of Deerfield; and since they had no daughters with names beginning with a W, this chest is thought to have been owned by William Arms (1692–1774), who married Rebecca Nash of Hatfield in 1720. Chests bearing male initials are most unusual, but could not they, too, have hopes?

360. Chest with drawer, oak with hard pine top and back with white pine in drawer, Hadley type, 1700–1720. Owned by Arms family of Deerfield, possibly by William Arms (1692–1774). Originally painted red and black. H. 34″, W. 44″, D. 19½″. P.V.M.A., gift of Aaron Arms.

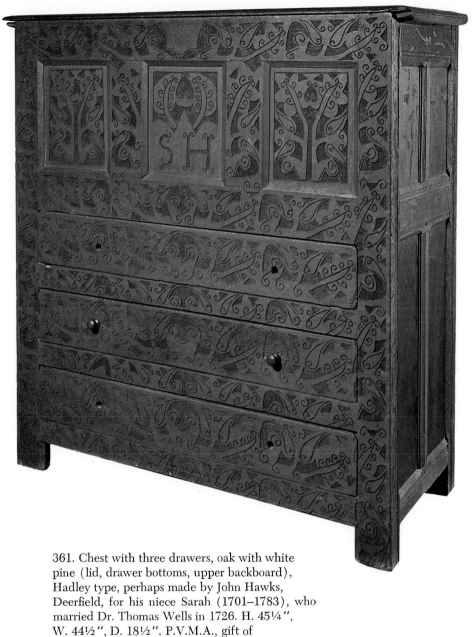

361. Chest with three drawers, oak with white
pine (lid, drawer bottoms, upper backboard),
Hadley type, perhaps made by John Hawks,
Deerfield, for his niece Sarah (1701–1783), who
married Dr. Thomas Wells in 1726. H. 45¼",
W. 44½", D. 18½". P.V.M.A., gift of
George Sheldon.

There are many similarities between the decoration of the chest above and the Arms chest (360),
including the inverted heart in the central panel. The Arms chest also has this feature repeated
near the base of the front stiles. Figure 361 retains much of its old black and red colors and is one
of the few three-drawer Hadley chests known (see Luther, no. 41; Nutting, I, no. 76). This chest
descended in the Hawks and Wells families of Deerfield and was owned originally by Sarah
Hawks. Dating from 1710 to 1726, the chest has been linked to the carpenter-joiner John Hawks
(see the Rev. Clair F. Luther, "John Hawks as a Hadley Chest Maker," P.V.M.A. *Proceedings*,
VIII, 69-70), as has the Arms chest on the preceding page. However, Hawks, who had come to
Deerfield from Hatfield about 1680, retired to live with his daughter in Waterbury, Connecticut,
some time between 1714 and 1721 and may not have been in the area at the time this chest was
made. White pine is the only pine used with oak in this chest.

362. Chest with drawer, oak and hard pine (lid, back, drawer bottom), possibly made by Ichabod Allis for his daughter Abigail (born in 1700, married Nathaniel Smith), Hatfield, Massachusetts, 1710–1720. Later owned by Stebbins family. Red paint with some moldings in black. H. 35½", W. 50⅜", D. 20". P.V.M.A., gift of Moses S. Ward.

The carved decoration on the chest above is confined to the three front panels, with few of the incised, squiggly scrolls that are seen on most Hadley-type chests. This plainer decoration is found on other chests which come from Hatfield, a town that was once a part of Hadley. The plainer carving can extend completely over the front of a chest (Luther, no. 2) and is also found on chests with turned legs (Kirk, *Connecticut*, no. 21). Turned legs also occur on uncarved, painted chests made in Hatfield (page 176). The carved examples were considered by Luther to be the work of John Allis and his son Ichabod. Another chest almost identical to 362 is known, with initials "LA" (Luther, no. 7). This was made for Lydia Allis, the sister of Abigail, who owned the chest above. The initials are placed in the outer panels, rather than in the center. Both girls were the daughters of Ichabod Allis, a joiner-carpenter, and there is a possibility that he made both chests. The combination of carving and heavy moldings on the "AA" chest (Luther, no. 3) is pleasingly unusual. This Hatfield type, together with a small group made in the Northampton area (Fales, *Painted*, no. 17), are the two most recognizable local types of Hadley chests made in the Massachusetts Connecticut Valley.

One can spend hours studying the details of their construction and minute vagaries of their carving, the result usually consisting of a trip to the optometrist rather than the possession of a pat set of theories as to their makers and locales. (For their proper classification, see the article by Patricia E. Kane cited in note on page 168).

363. Chest with drawer (missing), oak with hard pine lid and bottom, upper Connecticut Valley, 1700–1740. Initials "MND" in nails on bottom rail. History unknown; donor lived in Dummerston, Vermont. Another non-Hadley paneled chest (with turned legs) from Deerfield is shown in *Antiques*, September 1959, p. 194, confirming that other types of chests were made in the upper Connecticut Valley. H. 30¼", W. 47", D. 18". P.V.M.A., gift of James A. Reed.

The unadorned, handsome joined chest (364), with four panels on the front, is almost identical to another example in Memorial Hall. Both have histories of use in the Old Indian house and escaping the conflagration of 1704 (see page 32). This chest was given to Miss C. Alice Baker by Mrs. Catherine W. Hoyt. The top and lock are replacements, and Miss Baker scraped the old red paint off the chest on the "yellow day" in September, 1881, when President James A. Garfield, fatally wounded, was being carried to the seashore, where he died on the nineteenth at Elberon, New Jersey. This history shows it was a bad day for both man and chest. This example has similarities to the plain Hadley chest on page 169, figure 358.

Few museums preserve the ordinary, run-of-the-mill, nailed chests of the eighteenth century. They could be decorated in various ways, and some used molded boards to do this (*Antiques,* January 1957, p. 22). Shadow molding is used on 365 (right) to dress up the front of a plain, large chest with two drawers added at the bottom. The shadow molding is similar to that used in earlier architectural interiors (367). This chest was owned by the Hitchcock family of Deerfield; they came up the Valley from Springfield in 1774.

The box below (366) has a field of trellised carving on the front and the initials "ES" under the later lock. It resembles two boxes with fronts entirely carved, one from Connecticut (Nutting, I, no. 147) and the other from Bedford, Massachusetts, in Middlesex County (Kettell, no. 106).

364. Chest, oak with pine, Connecticut Valley (probably Massachusetts), 1685–1705. Originally painted red, refinished in 1881. Owned in Hoyt family; from Old Indian house. H. 30¼", W. 47", D. 18".

365. Chest with drawers, hard pine and white pine, possibly Springfield, Massachusetts, 1700–1770. Painted red. Hitchcock family. H. 37", W. 51", D. 19½". P.V.M.A., gift of Nathaniel Hitchcock.

366 (right). Box, hard pine with white pine bottom, Massachusetts or Connecticut, 1680–1720. Refinished. H. 8½", W. 21½", D. 15¾".

367 (left). Detail of shadow-molded board from interior of the Old Indian house, built for John Sheldon in Deerfield in 1698.

173

368. Chest of drawers, oak and tulip, with pine, chestnut and whitewood.
Guilford-Saybrook area, Connecticut, 1700–1720. Feet restored.
Paint original. H. 43½″, W. 44½″, D. 19½″.

Two fine examples of the earliest types of painted American decorated chests are shown on these two pages. They have no carving, and no split spindles or bosses, since they were made to be decorated. The chest above is one of a group of case pieces featuring roses, thistles, fleurs-de-lys, and urns of flowers in their decoration, frequently with large tulips or birds on their paneled ends. This chest of drawers has a black ground, with ochre, red, yellow, green, black, and white colors also used. It is rather sophisticated, and the piece itself is an early example of a full-fledged chest of drawers. It is similar to another at the Wadsworth Atheneum (Fales, *Painted*, nos. 22, 22a). Boxes, chests, chests with drawers, and high chests were produced with this type of painted decoration. Charles Gillam of Saybrook, a joiner who died in 1727, may have been the maker of some of these (see William L. Warren, "Were the Guilford Painted Chests Made in Saybrook?" *Bulletin*, the Connecticut Historical Society, January 1958, pp. 1–10; and Fales, *Painted*, pp. 24–31 and notes). These Guilford/Saybrook chests constantly rank high in their painted decoration.

369. Chest with drawers, oak, white pine lid, hard pine back
and drawer linings, Hadley area, Massachusetts, 1695–1720. Old paint.
H. 47″, W. 45″, D. 19½″. P.V.M.A., gift of George Sheldon.

The SW chest of drawers (above) is one of a handful of case pieces with highly spirited painted decoration that were probably made in the Hadley area of the Massachusetts Connecticut Valley. Several chests and a press cupboard exist (Fales, *Painted,* pp. 22, 23). A chest from Hadley similar to this one, but unfortunately completely shorn of all its paint, has a pathetic jay-bird quality (*Antiques,* September 1929, p. 202).

The ground color is now cream but it was undoubtedly white lead that has darkened over the years. The decoration, consisting of stylized vines and a variety of doodlish geometrical shapes, is painted in shades of blues and reds, as well as yellow, black, and white. The dart-board motif on the outer panels is accompanied by inverted hearts on the stiles, carrying on a feature of the carved Hadley chests. Bought by George Sheldon from Jonathan A. Saxton about 1870, this chest was once thought to have been owned originally by Susanna White of the *Mayflower* (Sheldon, *Guide,* p. 66). The drawers have single heavy dovetails at each corner with the early type of side runners.

370. Chest with drawers, hard pine and oak, Hadley to Deerfield area, Massachusetts, 1700–1725. Original paint; brasses replaced. H. 47″, W. 48″, D. 18¼″.
Gift of William W. Newton and Mrs. Benjamin Childs in memory of Mrs. Herbert Newton.

Related to the SW chest on the previous page and the three chests on the next page, this chest is an important recent addition to the Deerfield collections. Painted on a black ground, the decoration (mostly in red and white) is made up of geometric forms including diamonds, circles, triangles, and scrolls. The initials "KK" on the upper drawer cannot be traced back to an earlier owner at this time. The construction of the legs is interesting; they are continuations of the square stiles which are set inside the junctures of the front, sides, and back. Normally early stiles are exposed at the corners of a case piece, but in this chest they are hidden. On the so-called Deerfield chests on the next page, they are visible but nearly hidden by moldings and paint. Turned legs that are continuations of the stiles are occasionally found in Hadley chests from the Hatfield, Massachusetts area; and one of the polychrome chests from the Hadley area, at Winterthur, also has this feature (Fales, *Painted*, no. 20). Since these towns are within an area not more than fifteen miles south of Deerfield in the Connecticut Valley, it is logical that they would all share certain common characteristics of furniture styles and techniques.

371. Chest with drawers, hard pine and maple, possibly made by John Hawks, Deerfield, 1700–1715. Refinished. H. 45¼″, W. 38″, D. 18¼″.

372. Chest with drawers, hard pine and maple, Deerfield type, 1700–1720. Refinished. H. 54½″, W. 40¾″, D. 19¾″.

These Deerfield chests appear to have been inspired by molded chests with turned legs and sides bearing fielded panels that were made in the Hatfield area (Kirk, *Early*, no. 193; and *Antiques*, February 1944, p. 74). The Deerfield versions have plainer sides with moldings and no fielded panels, and their legs are often turned less effectively. There is a possibility that John Hawks, the joiner-carpenter believed to be a maker of carved Hadley chests, made this plainer type also. Of the six chests associated with his name in the Rev. Clair F. Luther's paper, "John Hawks as a Hadley Chest Maker" (P.V.M.A., *Proceedings*, VIII, 63–74), the chest above (371) presents the best chance of being made by him. On the inner lid are inscriptions indicating that the chest was owned by Sarah Mattoon. She was a neice of John Hawks and was born in 1687. In 1711, she married Zechariah Field; and this date, which ties in with Hawks' working dates in Deerfield, could be that of the chest. Finding an early joiner in an area where existing examples have been located can be an exercise in walking on the lily pads of attribution, but the possibility is a strong one in this case. The Deerfield chests are made of maple and pine, and details of construction can vary, suggesting more than one hand at work. They were all painted (or even decorated) originally, and traces of old red can be found on 371 and 372. Examples at the Petersham (Massachusetts) Historical Society and Yale have nineteenth-century decorative graining, while another, privately owned, has graining in red and black of the eighteenth century.

373. Chest of drawers, hard pine and maple, Deerfield type, 1700–1720. Refinished. Compare *Nutting*, I, no. 241. H. 45¼″, W. 40⅜″, D. 22″.

177

374. Chest of drawers, oak and pine, Boston area, 1690–1710. Traces of old black and red paint. Brackets above feet probably added later. H. 37″, W. 38½″, D. 20½″.

The handsome chest above (374) has bold geometric panels on its drawers and heavily molded side panels. It is one of a group of chests made in the Boston area around the turn of the century. The side panels and fronts of the drawers are made of pine, while the framing of the ends, the stiles, and the side-runner drawers are of oak. The chest was painted with black and red paint originally and could even have been decorated. A walnut-grained example is at The Brooklyn Museum (*Johnson Wax Album of American Furniture Classics,* Marvin D. Schwartz, compiler, Racine, 1967, pp. 20, 21). Another with decorative painting is at The Metropolitan Museum of Art (*An-tiques,* February 1952, p. 165); while two others with plain painting are very similar to the Deerfield chest (Kettell, no. 34; *Antiques,* February 1963, p. 164). The brasses are original and, with the exception of some work at the base, the chest has retained its original feeling of strength.

While painted graining could attempt to emulate finer woods, the woods themselves were king. Walnut became the elegant wood of the first half of the eighteenth century; and the small case below, used perhaps as a jewel box or receptacle for mementos, is finished with highly patterned veneers of black walnut framed with walnut herringbone inlays.

375. Small case with nine drawers, walnut veneers on white pine, Boston, 1700–1730. Original brasses; one rear walnut ball foot restored. Owned by Whitcomb family of Massachusetts and used by Colonel Asa Whitcomb (1719–1804), who fought at the Battle of Bunker Hill. H. 17″, W. 16″, D. 12⅛″.

376. Chest with drawer, oak and pine, probably eastern Massachusetts, 1690–1720. Red ground with decoration in black. Initials "SN." H. 30½", W. 44½", D. 18¾".

A slightly simplified cousin of the paneled front chests-on-frame made in eastern Massachusetts (Nutting, I, nos. 213, 215), the chest above (376) has charming black decoration with pine trees and birds on the front panels and black curlicues and moldings elsewhere, all painted on a red ground that has practically disappeared. The black paint has been restored, and the name of the original owner, "SN," is not known. All of the panels and lid are of pine, and the drawer has side runners and is nailed together (not dovetailed). Whether or not the ball feet are original is hard to say, but a similar chest (lacking its original drawer) at the Wadsworth Atheneum with similar decoration has such feet (Nutting, I, no. 53).

The chest below is fascinating, since it is an old chest that has been altered considerably. The moldings have been changed, and even the front panels have been reworked. It was owned by James L. Little

of Brookline, Massachusetts. He was collecting early furniture by the 1870s and was an accomplished amateur joiner. Both he and his brother, David Mason Little of Salem, enjoyed fixing up and "reviving" (James' term) old pieces of furniture. They had home workshops equipped with lathes, band saws, and other tools. Of significance is the fact that they were interested in early furniture before the heyday of the Colonial revival. They handled "pieces with varying, perhaps, success, but with what they must have thought sympathetic treatment, entirely for their own recreation" (letter from a son of David Mason Little, June 19, 1973). James Little married a descendant of the Revere family; and after their daughter Laura Revere Little died, this chest and other pieces were sold at auction with the Revere name featured. Today, the importance of this chest lies in its early dates—both of manufacture and of revival.

377. Chest with drawer, red oak, white pine and pine, Boston or Salem, 1690–1710; restored and "revived" by James Little, Brookline, Massachusetts, late nineteenth century. See text above. H. 20¼", W. 29⅜", D. 17⅝".

378. Chest with drawers, white pine with maple bracings and feet, Massachusetts, 1700–1750. Painted red, with black moldings and feet. H. 37″, W. 38¼″, D. 19⅜″.

379. Chest of drawers, white pine and oak, southeastern Massachusetts, 1700–1750. Painted graining on front. H. 33½″, W. 27½″, D. 16½″. Lucius D. Potter Memorial.

The two chests on this page are interesting to compare. The larger one (378) has a lift top with cotter pin hinges, a storage area, and two drawers below. Single-arch moldings make up the drawer divisions on the front, simulating two drawers in the chest area at the top. The chest has its original tear-drop brasses and escutcheons, except for two pulls that are missing. Found in eastern Massachusetts, the chest retains its old red color, with the moldings and feet painted black. The rear legs are inset and square, and not visible from the front.

Below is a chest of drawers of small size. It is grained, but the years have altered the original appearance of the paint considerably. Double-arch moldings are used on the faces of the drawer dividers; both these and the bolder single-arch moldings are found on ball foot chests. The feet have discs below the balls that taper inward slightly. These are sometimes called turnip feet, a relatively modern term. While the engraved bail-handled brasses are old and appropriate, they are not original to the chest. Frequently, small size case pieces can be lacking in proper proportion, but this chest has a good sense of scale, as well as a crisp, upstanding feeling. It was owned in Nantucket, according to a label pasted inside the right-hand upper drawer, by Micajah Coffin in 1740 and exhibited at a show of Nantucket heirlooms at the Charles G. Coffin mansion in 1935. Whether the chest was made on the island or on the mainland is undetermined.

380. This chest with drawers is one of the few known American examples with carved Spanish feet. Made of pine in Connecticut between 1720 and 1785, it retains its original tear-drop brasses and red paint. Three rows of simulated drawers, separated by single-arch moldings, are over two real drawers. The chest is in excellent condition, with only the edge moldings of the top missing. Formerly owned by Mr. and Mrs. Arthur G. Camp, the chest was illustrated in their home in *Antiques*, December 1943, p. 290. H. 42⅜″, W. 38½″, D. 17⅛″.

381. Chest with drawer, white pine, probably
Essex County, Massachusetts, 1710–1760.
Original painted decoration. H. 40⅜″, W. 43⅜″,
D. 19¼″.

382. Chest with drawer, pine, Milford,
Connecticut, area, 1710–1760. Original paint.
H. 37½″, W. 39½″, D. 16″. P.V.M.A., gift of
Henry Shepherd.

383. Chest with drawer, pine, eastern New England, 1720–1780. Original painted decoration in black and red. H. 30¼", W. 46½", D. 17".

On these pages are three decorated chests of the eighteenth century that make use of the brown and red earthen pigments that were available and popular at the time. Black (from lampblack) and white lead, the basic material in which the other pigments were most often ground, were also used.

On the opposite page, 381 has three simulated drawers over a real drawer (the brasses are later). The decoration consists of leaves and abstract rounded forms in vermillion and white, with flowers on the top and bottom "drawers." A small group of chests and one high chest of drawers are known with similar decoration, some of them also having buildings or birds in the decoration (Fales, *Painted*, pp. 36–38). Two of these were found in the Georgetown-Andover area of interior Essex County. Their samplerlike decoration could have been inspired by textiles and high-style, urban japanned furniture. This chest was once owned by William W. Wood, III (*Antiques*, November 1936, p. 206).

The chest below (382, opposite) has no simulated drawers or single-arch moldings. The real drawer is raised up from the base, and the bottom molding becomes a red stripe along the ends of the chest. In the P.V.M.A. *Catalogue*, it was referred to as a "Lily chest . . . An old and odd affair" (p. 138). Its donor's family was from Connecticut, and other chests with similar decoration have been found with Milford, Connecticut, histories (Kirk, *Connecticut*, no. 49). A one-drawer chest from the Scofield house is at the Darien Historical Society, and another, privately owned, had a Woodbury, Connecticut, history. All these point to Milford as their original home base.

The chest on this page (383) is simply constructed, with no moldings on the body and simple "boot-jack" ends forming the legs. Indian red and black are the only colors used, and the decoration is not well unified, with flowers on the upper section, geometrics on the drawer front, and squiggly trees on the ends. Not every early decorated chest was painted by a professional, and this homey example shows how even the simplest piece could be transformed into something a bit special through paint. It was found in southeastern Massachusetts.

384. H. (overall) 71¼″, W. 41″, D. 20¾″.

High chests and chests with stepped tops were made occasionally in eighteenth-century Connecticut (see Edith Gaines, "The Step-top Highboy," *Antiques*, October 1957, pp. 332–334). This chest is made of maple and pine, and atop its Wagnerian seven-drawer facade is a stepped-top case with drawers that was made to slide on the top of the chest in grooves. The carved fan at the base is the only decoration on the chest, and its paint, though original, has been cleaned when later decoration was removed from the surface of the chest. It never had brasses or pulls originally, like quite a few other painted chests and tables with drawers that started off life pull-less. Made between 1750 and 1800, this imposing chest was made either in Connecticut or possibly in neighboring New Hampshire (*Antiques*, October 1960, p. 346).

385. Chest with drawers, pine, probably New York, 1720–1770. Painted blue. H. 37″, W. 50¼″, D. 20½″.

Two plain-painted chests are shown on this page. Figure 385 is painted blue, and its fielded panels, bold moldings, and feet relate it to an earlier type of ball-foot chests made on Long Island (*Antiques,* January 1939, pp. 14–15). Since its distinctive shade of blue is seen on other Hudson Valley pieces, the chest could have been made there also.

The blanket chest below (386) is of a neutral type which could have been made anywhere in New England in the eighteenth century. It has its old red paint and double-arch moldings around two real and three simulated drawers, none of which ever had any brasses. An identical blanket chest (figure 577, page 287) which has been refinished and fitted out with new brasses, was given to Miss C. Alice Baker years ago by Miss Electa Mather (1816–1890). Her uncle William Mather was a handyman-housewright-cabinetmaker who came from Lyme, Connecticut, to Whately, Massachusetts (the next town south of Deerfield), in the late 1780s or 1790s. He worked in Whately until about 1825, when he moved to Ontario County, New York. Some of his account books are at both Deerfield and Winterthur (see Philip Zea, "William Mather: A Specialist in Specialties," unpublished Historic Deerfield Fellowship Program paper, 1973). Considering the histories of the two chests, there is a possibility that both could have been made by Mather.

386. Chest with drawers, white pine, possibly made by William Mather, Whately, Massachusetts, 1790–1805. Old red paint. H. 45″, W. 37¾″, D. 18½″.

387. One of the most pleasing and well proportioned case pieces at Deerfield, this chest-on-frame was traditionally a gift of David Hoyt (1772–1814) to his daughter Mary for her wedding to Dr. William Stoddard Williams of Deerfield in 1786. It is made of cherry with white pine and was probably manufactured locally. A detail of the scalloped top is shown on the next page (387a). A related chest-on-frame is shown in *Antiques,* January 1961, p. 52; and two dressing tables with the same shaped top are at Winterthur (Downs, no. 327) and at Deerfield (see page 219). Above the chest is a portrait of its original owner, Mary Hoyt Williams (1760–1821), painted in 1801 by William Jennys. Dr. Williams paid $24 for portraits of himself and his wife, $2 to Daniel Clay of Greenfield for the frames, and $1.50 to Jacob Wicker for painting and gilding them. Chest: H. 35½″, W. 36″, D. 24″. Portrait: 35″ x 30″.

388. Chest of drawers-on-frame, cherry and white pine,
upper Connecticut Valley (Massachusetts), c.1769.
H. 35¼", W. 39½", D. 23⅜". P.V.M.A., gift of George Sheldon.

Scalloped-top chests, dressing tables, and tea tables are among the most exciting furniture found in the Connecticut Valley; and many of these pieces were made in the area including Northampton, Hatfield, and Deerfield. More than one maker was responsible for them, since they vary considerably in construction, and they were made over a rather long period of time, from about 1740 to 1800 (see Michael K. Brown, "A Study of Scalloped Top Furniture from the Connecticut River Valley . . . ," unpublished Historic Deerfield Fellowship Program paper, 1974, pp. 1–63). Among the chests that can be dated are three which were given by David Hoyt to three of his daughters as marriage presents in 1769, 1779, and 1786, according to family tradition. Earliest of these is the example above (388). With the exception of missing knee

387a.

brackets at the juncture of the legs and frame, as well as some missing hardware, the chest is all original, even to its old dark finish, which was not helped by a fire in some of the drawers. The drawers are lined with old newspapers from Boston and Hartford, dated from 1812 to 1815. While this chest is less sophisticated than 387 (opposite), the carved fan on the central, upper drawer is well executed, with oval "eyes" at the ends of the ribs. The second chest, probably made for Mercy Hoyt in 1779, has some similarities in the arrangement of the drawers but is not made on a frame and has molded bracket feet (privately owned; somewhat like the chest in *Antiques*, September 1964, p. 266). The best of the three is 387 (opposite). With splashy brasses, a triple flattened-arch skirt, and delicate, pointed ribbed feet, this chest of drawers-on-frame is the quintessence of cabinetmaking in the Connecticut Valley.

The chest above (389) has a verticality that is accented by the tucked-in quality of the claw feet as opposed to the wide overhang of the top. The shape of the top is much like that of blockfront bureau tables (391). Large brasses on the front and fluted chamfered corners add to the elegance of this small chest. A similar, larger chest of this rare type has molded bracket feet (*Antiques,* November 1957, p. 384).

At the right is a scalloped-top chest that is a watered-down version of those on the previous two pages. Found in or near Deerfield, it was sold in the auction of Miss Susan Hawks' effects over thirty years ago. Its later bail brasses are original; and, in spite of the small cabriole legs with pad feet, the chest was made probably in the Federal period. The pull-out slide between the upper drawer and top is highly unusual. Traces of stain remain that indicate the chest had a dark, mahoganylike finish when it was made. Its lipped drawers are of a type that came in with the Queen Anne style. Both chests on this page look like they could be chests-on-frames, but the feet are attached directly to the bases and are not in separate frames.

389. Chest of drawers, maple with pine, tulip and whitewood, Connecticut, 1765–1800. Mahoganized finish, original brasses. H. 30⅜″, W. 29½″, D. 18½″.

390. Chest of drawers, birch and pine, upper Connecticut Valley, 1790–1805. Originally had mahoganized finish. Original brasses. H. 35¾″, W. 41″, D. 18⅞″.

While blockfront furniture was produced in the Boston area as early as the 1730s, it was during the 1760s and 1770s that the design became more widespread, glowingly localized in Rhode Island, and continuing in Connecticut to the next century. The drawer fronts were usually made from a single, thick piece of wood, although on occasion the concave or convex sections could be applied to save stock.

One of the earliest blockfront forms was the bureau table (391). Used as a dressing table in bedrooms primarily, this form was mentioned in Boston inventories as early as 1739 (see Nancy A. Goyne, "The Bureau Table in America," *Winterthur Portfolio III*, 1967, 25–36). With the rounded blocking of the drawers, the shaped brackets at the base, and the raised arched panel on the recessed door, the entire piece exudes a Queen Anne spirit. The top follows the shaping of the front, and the entire cupboard section slides out. Bureau tables were made in the Boston-Charlestown-Salem area. Other examples have square, blocked drawers (*Antiques*, August, 1970, p. 212). The chest at the right has shallow, rounded blocking, with a shaped central ornament and high feet of a type found in northern Essex County.

391. Bureau table, mahogany and white pine, eastern Massachusetts, 1750–1780. Brasses old but not original, Refinished. H. 30¼", W. 37¾", D. 19½". Lucius D. Potter Memorial.

392. Chest of drawers, mahogany and white pine, possibly Newburyport, Massachusetts, 1765–1795. Brasses replaced; refinished. H. 31¾", W. 36¼", D. 21".

393. Chest of drawers, mahogany with white pine,
eastern Massachusetts, 1760–1790. Brasses replaced.
H. 32″, W. 36″. D. 21¼″. Lucius D. Potter Memorial.

394. Chest of drawers, cherry with white pine,
possibly by Samuel Loomis, Colchester, Connecticut,
1770–1805. Ex colls. A. W. Steel and Mr. and Mrs.
Ellerton M. Jetté. H. 38″, W. 38″, D. 20″.

395. Chest of drawers, mahogany with
white pine, Boston area, 1770–1790.
Brasses original. H. 32″, W. 39″, D. 21″.

The chest at the top of the opposite page (393) has
flattened blocking on its drawers. Its top conforms
with the shaping of the front, as is usual in Massachusetts work. The front brackets have been restored,
but the feet are original—and unusual in that they
combine claw front feet with molded bracket feet at
the rear. The chest was made in the Boston-Charles-
town area.

Below is a chest of drawers (394) of unmistakable Connecticut origin. Made of cherry, it is framed
by rope-carved columns, and the straight edge of the
top and swirling spiral brackets at the molded feet
lend a delightful exaggerated quality to the chest.
Even the oversize brasses contribute to a caricatur-
able, charming feeling. Many of the characteristics of
this chest tie in with those of a double chest and a
desk made by Samuel Loomis of Colchester, Connecticut (Myers and Mayhew, nos. 35, 36, and p. 121).
Loomis (1748–1814) worked in Colchester from 1769
until sometime after 1800 when he moved to Essex,
Connecticut, where he lived until his death. His other

two case pieces have much more carving and importance, but this chest has molded bracket feet which
are better executed.

Among the most unusual types of case pieces
made in the Colonies were the bombé chests and
desks of eastern Massachusetts. With their curved
sides, and occasionally with serpentine fronts, these
pieces put great demands on the abilities of their
makers. Bombé case pieces were made mostly in
Boston, although there is a Salem type that features
a scallop shell at the center of the skirt and brackets
with complicated outlines. A Salem example, owned
by the Osgood and Waters families, is at Winterthur.
(Downs, no. 166). The chest above (395) is from the
Boston area. Almost identical to an example at the
Ford Museum (*Antiques*, February 1958, p. 158, no.
25), this chest is a simpler version of one attributed
to John Cogswell at the Boston Museum of Fine Arts
(Randall, no. 30). The side claws on the feet sweep
back vividly in typical Massachusetts fashion, and the
top has the generous overhang needed with this form.

396. Chest of drawers, mahogany and white pine, Boston area, 1775–1800. Old brasses. H. 32⅜″, W. 35½″, D. 21″.

397. Chest of drawers, mahogany with pine and hard pine blocks, Connecticut, 1790–1805. Original bail handles. Inlay on edge of top. H. 31¾″, W. 37¼″, D. 20⅝″.

The undulations of the serpentine front in a case piece result in one of the most satisfying methods by which a cabinetmaker can demonstrate his ability and create a pleasing work of art at the same time. The chest at the bottom of the opposite page (397) has heavy claw feet, which successfully anchor the motion of the case. This form was produced in all the major cabinetmaking centers, including the Connecticut Valley. The firm of Kneeland and Adams made a handsome serpentine chest with fluted pilasters at the front corners in 1793 (Downs, no. 373); and another example has inlaid corners (*Antiques*, April 1974, p. 671). In 1792, the cabinetmakers of Hartford listed four variations on this type of chest, ranging from a plainer type to one with "columns, claw feet and carv'd mouldings" (Lyon, p. 268).

When the front is reversed so that the ends do not project forward but retreat, this is known as a reverse-serpentine, or "oxbow," front. The two examples at the tops of these pages (396 and 398) are of this type. They lack a bit of the strength of the true serpentine front. Figure 398 has "blocked" ends which continue down to the front knees. Reverse-serpentine chests made in Massachusetts invariably are fitted with large brasses, recalling a 1756 Boston advertisement of a chest "brass'd off in the best Manner" (Dow, p. 115). Several chests of this type exist that were signed by Boston-area cabinetmakers; and a reverse-serpentine front chest at the Connecticut Historical Society, replete with Boston-type swept-back claws on the feet, was made by John I. Wells, who worked in Hartford from 1789 into the nineteenth century (Houghton Bulkeley, *Contributions to Connecticut Cabinetmaking*, Hartford, 1967, frontispiece).

The small box at the right (399) is perched on four claw-and-ball feet and was made in the Federal period. It has stringing on the front and ends, but not the top. It could have been used as a jewel box, since the drawer has a lock. The grain of the top runs fore-and-aft, rather than at right angles to the front, as is usually the case.

398. Chest of drawers, mahogany and white pine, eastern Massachusetts, 1775–1800. Original brasses. Claw front feet, molded bracket rear feet. H. 31¾″, W. 33½″, D. 19½″.

399. Box with drawer, mahogany and white pine, Boston area, 1785–1820. Stringing on drawer and ends. Inlaid escutcheon; initials "LN" (?) on pointed oval underneath. H. 8¼″, W. 12″, D. 13½″.

400. Chest of drawers, cherry and white pine, upper Connecticut Valley, 1780–1810. Refinished; originally mahoganized. Brasses replaced. Owned by Stebbins or Hitchcock families of Deerfield. H. 59½″, W. 38¼″, D. 18¾″.

The tall chest of drawers above has long bracket feet with simple shapings on the skirt often found on furniture in the Deerfield area. The form itself, sometimes with as many as eight banks of drawers, is often found in New Hampshire and is usually considered a northern New England type. The chest was bought by Miss C. Alice Baker in 1891 from Mrs. Maria (Stebbins) Hitchcock. Justin Hitchcock, her husband, was the grandson of another Justin (1752–1822) who constructed a bass viol that is now in the P.V.M.A. collections in Memorial Hall.

Another northern New England form is the simple chest of drawers with straight bracket feet and a bold cornice at the top (401). Curled maple is used on the front of this chest, and the old black paint that remains highlights the figure of the wood. The brasses are engraved and are much earlier. They must have come to the cabinetmaker by inheritance rather than purchase. The top and ends are joined by exposed dovetails located next to the cornice.

The mahogany chest (402) is the work of an accomplished cabinetmaker. The drawers have simple beading, rather than the lipped types of the other two chests shown here. The lid has two end cleats, much in the manner of desk lids. The brasses are original, with two wonderful large carrying handles on the ends. Inside the chest area is a till on one end with a secret drawer and three arched cubbyholes underneath—once again reminiscent of a desk. This chest was owned in the family of Miss Susan Lane, a friend of Miss Baker. While this is a Boston area chest, it is somewhat like a chest bearing the label of William Savery of Philadelphia (*Antiques*, February 1929, p. 137).

401. Chest of drawers, curled maple and maple
with white pine, probably New Hampshire, 1775–1810.
Originally painted black. Original earlier brasses.
H. 44¼″, W. 39″, D. 19″.

402 (below). Chest with drawers, mahogany and
white pine, eastern Massachusetts, 1780–1805.
Original brasses. H. 32½″, W. 40¼″, D. 17¼″.

403. Chest of drawers, cherry and white pine, labeled by Daniel Clay, Greenfield, Massachusetts, c. 1794. Label identical to that on clock on page 266. Brasses original. Refinished. Ex coll. William E. Green. H. 34″, W. 41½″, D. 19¾″. Gift of Mr. and Mrs. William H. Murdoch, Jr.

404. Chest of drawers, cherry and white pine, western Massachusetts, 1800–1825. Original brasses. H. 38″, W. 40¼″, D. 22″.

405. Chest of drawers, or round-front bureau, cherry and whitewood, Connecticut Valley (Massachusetts), 1795–1815. Original brasses. H. 38¼″, W. 40½″, D. 25½″.

406. Chest of drawers, cherry (inlaid) and white pine. Northampton, Massachusetts, area, 1790–1810. Brasses original. Refinished. H. 33½″, W. 40½″, D. 21½″.

The chests of drawers on these two pages represent the shift from the Chippendale to Federal styles in western Massachusetts. A recent acquisition by Historic Deerfield, Inc., is the very handsome reverse-serpentine front chest shown on the opposite page (403). With fluted quarter columns, molded bracket feet, bail brasses and gadrooning along the base, it is mostly Chippendale in feeling. The earliest known chest made by Daniel Clay, it was discovered in Orford, New Hampshire, in the early 1930s (see page 124, references; also shown in color in *Antiques,* January 1973, p. 89). Other Chippendale-style chests are attributed to Clay, and he is known to have made a later example in the Sheraton style about 1816 (*Antiques,* June 1966, pp. 840–841).

The chest at the lower left (404) has a straight front and heavy, well-shaped legs. The center ornament is unusual. The latest feature of the chest is the reeded edge of its top, a nineteenth-century feature as are the double-oval brasses. The drawers still retain the earlier-type lipped edges. Both this chest of drawers and 405 were owned by Miss C. Alice Baker in the Frary house in Deerfield.

Having a bowed front, oval brasses, and drawers with thin strips of cherry edgings—all Federal influences—405 retains bracket feet and fluted quarter columns of an earlier period. The shape of the brackets is similar to the cutouts on ears of Chippendale looking glasses, and there is an inverted heart at the center of the skirt. The chest was originally mahoganized (stained and finished dark).

On this page, the chest above is an example of a lively type made in the Northampton, Massachusetts, area. With serpentine fronts, conforming tops with rounded corners, high molded bracket feet, and wild inlays, these chests bring together Chippendale and Federal influences in a highly individual manner (see *Antiques,* February 1948, p. 110). In addition to the stringing on the drawers and on the edge of the top, there are quarter-fan inlays on the drawer ends and three propeller-like quatrefoils on the ends and center of the top. This chest was retrieved by the Flynts and returned to its native area from Brooklyn, New York, where it had been for some time.

407a

407. Chest of drawers or bureau, mahogany and mahogany veneers with white pine and whitewood, made by Erastus Grant, Westfield, Massachusetts, 1795–1820. Band of stringing around base. Brasses old but not original. H. 34¾", W. 42", D. 20½". Gift of David Stockwell.

A feeling of delicacy and attention to minute detail characterized furniture made in the new classical taste after the Revolution. Chests (which were often called bureaus—Montgomery, pp. 179–180) made use of delicate, outward-flaring French feet (407–409) or, slightly later, turned legs (410). Rounded fronts became highly fashionable, and veneered and inlaid surfaces were used more often than solid woods. Brasses changed in shape, and they could be counterpoints to the veneers (410) and be highly instrumental in the decoration.

The bureau above is of the basic sort, with a straight front and a single strip of banding around the base. It has French feet and veneered surfaces, but its claim to fame is the fact it is labeled by its maker, Erastus Grant (1774–1865) of Westfield, Massachusetts (just west of Springfield). Other furniture by Grant is known, including a distinctive secretary and bureau (see Houghton Bulkeley, "George Belden and Erastus Grant," in *Contributions to Connecticut Cabinetmaking*, Hartford, 1967, pp. 72–81). The label on 407 states: "CABINET FURNITURE/ OF ALL KINDS/ MADE AND SOLD BY/ ERASTUS GRANT/ WESTFIELD, MASS."

On the next page, the bureau at the top (408) is a typical eastern Massachusetts example, using well matched veneers on the drawer fronts and simple lines of banding at the base and edge of the top. The rounded front is reflected in the sweep of the skirt. It was owned by the Fuller family before they moved to Deerfield.

Figure 409 is less urban. Like a movie starlet, this bureau really tries and puts everything out front. The bandings do not continue around the ends of the case, the feet lack the flare of certainty, and the construction is on the heavy side. Its rating, however, should be A for effort.

Figure 410 has everything a good rural piece should have—individuality, spirit, and style. The oval and rectangular panels of inlay splash across the front, the engaged colonettes end in long legs with ball feet, and the smaller details, such as the brasses, banding on the top edge, and shaping of the apron, all add to the snap of the bureau. It relates to the so-called drop-panel furniture of New Hampshire (George Michael, "A Study in Identity: Drop-panel Furniture," *National Antiques Review*, March 1972, pp. 16–33, esp. fig. 46). However, the treatment of the skirt and top banding is like that on a French-footed bureau labeled by Spooner and Fitts of Athol, Massachusetts (see *Antiques*, October 1952, p. 263).

408. Chest of drawers or round-front bureau, mahogany and mahogany veneers on white pine, Boston area, 1790–1805. Bands of stringing around base and edge of top. Brasses original; ivory escutcheons. Owned in Fuller family of Brighton, Massachusetts who came to Deerfield in the 1820s and settled at The Bars. H. 36¾″, W. 41½″, D. 22¾″.

409. Chest of drawers or round-front bureau, mahogany veneered front, cherry sides, with white pine and whitewood, Connecticut Valley (Massachusetts), 1795–1820. Original brasses; inlays at front of base and top, around drawer edges. Probably owned by Sheldon family of Deerfield; sold at Hawks' auction. H. 36¾″, W. 40″, D. 22½″

410. Chest of drawers or elliptic-front bureau, cherry with mahogany, birch and birdseye maple veneers, with white pine, New Hampshire or Massachusetts, 1805–1820. Original acorn brasses with Greek key motif on borders. Similar chest shown in *Antiques,* January 1970, p. 29. See text at left. H. 42½″, W. 40″, D. 21¼″.

411. Chest, pine, probably Connecticut, 1800–1830. Original paint: red ground, black feet and molding, yellow columns, with decoration in yellow, white, and green. H. 25⅝″, W. 50″, D. 21½″.

Many simple six board chests were made of pine in New England in both the 1700s and 1800s. They were all painted originally—with plain paint or with imitative or decorative painting. The two examples on this page are in the latter category. With stylish, flaring French feet and painted columns and urns, the chest above (411) fits right in with the classical revival of the early nineteenth century. The bright red ground is eye-catching, and another identical chest which is privately owned demonstrates that professional decorators usually made more than one piece with the same designs (*Antiques,* June 1957, p. 543).

The later part of the Federal period, from about 1815 through the 1830s, became the great age of painted decoration in American furniture. Frequently, earlier-looking pieces of furniture were still made; and while the two chests on this page appear to be eighteenth-century examples, their construction indicates that they are later. The moldings at the base and on the edge of the lid of 412, for instance, are nineteenth century moldings, and even the straight bracket feet have a squat quality that one would not expect to find in an eighteenth-century example. The chest is dovetailed, and it ties in with sea chests which were widely made after 1815 throughout coastal New England. The tulips in the decoration are echoes of those on the chests made earlier in the Milford, Connecticut, area (see page 182). The circle in the middle of the front is not quite centered, and the painted decoration is more naive than that on the other chest, indicating that this example could be the work of an amateur painter.

412. Chest, white pine, probably Connecticut, 1800–1835. Original paint: blue-green ground, with decoration in white and red. Initials "MM." H. 21″, W. 43″, D. 16½″.

413, 414. The two most used types of
painted wall decoration—graining and
stenciling—can be seen in these two
Deerfield interiors. The south chamber
of the Dwight-Barnard house (413) has
cedar graining on its fireplace wall. This
two-toned imitative painting was a
favorite method of decorating both paneling and furniture before the Revolution.
In the nineteenth century, stenciled decoration, easier to apply, was introduced to
furniture about 1815 (see page 93), and it
was used also on walls. The ballroom of
the Hall Tavern (below, 414) is stenciled
on a yellow ground, with two horsemen
and a willow tree over the mantel. Many
Deerfield area houses have stenciled rooms
(see P.V.M.A. *Proceedings*, VI, 272–279
and VII, 130–133), although not everyone
could afford stenciling (VI, 46). When the
temperance movement swept through Massachusetts in the nineteenth century,
Augustus Hall, grandson of the original
innkeeper Joel Hall (see page 157), was
running the old tavern in East Charlemont.
He became a convert, removed the old lion
sign from the tavern, sold no liquor, and
raised silkworms in this ballroom, filling
it with mulberry leaves.

413

414

416. Box, mahogany, probably New England, 1800–1835. Decoration in green, white, and yellow paint. Lined inside with salmon-colored wallpaper. H. 3⅛″, W. 6″, D. 3½″.

415. Trunk, whitewood, New York state or western Massachusetts, 1825–1850. Ochre ground, decoration in green, brown and red paint. H. 16¼″, W. 34″, D. 18⅜″.

The trunk above (415) has a rich pumpkin ground, with a patera-like motif on the top which becomes more knotty on the ends and front. While trunks of this type have been found in New York state (Fales, *Painted,* p. 212), a similar example at Deerfield in poorer condition came from a house in Conway, Massachusetts, the town just to the west of Deerfield.

The small box (416), made of mahogany and painted, is unusual, although painting on mahogany did occur occasionally. The swag-and-tassel decoration is in the Federal style, as is the diamond-shaped escutcheon and simulated stringing, all done in paint.

The chest below (417) is full of action, with scenes on the front and ends. The colors are mid-century in tone and the number "18" over the door of the house at the end must refer to an address or century (the nineteenth) but not the year 1818. The barn on the front has a slanted sash window of the type often seen in Vermont and northern New England; but the chest was found in Massachusetts (Jean Lipman and Eve Meulendyke, *American Folk Decoration,* New York, 1951, no. 8). The chest has trestle feet to raise it slightly off the floor.

On the next page are two spirited examples of decorative painting of the nineteenth century. These simply made six-board chests of nailed construction were raised far beyond the realm of the ordinary through the simple medium of paint.

417. Chest, white pine, western New England, c. 1850. Pink background, with scenes in green, black, brown, and white. Cows, ram, hunter, and trees on left side. H. 17″, W. 36½″. D. 19″.

418. Chest, pine, New England, 1820–1840. Painting on front in blue-green, pink, and brown on off-white ground. Sides and top grained. One bird sits on flowers in vase. Initials "SM" and two trees at bottom. The decoration on this chest is much like that on fireboards (see Nina Fletcher Little, *American Decorative Wall Painting, 1700–1850*, New York, 1972, pp. 66–76).

419. Chest, white pine, probably Nantucket, Massachusetts, 1820–1840. Indian red ground, with bird at left in black, white, pink, and red; bird at right in blue and white paint. Found on Nantucket. H. 17″, W. 24½″, D. 12″.

High Chests and Dressing Tables

420. Japanned furniture was imported to the Colonies by the early eighteenth century, and craftsmen in Boston and New York produced an American version of this art from the early 1700s to the Revolution. Many varied forms were made in Boston, and over a dozen Colonial japanners working there produced chests, high chests, dressing tables, and looking glasses. This high chest of drawers is made of maple and pine, with a black ground bearing built up gesso-like fanciful chinoiserie decoration which is gilt. Made in Boston between 1710 and 1735, this high chest has scenes that are closely spaced, in the manner of the later japanning of the 1730–1760 period usually seen on high chests with cabriole legs (Downs, no. 187). The decoration on this high chest was vastly restored at a later date, a frequent fate of fragile japanning, and extensive restorations were made to the base. In spite of all these vicissitudes, the high chest remains a rare example of a highly prized type of Boston furniture. It was owned by the Swett family. (See Fales, "Boston Japanned Furniture," in *Boston Furniture*, pp. 49–69.) H. 67″, W. 40″, D. 22″.

As comfort increased in upholstered chairs early in the eighteenth century, this new quality became apparent in case furniture also. The chest of drawers was often made on a frame and brought higher for greater accessibility. The frame could also contain one or more drawers. These high chests of drawers were made throughout the Colonies before the Revolution, persisting here long after their popularity had waned in England. Through their development and refinement, they became one of the most pleasing and important forms in all of early American furniture.

The earliest high chests of drawers (421) had four tiers of drawers (the upper one normally with two half drawers) in the upper section on a frame with one long drawer, all surrounded with single-arch moldings, a straight apron, and rounded trumpet-turned legs. The front and side stretchers were flat and could be curved on the front and sides. As the form developed, the trumpet turnings of the legs became more angular and scalloping more widespread on the apron and the stretchers (422, 424). Frequently the shapings of the apron were repeated in those of the stretchers (424).

The high chest of drawers at the right (421) was traditionally owned by Elnathan Chauncey of Durham, Connecticut. Since it has white pine as its secondary wood, it probably came from eastern Massachusetts. With the exception of the legs, it has many similarities to a scrolled-leg high chest made by Edmund Titcomb of Newbury, Massachusetts (*The Antiquarian*, June 1931, p. 15), and to other eastern Massachusetts examples (Albert Sack, *Fine Points of Furniture: Early American*, New York, 1950,

421. High chest of drawers, walnut and white pine, probably eastern Massachusetts, 1695–1720. Original brasses (except on two lower drawers). H. 51¾", W. 40¼", D. 23".

p. 176). It has few similarities in woods and execution to early Connecticut high chests of drawers (Kirk, *Connecticut*, nos. 72–74). Most of the brasses are original, and the heavy molding at the top of the frame is typical of the earliest high chests of drawers.

The tiny high chest at the left (422) has double-arch moldings and an elaborately scrolled apron. It was probably used for storing valuables or jewelry. While its pulls and door have been replaced, its legs and serpentine stretchers with a finial are original. An 1845 inscription indicates that this high chest was owned by Benjamin A. West of Salem. A similar small high chest is shown in Nutting, I, no. 357.

422. Small high chest of drawers, walnut and white pine, eastern Massachusetts, 1700–1735. H. 31⅝", W. 19¼", D. 10¼".

423. Dressing table, maple legs and pine case, Massachusetts, 1710–1735. Restained red; probably painted or grained originally. Brasses old but not original. Owned by Williams-Billings families. H. 29½", W. 35½", D. 21¼".

While the two pieces on this page have good Deerfield histories, they could have been made in the eastern part of the Colony as easily as in the Connecticut Valley area. The dressing table has single-arch moldings and a serpentined-X stretcher, with cutouts on the apron and sides like those on the high chest at the right. Owned by the Williams and Billings families of Hatfield and Deerfield, this dressing table has a red color indicating that it was painted red—or more likely grained—originally. A William and Mary high chest with old graining is at Old Sturbridge Village (Fales, *Painted*, p. 33).

The high chest (424) has traces of black, indicating it was painted black or even japanned when it was made. Graining can be ruled out, since red or brown was the usual base coat of a grained finish. Occasionally Boston japanned high chests with deep bases like this were made; a cabriole-leg example is at the Shelburne Museum (*Antiques*, February 1954, p. 103). This high chest has double-arch moldings and, like the japanned high chest (420), has a drawer behind the torus molding at the top of the upper case. Missing ball turnings above the "trumpets" on the legs indicate they have been repaired and shortened several inches. The names of Eunice and Obadiah Frary, likely grandchildren of Samson Frary who built the Frary house, are inscribed on the bottoms of several of the drawers (see Sheldon, *History*, II, 165–166). Obadiah made clocks in the 1740s and possibly could have made this high chest also.

424. High chest of drawers, pine case with ash legs, Massachusetts, 1700–1745. Originally painted or japanned; traces of black remain. Brasses original. Owned by Frary family. H. 69½", W. 41", D. 22¾".

425. Chest with drawers-on-frame, pine with maple legs, chestnut drawer linings and back of frame, Connecticut or Rhode Island, 1750–1800. Originally painted black. H. 42¾", W. 25½", D. 11½".

426 (below). Double chest of drawers, white pine, Newburyport, Massachusetts, 1700–1745. Painted blue-green (partially restored); one ball foot replaced. Owned by Perkins family. H. 78½", W. 35", D. 17¾".

The two chests on this page were made probably for a doctor or an apothecary. The example above (425) is in the Queen Anne style, with nearly straight legs and pad feet on minute discs, similar to those on a more elaborate chest-on-frame owned by Dr. Reuben Warner of Litchfield, Connecticut—now at Williamsburg (Greenlaw, no. 78). It was painted black (and possibly decorated) originally. The grand chest-on-chest at the right is plain-painted in a warm blue-green. It is made in two sections, with twenty-four small drawers in the upper part and three large drawers below, the upper one slanted to resemble a desk lid and to reduce the bulk of the base. This chest was owned by the Perkins family of Newburyport and came from the State Street home of a descendant.

The best paints were those ground in linseed oil. While buttermilk could have been used after 1800 on occasion, casein paints did not have the permanence of oil-based paints (see Richard M. Candee, "The Rediscovery of Milk-based House Paints and the Myth of 'Brickdust and Buttermilk' Paints," *Old-Time New England*, Winter 1968, pp. 79–81).

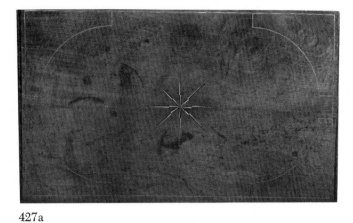

427a 428a

427. H. 30″, W. 35″, D. 20½″.

These two Boston-area dressing tables are representative of the best of the Queen Anne style made there. While 427 is made of solid walnut, 428 makes use of walnut veneers and walnut herringbone inlays on the top and front. Both have white pine as the basic secondary wood, and both were made in the second quarter of the eighteenth century. The so-called star inlay case pieces, which actually feature a compass-type inlay on their fronts, sides, or tops, include dressing tables, chests, high chests, desks, and secretaries (see *Boston Furniture,* nos. 14, 16, 17, 19, 70; Warren, no. 63; and *Antiques,* July 1956, p. 13). Some, like 427, were made of solid walnut, with stringing outlining the drawers, borders, and tops. Carved, gilt shells indicate that carvers and gilders also worked on these pieces. While 427 has no history, the last owners of 428 were members of the Elder and Hoyt families of Boston.

428. H. 32½″, W. 33″, D. 21¼″.

428b. Detail of side.

One of the cabinetmakers working in the "star inlay" style was Ebenezer Hartshorne, who lived in Charlestown between 1721 and 1743 (Richard H. Randall, Jr. and Martha McElman, "Ebenezer Hartshorne, Cabinetmaker," *Antiques*, January 1965, pp. 78–79). While this dressing table (428) has many similarities to a high chest made by Hartshorne in 1739, an attribution is not valid, since the style was a regional one. The legs are heavy at the knees, and the ribbed feet resemble those on the Loring japanned high chest at Winterthur made by John Pimm (Downs, no. 188). The brasses are old replacements and the Herculean gilt drops are original. A matching high chest is in existence—alas, not at Deerfield.

Although the dressing table and high chest on this page do not exactly match, they show that these forms could be made *en suite* in the eighteenth century. Both make lavish use of walnut veneers and herringbone inlays to achieve a rich, decorative surface. While the moldings differ, both pieces have fillets that neatly outline their well shaped aprons. Their lines have the crisp delicacy of New England Queen Anne at its best. The high chest was owned by the Gerrish family of Newbury, Massachusetts, and the extra ridge on the pad feet of both pieces is sometimes found on Queen Anne feet in Essex County. The dressing table was owned in the Paige family. Both of these examples show how important the original engraved brasses were to the overall decorative effect.

On the next page, the dressing table is a classic example of rural Queen Anne line and simplicity. The rounded cutouts of the apron and sides are most pleasing. It was acquired from the Wetherbee family of Meriden, Connecticut, and was probably made in that area of the Connecticut Valley.

429. High chest of drawers, walnut and walnut veneers on white pine, eastern Massachusetts, 1730–1750. Original brasses (one replaced). H. 76″, W. 41″, D. 22½″.

430 (right). Dressing table, walnut and walnut veneers on white pine, eastern Massachusetts, 1730–1750. Original brasses. H. 32½″, W. 33¾″, (W. of case 29″), D. 20¼″.

The "square head" high chests below have Deerfield associations. Figure 432 was purchased by Miss C. Alice Baker. Since she lived in the age of refinishing in the early 1900s, the piece has had most of its black paint removed. The use of curled maple dresses up the facade considerably, although the rather out-of-date brasses were meant for a smaller piece of furniture.

The high chest at the right (433) has delicate legs and a narrow, vertical thrust. The shell on the lower drawer is original, but that at the top is a later "improvement." The high chest was traditionally part of the wedding outfit of Mary Stebbins of Belchertown, Massachusetts, who married Samuel Hindsdale in 1772. A high chest with similar treatment to the skirt was owned in nearby Chicopee Falls (*Antiques*, May 1968, p. 625).

431. Dressing table, cherry and white pine, Connecticut Valley, 1740–1790. Probably mahoganized originally. Original brasses. H. 30¼", W. 32", D. 22".

432. High chest of drawers, maple and white pine, probably Massachusetts or northern New England, 1730–1770. Originally painted black. Original brasses. H. 70", W. 39", D. 22½".

433. High chest of drawers, maple and white pine, Massachusetts, c.1772. Repainted black; red or grained originally. H. 78", W. 38½". D. 21½". P.V.M.A., gift of Fannie and Emily Hinsdale.

434. Dressing table, walnut and white pine, Essex County, Massachusetts, 1750–1790. Original brasses. H. 30½", W. 39¾", D. 20⅛".

The dressing table at the left has a generous three-and-one-half inch overhang to the top, large brasses and notched knees—all typical of Essex County. The use of carved claw feet is unusual in Massachusetts dressing tables.

Graceful, arched bonnet tops, or "scroll heads" as they were called in Hatfield in 1796 (page 286), were introduced to the high chest in the 1730s. Figure 435 has this feature as well as corkscrew finials which were often used in Massachusetts. It was owned in the family of William Dudley, son of Governor Joseph Dudley. William was a well known lawyer who was sent to Canada in 1705 to make arrangements for the return of the Deerfield captives.

435. High chest of drawers, mahogany and white pine, Boston area, 1730–1750. Dudley family. Original brasses. H. 93¾", W. 40¾", D. 21½".

436. High chest of drawers, mahogany and white pine, hard pine, and maple, Newport, 1745–1765. 1765 Marblehead account book pages pasted on back. H. 88", W. 39¼", D. 21½".

437. H. 87½″, W. 39½″, D. 21½″.

The high chest at the left (436) is a suave expression of the Newport school. Made of heavy mahogany, it has pointed slipper feet that were sometimes used in that area, often as foils to the bonnet tops. The finials and plinths have been added. Originally, there would have been a single finial at the top center. This high chest has many similarities to a flat-top example made by Christopher Townsend in Newport in 1748 (*Antiques,* May 1961, pp. 450–451).

With handsome walnut veneers, herringbone bandings, a blocked area in the apron under the lower shell, and intricate cutouts on the inside of the pediment, the high chest above (437) was made in Essex County. It is similar to two with Ipswich, Massachusetts, histories (*Antiques,* October 1950, p. 223; and December 1967, p. 833). White pine is its secondary wood, and it was made between 1730 and 1750. The brasses and lively finials are original.

438. High chest of drawers, cherry
and white pine, Connecticut, 1760–1800.
Ex coll. Mr. and Mrs. Ellerton M. Jetté.
H. 88¼″, W. 42″, D. 22″.

439. High chest of drawers, cherry
with white pine and chestnut, probably
Colchester, Connecticut, c.1781.
H. 84½″, W. 39⅝″, D. 21″.

While the unusual high chest above has been thought to be New London cabinetwork (Kirk, *Connecticut*, no. 89), it was owned in Woodbury, in the western part of the state (*Antiques*, October 1950, pp. 276–277). The two shells are carved in relief rather than intaglio—a rare feature in American furniture. Under the bold bonnet top on the tympanum are two painted birds sitting on an inlaid pendant seesaw. The inlay is birch. The legs do not easily flow into the pad feet and have a ridge running all the way to the tops of the feet. High in individualism, this interesting high chest of drawers has scattered moments of greatness in its execution.

This deep high chest (439), with the desk and bookcase shown on page 240, was owned by Julius and Dorothy (Champion) Deming, who had lived in Colchester, Connecticut, before their marriage in 1781 (see Houghton Bulkeley, *Contributions to Connecticut Cabinet Making*, Hartford, 1967, pp. 16–20). The finials and the swirling petals of the scrolled top are well carved. The pilasters of the upper part are stop-fluted, and the shells are outlined. The base is simpler, with a rounded apron. Ribbing and volutes are naively carved on the knees. The truncated cabriole legs support two claw feet on the front and two pad feet at the rear of the lower chest.

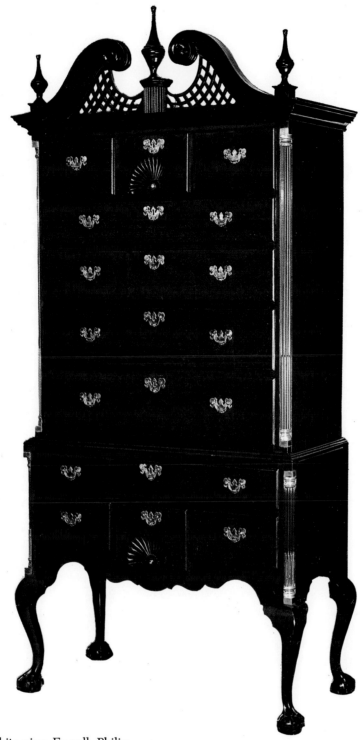

440. Cherry and white pine. Ex coll. Philip
Flayderman. H. 86½″, W. 40¼″, D. 20″.

This high chest of drawers is similar to one in the Garvan Collection at Yale considered to be the work
of Eliphalet Chapin of East Windsor, Connecticut, between 1771 and 1807 (Kirk, *Early*, no. 84). With
decided Philadelphia influences both in mass and in details such as the pierced pediment and outline of the
skirt, high chests of drawers of this type have long been associated with the Chapin name (see Aaron
Marc Stein, "The Chapins and Connecticut Valley Chippendale," *The Antiquarian*, April 1931, pp. 21–24,
62; Kirk, *Connecticut*, no. 93; and *Antiques*, October 1966, pp. 540, 542). This high chest was owned by
Governor Caleb Strong of Northampton along with a companion desk and bookcase (see page 241). The
brass flutes and capitals of the quarter columns may have been added a little later, while the brasses and
slightly Oriental finials are original. The use of the deepest bank of drawers at the top, above normally
graduated drawers, is daring.

441. High chest of drawers, cherry sides, mahogany front with white
pine and maple, probably Colchester-Norwich area, Connecticut, 1775–1795.
Brasses replaced. H. 87¾″, W. 40½″, D. 21″.

441a. Detail of top of 441.

The high chest of drawers (left and detail above) was the first important example of Connecticut cabinetmaking acquired by the Flynts—in 1947. It is a handsome, well balanced high chest. With a mahogany front and cherry sides, the latter wood was obviously finished darker originally. Carved details of all sorts are featured. In addition to the shells, rosettes and fluted pilasters, there is a ribbed type of carving on the knees and feet. Also, a minute, billowy series of scrolls borders the pilasters and is on the bonnet top molding and around the large shells. An area of horizontal fluting beneath the lower shell on the apron attempts to tie together the other flutes on the pilasters and legs. The design and details are well conceived in the best spirit of rural cabinetmaking.

Several other related high chests of drawers exist (see *Antiques*, October 1964, p. 440; Benjamin Ginsburg, "The Barbour Collection of Connecticut Furniture in the Connecticut Historical Society," *Antiques*, May 1974, pp. 1100, 1102; and Myers and Mayhew, no. 40). Whether they were made in Colchester or Norwich is not now known, but they are a most important group of New London County furniture.

The terms highboy and lowboy are relatively recent terms. Merely chest or high chest (of drawers) was used in the 1700s, with table or dressing table indicating the smaller piece.

Since Connecticut furniture is usually so distinctive, there has been a mild mania of attribution for many pieces—right or wrong. The dressing table below (442) once was considered the work of Benjamin Burnham of Colchester (*Antiques*, May 1959, p. 466). This could not be substantiated, and Houghton

Bulkeley felt that Brewster Dayton of Stratford might be its maker. A signed high chest by him exists (*Antiques*, July, 1970, p. 27; and another is shown in Kirk, *Connecticut*, no. 90 as probably Wethersfield). With square bold legs, outlined shell, and vine-carved knees, its appearance outdoes its anonymity.

442. Dressing table, cherry with pine and oak, Connecticut, 1770–1795. Original brasses. H. 31″, W. 35½″, D. 21½″.

443. Double chest of drawers, cherry and white pine, Deerfield area,
c.1800. Refinished; originally mahoganized. Brasses and two finials replaced.
H. 85″, W. 40″, D. 22½″.

As ceilings became higher in the eighteenth century, bonnet tops became more fashionable than flat tops on high chests, double chests and clocks. These were called "scroll heads" (as opposed to the earlier "square heads") in a 1796 price list issued by Hampshire County, Massachusetts, cabinetmakers (page 286). The example opposite, however, must hold some sort of record for the most ascending top in existence. Most of the cabinetmaker's efforts, in fact, centered on the upper section. The finials, which have been likened to pine trees on top of mushrooms, are spirited, as is the treatment of the pediment. Gadrooning which verges on rope carving frames the upper section and runs along the top edges of the lower section. An old inscription states "L. D. Allis, Conway." Lucy DeWolf married John Belding Allis of Ashfield in 1800, Ashfield and Conway being immediately west of Deerfield. This double chest could have been theirs, and the date of their wedding seems logical for the chest. A desk and bookcase at Deerfield was made by a Conway cabinetmaker, Israel Guild (see page 238), but there seems little structural connection between the two pieces. Later, this double chest was acquired by Doctor Edwin Thorn of Deerfield, retrieving each half from a different part of the family. Dr. Thorn, who lived in the Wells-Thorn house, was an amateur cabinetmaker and probably repaired and refinished the whole chest (see page 23).

The two dressing tables on this page are examples of the scallop-top school of the Hatfield-Amherst-Northampton area of the Connecticut Valley (see pages 186 and 187). Figure 444 lost its original brasses and pendant finials in the Victorian period, but it retains its fine top, scalloped skirt, and graceful legs with pad feet on discs. It relates to a dressing table at Winterthur found in Northampton (Downs, no. 327) and to another owned by the Allis family of Hatfield (*Antiques*, February 1958, p. 121), the latter having its old drops and brasses.

Figure 445 is simpler in effect, and its cabriole legs are squared off down to the feet. It was owned by the Billings family of Hatfield, along with a table with drawer that had a very similar scalloped top (*Antiques*, June 1961, p. 539). Another dressing table with a similarly shaped top is shown in *Antiques*, June 1939, page 269.

An interesting sidelight on the branding of furniture is contained in the will of David Hoyt (1722–1814), who gave scallop-top chests to his three daughters (see pages 186, 187). In his will he said, "I give and bequeath to my daughter Mercy, wife of Justin Hitchcock, one case with drawers, branded D.H. and one chest with drawers branded D.H." Owners sometimes branded or stamped their initials or names on furniture in the eighteenth century for easy identification.

444. Dressing table, cherry and white pine, Hatfield, Massachusetts, area, 1750–1800. Brasses replaced; pendants missing; refinished. H. 31¼″, top 39″ x 23½″.

445 (below). Dressing table, cherry and white pine, probably Hatfield, Massachusetts, 1750–1800. Refinished; escutcheon replaced. H. 29″, top 36″ x 24½″.

447 (right). High chest of drawers, cherry and
pine, probably Hartford area, 1765–1800.
Original brasses; probably mahoganized originally. Owned by the Trumbull-Hartshorne families of Hartford and Taunton, Massachusetts,
this high chest features swirled quatrefoils
on two drawers and a smaller one on the
plinth below the finial. A sunburst could
substitute for the latter (Kirk, *Connecticut*,
no. 85). Dressing tables with this effective
decoration are known, and they and the high
chests all use a distinctively shaped skirt
typical of Hartford County (see Kirk,
Connecticut, nos. 84, 158 and 177; and Albert
Sack, *Fine Points of Furniture: Early American*,
New York, 1950, p. 196). The placement
of the upper brasses in line with those of
the base is another feature of this quatrefoil type. H. 86½″, W. 38½″, D. 20½″.

447

446

446 (left). Double chest, cherry and white pine,
Connecticut or western Massachusetts, 1775–
1805. Original brasses; probably mahoganized
originally. This double chest combines a
blockfront base with a straight top framed by
reeded pilasters having carved capitals. The
rosettes, shells, and legs are also carved with
varying amounts of success. The claw feet have
an unusual overhang above at the knees, with
carved and punched decoration. This double
chest relates more in feeling than in detail to
another, formerly at the Metropolitan Museum of
Art, from the Trumbull family of Norwich,
Connecticut (Myers and Mayhew, no. 48).
The Deerfield double chest was found by the
Potters in Bernardston, Massachusetts—just north
of Deerfield. The base and top were owned by
two different branches of a family. Reunited,
this double chest bows to New London County
for its inspiration, if not its execution. H. 90½″,
W. 43″, D. 21″. Lucius D. Potter Memorial.

448

448 (left). High chest of drawers, cherry and white pine, probably Deerfield area, c.1775. Bonnet top restored; two original finials survive; some brasses replaced. While this high chest has undergone considerable restoration to remedy its "beheaded" condition, it is important to Deerfield, since it was owned by Dr. Elihu Ashley (1750–1817), one of Parson Ashley's sons who married Mary Cook Williams in 1775 (see Amelia F. Miller, *The Reverend Jonathan Ashley House,* Deerfield, 1962, pp. 42–51). The carved fans and quarter columns of the upper case add decoration to an otherwise plain form. (See N. Theresa Mellen, "Evolution of the Bureau as Illustrated by the Chests in Memorial Hall," P.V.M.A. *Proceedings,* VI, 290). H. 89½", W. 42¾", D. 21". P.V.M.A., gift of Mrs. Philena D. Trask.

449 (right). Double chest, maple and white pine, New Hampshire, 1785–1805. Finials and brasses replaced; refinished, originally painted dark red. The two fans on the upper and lower drawers are typical of those executed in New Hampshire (*Antiques,* June 1959, p. 539; and Charles S. Parsons, *The Dunlaps & Their Furniture,* The Currier Gallery of Art, Manchester, New Hampshire, 1970, no. 20). The top and bottom drawers are actually single but made to look like three smaller drawers, and the top two drawers of the base are actually a single, very deep one. A related double chest with very similar cabriole bracket feet is shown in Richard H. Randall, Jr., *The Decorative Arts of New Hampshire 1725–1825,* Manchester, 1964, no. 33, and another very similar double chest is at the Munson-Williams-Proctor Institute in Utica, New York. A "practice" fan is carved on the top of the upper chest behind the pediment. H. 90", W. 43½", D. 22¾". Lucius D. Potter Memorial.

449

221

450. Double chest, cherry and whitewood, possibly made by Daniel Clay, Greenfield, 1792–1805. Originally mahoganized. H. 74", W. 45", D. 18¾". Lucius D. Potter Memorial.

451. Dressing table, cherry and white pine, probably Deerfield, 1795–1810. Refinished; originally mahoganized. H. 30¾", W. 37½", D. 30½". C. Alice Baker Bequest.

The double chest at the left (450) was found in Greenfield by the Potters. Since the lamb's tongues and fluted, chamfered corners on the base relate to those on a clock case labeled by Daniel Clay (see page 266), and since the molded bracket foot was used by him on several chests (see page 124, references and 196), this double chest could be associated with his work. The secondary wood is a whitewood (basswood) like that found in his Pembroke tables and case pieces. His advertisements in the *Greenfield Gazette* between 1794 and 1806 frequently mentioned his need for white oak, ash, white maple and bass planks. Many details of construction are also similar to Clay's work.

Not everything old has to be glorious, and the latter-day lowboy (451) is an interesting hybrid. Looking as though the upper row of drawers had been liberated from a double chest and placed on spindly, square legs with stretchers to hold them together, this dressing table was made in Deerfield, according to tradition, by a member of the Hoyt family. Two other similar examples are known, one of which was owned by the Starr family who lived south of town on the road to the Bars.

On the next page is an important double chest with local associations. It has many similarities to the desk and bookcase shown on pages 242 and 243, and both of these pieces were owned by the Billings family of Hatfield and Deerfield. The cluster of herringbone inlays on the lower canted corners of the upper section is echoed faintly by a small band above the molded bracket feet. The feet themselves are distinctively carved in an almost-eastern-Connecticut manner (see Myers and Mayhew, no. 92). The crowning achievement, however, is the elaborately carved cornice containing a frieze of Gothic arches topped by delicate beading and dentils, all surmounted by an egg-and-dart molding. The beaded edges around the drawers are on the case of this double chest, while they are on the edges of the drawers themselves on the desk and bookcase. White pine is the only secondary wood used in this chest, the desk and bookcase also making use of whitewood in its interior.

452. Double chest, cherry (inlaid) and white pine, Connecticut Valley (Massachusetts), 1790–1805. Probably made in the Northampton-Hatfield area. Refinished; brasses not original. Compare with desk and bookcase, pages 242–243. H. 81", W. 39¾", D. 21".

453. Dressing table, cherry and white pine, probably eastern Massachusetts, 1795–1805. Old mahoganized finish. This has been published as Connecticut; however, a very similar dressing table in cherry was found in the greater Boston area recently. See Elizabeth Stillinger, "Beau-Brummel Dressing Tables in America," *Antiques*, September 1973, pp. 446–451. H. 34¾", W. 29", D. 21½".

454a

Three chamber pieces are shown on this page. "Ladies Dressing Tables" was the term given by George Hepplewhite to the multidrawered and compartmented table above (453; see *The Cabinetmaker and Upholsterer's Guide*, plate 73, dated 1787).

Tables like the one below (454) have been called serving tables, but convincing research shows they were known as chamber tables (Montgomery, nos. 335–336). With its serpentine front, simulated tambour area on the lower drawer, and well carved legs, this chamber table is typical

of a kind favored in Salem (Montgomery, no. 336; and Fales, *Essex*, no. 65). The carved area has a star-punched background in the leafage. While it is tempting to conjure up the names of William Hook, Joseph True, or Samuel Field McIntire as the maker or carver of this chamber table, it must be remembered that there were many craftsmen working together in Salem during the Federal period.

The commode came from the Chapin family of Springfield, Massachusetts. Its front is hinged to its swinging top.

454. Chamber table, mahogany and mahogany veneers with white pine, Salem, 1810–1815. H. 34¾", W. 37⅛", D. 19¼".

455. Commode, mahogany, mahogany veneers and white pine, possibly Springfield, Massachusetts, c.1830. H. 27", W. 23¼", D. 18⅜".

Desks, Secretaries, and Bookcases

456. Desk and table with drawer, pine
and maple, Massachusetts, 1720–1750.
Old green paint. Williams family. H. 38",
W. 28½", D. 21½". Gift of Elizabeth Fuller.

The development of the desk from an early box to a box on frame and finally to an enclosed, lidded case with drawers is well known (see Lyon, pp. 109–136). The terms scrutoire and bureau were used before the word desk became the generic term in the latter 1700s. The desk—and especially the desk with a bookcase added above—was a favorite form in New England, in both the towns and rural areas. The Deerfield collection shows the wide range of these types which include some of the finest examples of New England cabinetmaking.

The desk above is actually a desk box, with a slanted lid and lift top, which fits on an early stretcher-base tavern table. While the two parts were not necessarily made at the same time, the history of this piece shows they were used together at an early date by Dr. Thomas Williams (1718–1775), the first of the three Doctors Williams to serve Deerfield (see page 24). The Williams family had moved to Stockbridge from eastern Massachusetts in 1738, coming to Deerfield a year later (Sheldon, *History*, II, 378–381). Dr. Williams served as an army surgeon several times in the 1740s and 1750s, and family tradition has always stated he had carried the desk part with him on these expeditions, reuniting it with the table upon his return home. He was surgeon in the regiment of his older brother, Colonel Ephraim Williams at the battle of Lake George in September, 1755. It was near there that his brother, the founder of Williams College, was killed (Chamberlain and Flynt, p. 160).

457, 457a. Desk on frame, pine with maple legs, New England, 1710–1750. Old red paint. Interior has well and single vertical document drawer above. H. 40″, W. 26½″, D. 18½″.

458. Desk on frame, pine with maple legs, eastern Massachusetts, 1715–1740. Repainted red; brasses not original. H. 37½″, W. 25¾″, D. 20⅜″.

459. Desk on frame, cherry and white pine, probably Connecticut Valley of Massachusetts, 1735–1790. Originally mahoganized. H. 40¼″, W. 38″, D. 20″.

460, 460a. Desk with drawers, maple and pine, probably eastern Massachusetts, 1700–1730. Original red paint and brasses. Well in interior. H. 42½″, W. 37″, D. 18½″.

Three of the early type of desks on frame are shown on the opposite page. The earliest (stylistically) is 457, with a well in the interior that provided access, thereby obviating the need for a drawer in the upper desk section. The legs have extra ring turnings to make them a bit higher than those used on tavern tables, and the pullouts that support the lid are the early, square type. An almost identical desk is shown in Kettell, no. 113; and one at the Shelburne Museum is very similar to this example.

Although repainted and slicked up, 458 is another early desk on frame. It was owned in the Minot family of Dorchester and (later) Minot, Massachusetts, and was exhibited long ago at the Dorchester Historical Society. An old label has the address of Edward A. Huebener, the colorful antiquarian and amateur artist who was president of the Society at the turn of this century.

The third desk on frame (459) is the latest of the three. It has no well, the turnings of the legs are not of the early type, the construction is much lighter,

and the supports for the lid are the vertically rectangular type that developed after the square supports had been found to be less efficent. The interior is plain, save for the scalloping under the central upper drawer.

The desk above (460, 460a) is the earliest type of a fully developed desk with drawers. It retains the early well inside; and, as a result, there is a wide space in the top of the base before the drawers begin. The original brasses are engraved; and double-arch moldings extend not only around the front of the case, but right up the slanted ends and across the sides of the top. The heavy ball feet are old, but, like many of these early feet, may be replacements. The desk still retains much of its old reddish-brown (or Indian red) paint. The interior has drawers, shelves, and rather rudimentary pigeon holes. The entire desk is important, since it sets the stage for the hosts of slantfront desks that were to blossom everywhere from the middle of the eighteenth century well into the 1800s.

461. Desk on frame, maple and white pine, northeastern New England, 1740–1800. Originally painted red; original brasses. H. 41½", W. 31", D. 16¾".

462. Desk on frame, cherry and white pine, Hartford County, Connecticut, 1730–1775. Original engraved brasses. H. 38½", W. 33¾", D. 21".

On these two pages are three Queen Anne desks on frame, one of the most graceful types of desks made in New England. At the top (461) is a very small, straight-legged example. The cutout of the skirt, especially the small half-round element at the center, is often associated with Queen Anne examples from New Hampshire and Maine. The interior is very simple, with two drawers under the lid. The desk was owned in the Codman family of Camden, Maine. They were among the first families to exchange the salubrity of Massachusetts for that of Maine.

This desk on frame was the first case piece bought by the Flynts in January, 1947, when their dream for Deerfield had started to become a reality.

Below, a Connecticut Valley desk on frame (462) with highly spirited cabriole legs has a shaped skirt that seems a forerunner of a more refined type found on later Hartford County high chests and tables (Kirk, *Connecticut*, nos. 177–179). This desk on frame was owned by the Loomis family of Windsor, and on a small drawer of the interior is inscribed "Home shelf/Charlotte Mecklenburg." While the desk was made sometime around the middle of the eighteenth century, the engraved brasses and "square" pullout supports for the lid are features of a slightly earlier period. Like most cherry pieces, this desk was mahoganized originally.

Desks were rather precious furnishings in the eighteenth century. When Joseph Barnard was purchasing furnishings between 1750 and 1760 (before he built the Manse), he paid Benjamin Munn, Jr. of Deerfield £9 for a table and £11 for a chest, while a desk made by the Northampton joiner-merchant James Couch cost £20 (Barnard, Munn family Mss., P.V.M.A.).

463, 463a. Desk on frame, cherry and white pine, probably Newbury or Newburyport, Massachusetts, 1750–1790. Originally mahoganized; brasses replaced. Currier family. H. 42⅝″, W. 37½″, D. 18¾″. Lucius D. Potter Memorial.

463a

The desk on frame above is a highly developed example of this form, made during the Chippendale period. The pad feet on high discs indicate that they were made after the middle of the eighteenth century, as do the fluted, beveled corners with lamb's tongues which appear only rarely on Massachusetts case pieces. The interior (463a) is rather elaborate, with scalloped tops to the pigeon holes, blocked drawers, and two document drawers with fluted, half-round pilasters. There are many later inscriptions on the

interior, including "Amos Currier, Aged 13 March . . . Newbury." The Curriers were a large clan in the Newburyport-Amesbury area of northern Essex County, and many of the family were craftsmen. While the maker of this desk on frame is unknown, it represents an eloquent statement of the abilities of a maker from a smaller town. While cherry is not a wood normally associated with this area, there is a considerable group of early furniture made of this wood from the Newburyport-Portsmouth region.

464. Desk, mahogany and white pine, labeled by Benjamin Frothingham, Charlestown, Massachusetts, 1770–1775. Brasses, lid, and center door in interior replaced; feet original. H. 49¼", W. 45½", D. 25½". 464a. Frothingham's label, engraved by Nathaniel Hurd of Boston in the late 1760s.

One of the most famous Massachusetts cabinetmakers was Benjamin Frothingham (1734–1809) of Charlestown. His working dates, 1762–1775 and 1783–1809, were interrupted by two lengthy periods of military service; but during his career, his documented examples include pieces in the Queen Anne, Chippendale, and Federal styles. Some are elaborate, while others are quite simple; but they all form as important a group of furniture as exists to demonstrate how a craftsman fulfilled the desires of his clients in the Colonies and early republic (see Richard H. Randall, Jr., "Benjamin Frothingham," *Boston Furniture*, pp. 223–249). The blockfront desk on this page, despite having barely survived Victorian indignities such as a recarved lid and the interior door, is a strong statement of Frothingham's abilities. It is the only instance of a documented case piece of his making use of hairy claw feet (464b). The mahogany of the drawer fronts is nicely figured and the interior is an especially handsome one with blocked sections topped off by fans alternating with reverse-blocked drawers and pigeon holes. This arrangement was a favorite of Boston-area cabinetmakers working in the Chippendale style.

464b

464c

465a

465. Desk, mahogany and white pine, Boston area, 1765–1775. Brasses original. Later owner's stamp "J. S. Ingraham" (465a). Primary wood is a heavy Cuban mahogany darker than the photograph indicates. H. 46″, W. 44″, D. 26″. Lucius D. Potter Memorial.

In addition to the blockfront desk on the opposite page, Benjamin Frothingham also made reverse-serpentine front desks with ogee bracket feet (Randall, article cited; and Brock Jobe, "A Desk by Benjamin Frothingham," *Bulletin 1976*, The Currier Gallery of Art, Manchester, New Hampshire, 1976, pp. 3–23).

Since a great many of the forms made in a given area were so similar in detail and even execution, it is safer to think of the desk on this page as the work of a Boston area cabinetmaker rather than that of Frothingham. This desk (465) really sings! The bold blocking of the facade is reflected by the strong grain of the mahogany and the splashy brasses, and all is firmly held to the floor by a most wondrously rugged set of claw feet. The interior is similar to that of 464, with a carved shell in a blocked center door flanked by three sets of pigeon holes on both sides, and three blocked drawers with a fan on top at both ends. This form was a favorite in the Boston area, although most other examples do not have such really bold feet (see Margaretta Markle Lovell, "Boston Blockfront Furniture," *Boston Furniture*, pp. 77–135). The primary wood in these handsome desks is invariably a strong, heavy mahogany.

"J. S. Ingraham" is stamped many times on the drawer sides and bottoms. While they might be maker's marks (Lovell, see above, p. 93), they probably signify an owner. This stamp is also on a Chippendale desk on frame with carved knees, from the Boston area (Randall, no. 57).

466. Desk, cherry and pine, probably
Deerfield, 1780–1805. Brasses replaced.
Allen family. H. 40⅛″, W. 38½″, D. 18¼″.
Gift of Miss Cora C. Vawter in memory
of Miss Ellen Gates Starr.

467. Desk, cherry and pine, Deerfield area,
1785–1810. Brasses replaced; highly
refinished. Feet partially restored.
Stebbins-Hitchcock families. H. 43″,
W. 38″, D. 19″.

The two desks on this page have local histories. Figure 466 was owned by Caleb Allen (1737–1807), who lived at the Bars, south of Deerfield. His daughter Lavina married Oliver Starr, and two of Caleb's sons, Caleb, Jr. and Carlos Allen, wrote inscriptions on the document drawers of the desk. Its exterior is plain, but the interior has four blocked drawers and pilasters on the vertical document drawers that flank the paneled central door. A daughter of Caleb Allen married a member of the Bardwell family, and the house on the opposite page (470), now known as Allen House, was owned earlier by Thomas Bardwell (1691–1781).

The desk below (467) is worthy of a prize for the most refinished piece in Deerfield. The cherry has been so bleached in the process, that it now resembles a light maple in color. It was originally mahoganized, and, in spite of its bare escape, the desk is of interest since it was a family piece of Maria Stebbins Hitchcock, who sold it to Miss C. Alice Baker (see page 194). The treatment of the interior is unusual, with the sweeping, curved lower drawers and carved shell. Ogee feet finish off the base with more determination than plainer straight bracket feet.

On the next page are two small slant-top desks. The larger one (468) is an elaborate child's desk with carved fans splashed over the front, fluted ends, and ogee feet. It demonstrates an axiom of rural cabinetmaking—if one fan is good, ten fans are ten times as good! The interior has small drawers and pigeon holes. The desk came from the Gay family of Farmington, Connecticut. Small desks of this sort are sometimes thought to be cabinetmakers' samples, but this one is just right in size for use by a child. Figure 469 is much smaller; yet, while curled maple dresses up the front, the quality of the desk is not quite that of a sample desk. It could have been used by a small child—or in a large dollhouse.

468 (left). Child's desk, cherry and white pine, probably Hartford County, 1780–1810. Originally mahoganized. Gay family, Farmington, Connecticut. H. 12″, W. 20″, D. 11″.

469 (right). Miniature desk, maple, curled maple and white pine, New England, 1800–1815. H. 14½″, W. 12″, D. 7⅛″. Lucius D. Potter Memorial.

470. This southern view of the Allen house, taken in early spring, shows the sweeping back roof of the house and the ells and sheds. Owned by the Beaman-Bardwell-Allen-Flynt families, the house was built after the 1704 massacre, with each generation making changes in typical New England fashion. The house contains some of the best early furniture owned by Historic Deerfield, Inc. (see Chamberlain and Flynt, pp. 67–79).

471a

471. Desk, cherry and white pine, possibly made by Moses Stebbins (1731–1815) or his son Moses (1762–1800), Deerfield, c. 1800. Brasses replaced; originally mahoganized. Flutes and scrolls on document drawers, carved sunburst on center drawer (471a). Relates to case of tall clock by Preserved Clapp, page 260. Scrolls on side brackets; broken off on front. Stebbins-Wright families. H. 40½″, W. 36½″, D. 18″.

According to family tradition, the desk above was made by Moses Stebbins of Deerfield. The treatment of the interior is most unusual, with dividers that soar upwards. The desk is more shallow than most slant-top desks, and constructional details indicate that it was made about 1800.

The secretary below (472) is in the Federal style, with French feet, handsome veneered surfaces and unusual silvered brasses. The banded pillar inlays were often used in Newburyport, and a recently discovered David Wood shelf clock bearing the label of Rogers and Atwood features this motif at the base.

472

472a

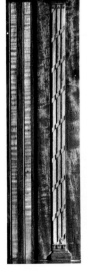

473b

472. Secretary, mahogany, mahogany veneers, maple and white pine, Newburyport, 1795–1810. Original silvered brasses; secret drawer behind fascia. H. 54¾″, W. 42″, D. 19½″. Detail of inlaid pillar with diagonal "breaks" at left (472a). The other details, below and right (473a and b) are from the Seymour secretary shown on the next page (473).

473a

473. Tambour desk, mahogany and mahogany veneers with white pine and elm, associated with John and Thomas Seymour, Boston, c. 1800. Ex coll. Mr. and Mrs. Ellerton M. Jetté. H. 45½″, W. 37¾″, D. 19½″.

Two tambour desks exist which bear the labels of John Seymour and Son of Creek Square, Boston (Montgomery, no. 184; and Vernon C. Stoneman, *John and Thomas Seymour: Cabinetmakers in Boston 1794–1816,* Boston, 1959, pp. 48–51). Several dozen others are attributed to or associated with the Seymours for one or more reasons. Lunette inlays (the three rows on this desk differ), the robin's-egg-blue paint in the upper section, and fine cabinetwork were all used by other cabinetmakers, but there are strong whiffs of the Seymours here. The banded pillar inlay is more delicate than its Newburyport counterpart (472). This desk (473) was owned originally by Rebecca Fessenden of Boston. She married Captain Archibald Anderson in 1803; and the desk was brought to their home in Warren, Maine, by Anderson on the brig *Alonzo* in 1812. It remained in their home until it was acquired by the Jettés in 1944.

474. Secretary, cherry and white pine,
New Hampshire, 1790–1810. Bail brasses,
finials original. Owned by family of Josiah
Bartlett of Kingston, Chief Justice of
New Hampshire and signer of the
Declaration of Independence. A nearly
identical secretary is shown in *Antiques,*
March 1966, page 359. A related example
at the Currier Gallery of Art was owned
by the Cilley family and is said to have
been made by Enoch Poor of Manchester
(see Richard H. Randall, Jr., *The
Decorative Arts of New Hampshire,
1725–1825,* Manchester, 1964, no. 50).
H. 80¼", W. 44", D. 21".

The addition of a bookcase to a desk in the Queen Anne and Chippendale styles resulted in the secretary, the most noble form in early furniture. The example above has a reverse-serpentine front, scalloped doors, and a well carved fret. The scale of the claw feet, the shaping of the flame finials, and the bail handles give clues to its later date.

On the next page is one of the most important pieces of furniture at Deerfield (475). This secretary has balance, variety, decoration, and everything that furniture of the highest quality should have. It was owned originally by the Ames family of Boston who later sold it to the Whitney family. The bombé base is made with the drawer sides conforming to the shape of the case, and the front is flat—not serpentined. The large brasses are notable, and the molded bracket (or ogee) feet are perfect foils for the shaping of the case. This is an instance where claw feet would not be as desirable from an aesthetic point of view. The

interior is a fine one typical of the Boston type with carved fans, blocked drawers, and secret drawers which are revealed when the center section slides out. The upper part has reeded pilasters and carved capitals framing doors with scalloped panels, and a carved frieze above leading to the broken pediment. Inside the top are a dozen small pigeon holes, six large ones for ledgers, two adjustable shelves, and three drawers below. There are two candle slides at the bottom of the upper section.

This secretary has many similarities to one at the Department of State traditionally owned by the Hancock family (*Antiques,* November 1970, p. 769). The treatment of the base (and other details) is similar to a bombé secretary attributed to the Boston cabinetmaker Gibbs Atkins and made for Martin Gay (see Gilbert T. Vincent, "The Bombé Furniture of Boston," *Boston Furniture,* pp. 137–196, especially no. 131).

475. Secretary, mahogany and white pine,
Boston, 1760–1785. Brasses original. Ames family.
H. 95″, W. 46¼″, D. 22¾″.

476. Secretary, cherry and white pine with maple inlays, attributed to Israel Guild, Conway, Massachusetts, c. 1799. Made for Nancy (Ann) Stoddard of Northampton who married John Williams (1767–1845) of Conway in 1799. H. 88¾", W. 41", D. 23".

The secretary at the left (476) is an outlandish, outdated, glorious example of rural cabinetmaking. From the feet and compass inlay of Queen Anne to the Chippendale stop-fluting on the quarter columns of the upper section, and the rope-carved columns and inlaid rosettes of the Federal period, it serves as a joyful review of eighteenth-century furniture. For instance, the capitals in the upper section have wisps of leaf carving that bring joy to the furniture historian while producing tears in the eyes of a classicist. The secretary was owned by Nancy Stoddard, and the heart on the interior door would indicate it was made at a time close to her marriage in 1799 (see Conway Vital Records; Stephen W. Williams, *The Genealogy and History of the Family of Williams*, Greenfield, 1847, p. 203). A painted inscription on the back of the base states "John Williams Conway Mass. Made by Israel Guild probably between 1791–1799. Known to have been in use before 1803. JAW." Israel Guild was born in Hatfield in 1767 and worked in Conway (west of Deerfield) from 1791 to 1831, when he moved to Michigan (see Michael K. Brown, "Israel Guild: Cabinetmaker of Conway," unpublished Historic Deerfield Fellowship Program paper, 1974, pp. 64–76).

On the next page is one of the best Boston blockfront secretaries in captivity (477). It has everything—from gilt flame finials to a blocked-shell interior, from fine mahogany to grand brasses, and from five secret compartments to two candle slides. The proportions of the secretary are noble, and its quality is outstanding. The bracket feet are more in keeping with the blockfront spirit than claw feet would have been. The piece has been attributed to Benjamin Frothingham of Charlestown (*Antiques,* June 1953, p. 505), and certain details do correspond with his documented work (*Boston Furniture,* nos. 160, 170). However, any final judgment should await further study of other makers of the area. The secretary was owned in the Marsh and then Dana families (see page 57; illustrated in Henry R. Stiles, *The History of Ancient Wethersfield Conn.,* New York, I, 1904, opp. 730).

477. Secretary, mahogany and white pine, Boston area, 1770–1775. All original, including brasses and gilt flame finials. According to family tradition, the secretary was purchased in 1775 by Ebenezer Grant of East Windsor, Connecticut, for the marriage of his daughter Ann(e) to the Reverend John Marsh of Wethersfield. Later owned by the Dana family of Cambridge, Massachusetts (see page 57). H. 97″, W. 43¼″, D. 23⅜″.

478. Secretary, mahogany, white pine and with
chestnut backboards, Colchester, Connecticut,
c. 1781. Finials original. Stop-fluted pilasters
on upper section; fluted quarter columns below.
Carved rosettes and dentiled bonnet top with
beading around openings. Deming family history
same as high chest in figure 439, page 214.
H. 85½″, W. 42½″, D. 22⅜″.

The secretary at the left (478) has many characteristics of Colchester cabinetwork and is similar to a serpentine-front secretary in the Barbour Collection (Myers and Mayhew, no. 39). This secretary differs from the norm in two ways—mahogany instead of cherry is the primary wood, and the feet do not have the usual exaggerated scrolls that normally appear on Colchester ogee feet (see Myers and Mayhew, nos. 35–39). In fact, the feet are almost identical to those on a double chest from the Lisbon area (Myers and Mayhew, no. 70). While it is tempting to think of this fine piece as the work of a known cabinetmaker, research (as is often the case) unwings fancy. In one of the best articles written on Connecticut furniture, Houghton Bulkeley removed Aaron Roberts of New Britain from contention ("The 'Aaron Roberts' Attributions," *Contributions to Connecticut Cabinet Making*, Hartford, 1967, pp. 7–23, especially pp. 18–20). Samuel Loomis, a Colchester cabinetmaker, is known to have made a double chest for Jonathan Deming in mahogany (Myers and Mayhew, no. 35); and while this secretary was made for Julius and Dorothy (Champion) Deming shortly after their marriage in 1781, there are differences in the construction of this scrutoir that make a definite attribution uncertain even if tempting. (See page 214, figure 439).

On the next page, the secretary at the top (480) was owned by Governor Caleb Strong of Northampton with the Chapin-type high chest shown on page 215, figure 440. While the two pieces were owned together, they were not made together. The secretary is obviously later, both in style and execution. A comparison of structural detail shows that while pine is the only secondary wood in the high chest, whitewood is also used in the secretary. The dovetails on the drawers are executed with finesse on the secretary, while they are more "squarish" on the high chest. The rosettes and finials vary slightly. It would appear that Governor Strong had a cabinetmaker—probably a local one—make the secretary to match the high chest he already owned. It was at this time that the brass flutes and capitals were added to the high chest to make the two pieces appear *en suite*. Similar brass trappings were used on clock cases in the Federal period.

480 (right). Secretary, cherry, pine, and whitewood, possibly Northampton, Massachusetts, 1790–1805. Refinished, originally mahoganized. Reeded quarter columns with brass flutes and capitals. Desk or scrutoir interior has two rows of eight small drawers over ten pigeon holes with scalloped tops. Owned by Governor Caleb Strong of Northampton, Massachusetts (see page 80), together with a high chest of drawers (shown on page 215, figure 440). Details of construction indicate the two pieces were made at different times by different makers (see text). Ex coll. Philip Flayderman. H. 96″, W. 45½″, D. 24″.

479 (left). Secretary, cherry and pine, with chestnut in drawer linings, probably Hartford County, 1785–1810. While this secretary was once considered the work of Aaron Chapin (*Antiques,* July 1942, p. 12), an association with either him or his cousin Eliphalet, a more likely candidate, would be tenuous at best. The final is delicate and airy, but it is a watered-down version of a type attributed to Eliphalet Chapin (Kirk, *Early,* no. 85). The shaping of the pigeon hole dividers is unusual—see the desk by Moses Stebbins on page 234 (no. 471) with this feature. H. 88″, W. 41¼″, D. 19⅞″.

481a

481b

481a-c. Details of secretary (opposite), cherry with white pine and whitewood, probably Northampton-Hatfield area, 1795–1800. Relates to double chest, figure 452, page 223. Owned by Billings family of Hatfield and Deerfield. H. 97″, W. 41″, D. 22½″. Bird 4″ high.

481c

A very small group of case pieces exists with bird finials, and most of them first left their nests not too far from Deerfield. This secretary shouts forth with a lavish wealth of ornamentation—both carved and inlaid—in the best, most exciting tradition of rural cabinetmaking. Everything—from stop-fluting to dentils, paterae, pilasters, rosettes, fretwork, leaf carving, drapery folds, and zigzag stringing—is here. The piece is abuzz with discordant bits of virtuosity, yet it achieves a harmonious whole after the initial shock of seeing it has worn off. Several pieces probably made by the same cabinetmaker are known. They include the double chest on page 223 and another secretary with less carving on the base but more on the bonnet top (see *Antiques*, May 1974, p. 979). This secretary is the only one of the group having a known history. It was owned in the Billings family of Hatfield and Deerfield. A plainer curled maple double chest with a different type of bird finial was owned in an early Greenfield collection (*Antiques*, December 1938, p. 288); and that piece might be a Greenfield echo of this more elaborate type made just to the south. Two other case pieces are known with bird finials, but they do not really relate to this type (*Antiques*, May 1968, p. 573; and June 1958, p. 511).

481

482. Cylinder secretary and bookcase, mahogany, mahogany veneers, and white pine, Boston, 1805–1815. H. 87″, W. 39¼″, D. 21¾″.

A predecessor of the rolltop desk of the late nineteenth century was the cylinder desk which was featured by both Hepplewhite and Sheraton (Montgomery, nos. 194–197). Their quarter-round tops rolled back to reveal a writing surface, which, in this case, could be lifted up for even greater convenience to the user. While this secretary might be considered to be the work of Thomas Seymour during his Boston Cabinet Manufactory period, there were other men in Boston making this type of furniture. The construction of this secretary is coarser than that of the Hepplewhite desk at Deerfield (473, page 235). Behind the glazed doors with Gothic arches are holes that indicate curtains originally hid the contents of the bookcase. Using the upper part for a display area is a modern custom. The ivory knobs are replacements, and a photograph taken of this secretary years ago shows it with old wooden knobs—perhaps original (*Antiques*, March 1930, p. 241). It was then in the collection of Dr. W. F. Temple, Jr.

483. Bookcase, cherry and white pine, probably Boston, 1805–1835. Original mahoganized finish. H. 85″, W. 79″, D. 14″.

While a large number of nineteenth-century bookcases survive, there are very few earlier ones remaining, especially with glass doors. Found in the Boston area, this bookcase is said to have been owned by Harrison Gray Otis (1765–1848), the famous Boston lawyer and real estate investor who built three of the finest Federal residences still standing in that city. Made in the early nineteenth century, it is of cherry, a wood that was used often (mahoganized) in Boston Empire furniture. Most of its old finish is still intact, as is its old glass. The knobs and key plates are replacements.

As a parenthetical note, William Emmons, a Deerfield cabinetmaker, advertised in 1813 and 1814 bookcases, all sorts of desks, including "cylinder, fall & Tambo" (tambour), sideboards, "Swing Cradles," and bureaus "sash corner and eliptic," as well as common, straight and swelled-front bureaus. He also listed a variety of light stands and tables in the *Greenfield Gazette*.

484. Sideboard, mahogany and mahogany veneers, inlaid, with white pine and elm, probably made by John and/or Thomas Seymour, Boston, 1800–1810. Inscription in right drawer: "Formerly owned by Hon. Asa French's grandfather." Asa French (1829–1903) was a noted jurist; and his grandfather Asa (1775–c. 1853) was town clerk, treasurer and first postmaster of Braintree, Massachusetts, in 1825. Ex colls. Mrs. Robert E. Warren: Mr. & Mrs. Ellerton M. Jetté. H. 39¾", W. 59⅜", D. 23¾".

Sideboards

The development of the sideboard coincided with that of the dining room in Federal homes throughout America. The earliest New England examples, made in the 1790s, had square, tapered legs. The sideboard above, in fact, has many similarities to a square-legged example (see Mabel M. Swan, "John Seymour & Son, Cabinetmakers," *Antiques,* October 1937, pp. 176–179, figs. 3–5). Carved and reeded decoration supplants inlays of the earlier type, but the tambour doors and scrolled drop with keyhole are retained. The details, woods, and construction warrant a strong association with the Seymours.

On the next page, 485 is a crisp, small sideboard with a most unusual combination of reeded legs and fluted engaged corner posts. While the elongated, bulbous feet are typical of Salem work at the turn of the century, the louder use of contrasting maple and mahogany veneers is a feature usually found on furniture to the north. This sideboard was owned by the Gerrish family of Newburyport, Massachusetts.

The sideboard below (486) proves that the glorious individuality of earlier times was not necessarily lost when the more national styles of the Federal period swept through southern New England. With rosewood banding at the top and ivory escutcheons, this sideboard features inlays of double-headed eagles on the doors and a patera on the backboard, which has an applied reeded edge. Backboards were introduced in cities just before 1810 and spread to more remote areas in the teens. The treatment of the bulging, leaf-carved capitals of the engaged legs and the round caps on the top is memorable.

485. Sideboard, mahogany, mahogany and maple veneers with white pine and maple, Essex County, Massachusetts, 1800–1810. Desk behind larger drawer. H. 40¾", W. 51", D. 19½".

486a

486. Sideboard, cherry with rosewood veneered band at top, with white pine and chestnut, Connecticut or Rhode Island, 1805–1820. H. 43", W. 55", D. 21½".

Cupboards

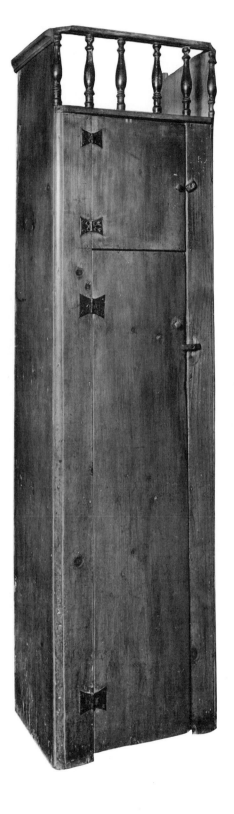

487. Livery cupboard, white pine with oak spindles, West Newbury, Massachusetts, 1717–1730. Originally painted red. H. 81⅝", W. 14¼", D. 22".

Two of the basic urges of man are collecting and then finding a place to store what has been collected. Household articles, clothing, food, and drink were collectibles, and cupboards became the receptacles for all of them. Cupboards are closely related to architecture, and many were actually built into walls like closets with their fronts exposed (487), while others were made as free-standing pieces of furniture that could be moved about (488). Cupboards were made from the earliest times to the present, and, while their uses and styles changed, their basic purpose, that of shelter and protection, did not.

The cupboard on this page is a survival of a rare type, a livery cupboard. Livery cupboards were designed originally with various types of openings so that air could circulate for proper food storage. The term appears in Massachusetts inventories as early as 1655, and there are several seventeenth-century examples known (Nina Fletcher Little, "Livery Cupboards in New England," *Antiques*, December 1963, pp. 710–713). In Dedham, Massachusetts, livery cupboards appeared in inventories of Daniel Fisher (1683) and John Richards (1688), and they were in the parlors of both houses (Cummings, pp. 46, 51). The cupboard at the left is from the Thomas Hailer house, constructed in 1717 in West Newbury, Massachusetts. The cupboard was built in under a beam sometime in the first half of the eighteenth century, and it has a closed top, so that the turned spindles form a decorative rather than a practical grille. The old butterfly iron hinges are original.

On the next page is an early cupboard owned by the Saltonstall-Lyman families of Massachusetts. While it was rejuvenated earlier in this century, it remains a noble late-seventeenth-century eastern Massachusetts cupboard. The term court cupboard was not in common usage in the Colonial period, although a related cupboard, the Prince-Howes cupboard at the Wadsworth Atheneum, was referred to as "the court cubberd that stands in the new parlour with the cloth and cushion that is on it" in the 1673 will of Thomas Prince (Nutting, I, no. 455; Randall, no. 19). Today, this type of cupboard with the base full of drawers is referred to as a press cupboard, while the term court cupboard indicates one with an open shelf in the lower section. Such are the vagaries of furniture terminology. The Deerfield cupboard is similar to the Alden family cupboard at the Museum of Fine Arts (Boston) and the Tracy family example from Plymouth (Randall, no. 19 and Nutting, I, no. 462), although not as fully developed.

488a

488. Cupboard with drawers, oak and pine, eastern Massachusetts, 1675–1695. Repainted black and red. Restorations include some applied spindles and turnings, drawer pulls, and possibly front feet. Serrated dentiling like earlier Plymouth "court" cupboards (see text, opposite), but other details differ from that type. Owned originally by the Saltonstall family, with their arms painted on an oval metal boss on central door of cupboard (488a, left). Later owned by the Lyman family. H. 58″, W. 52¼″, D. 22¾″.

Four non-New England cupboards stand on these two pages. Furniture, like people, crossed the American-Canadian border frequently, and the crisp *armoire* at the left found its way to Massachusetts. It has invected fielded panels and "fische" lift-off hinges that are often found in Quebec (Palardy, nos. 50, 56). The heavy molding at the base and the stiles continuing down to form the legs are early features.

Below is a related form with diamond panels in the doors and ends. It also has lift-off hinges and retains its old red paint. The moldings and construction are somewhat lighter than in the armoire above, suggesting a slightly later date of manufacture. This type of buffet was often used as a food locker (Palardy, no. 129). The history of this buffet is not recorded, but it came from a dealer just south of Deerfield. A similar buffet, with two drawers above the diamond doors, was owned by a Northampton dealer in 1930 (*Antiques,* July 1930, p. 60), indicating a number of early Quebec pieces were owned in Franklin County and other northern New England locales over the years.

489. *Armoire,* pine, Quebec, 1690–1730. Originally painted red, then green, then other colors. Owned by Higginson family of Essex County, Massachusetts, at one time. H. 48½", W. 36½", D. 15½".

490 (right). *Buffet bas* (low buffet), pine, Quebec, 1710–1750. Original red paint and hardware. No history known, but found in New England. Stile feet continuations of the corner posts, as in figure 489. H. 39¾", W. 41⅝", D. 19".

The handsome cupboard at the right (492) was found at Chincoteague, off the eastern shore of Virginia, but was probably made in the James River area. The panel is striking and also similar to that on an outside door at Tuckahoe, the great mansion in Richmond, Goochland County (letter from Frank L. Horton, January 4, 1973). A similar paneled chest is at Williamsburg, and another cupboard (found in Danbury, Connecticut) is shown in Kettell, figure 143. The Deerfield cupboard appears to be earlier than the others.

The *kas* below (491), influenced by solid Dutch prototypes, is one of a number of American examples that were made of walnut, maple, red gum, or cherry over a wide area of Long Island, the Hudson Valley, and even New Jersey throughout the eighteenth century. A similar *kas* from Bergen County is shown in *Antiques,* August 1965, p. 193; and one labeled by Matthew Egerton, Jr., of New Brunswick had to be made after 1785, when he started working. Except for the bracket feet, it is very much like the Deerfield *kas* (*Antiques,* February 1958, p. 141).

492. Cupboard, loblolly pine, Virginia, 1710–1740. Originally painted red. Found on Chincoteague Island. Ex coll. Edward C. Wheeler, Jr. H. 65½″, W. 39¾″, D. 18¾″.

491 (left). *Kas,* maple, with walnut panels and diamonds on front, New Jersey or New York, 1750–1800. Originally stained red and black. Feet and pulls original. H. 74½″, W. 72″, D. 21″. (Width of case, 57½″). Gift of John B. Morris, Jr.

493. Cupboard, pine, Connecticut Valley (Massachusetts), 1725–1780. Outside repainted red, old gray on shelves and interior. H. 69½″, W. 47½″, D. 20½″.

The great cupboard on the next page was removed from the Elijah Williams house in Deerfield. Now owned by Deerfield Academy, the house was built for Elijah Williams (1712–1771), the son of the Reverend John Williams, before 1762 (Chamberlain and Flynt, pp, 123–124). With its massive carved shell, panels, and fluted pilasters, the cupboard represents the best in Connecticut Valley work of the eighteenth century. On top of the pilasters are two weird finials which, while not original, show in photographs which were taken well over one hundred years ago. The 1920 *Catalogue* of the objects in Memorial Hall lists 495 as a "Corner Cupboard or Buffet," mistakenly pushing its original owner back a generation, but stating "*This* is the *only article* in Memorial Hall for which any money has been paid by the P.V.M. Association" (p. 123). The 1936 annual report noted that glass had replaced chicken wire to protect the rare china inside, thus obviating its annual washing (P.V.M.A. *Proceedings*, VIII, 132).

494. Cupboard, hard pine, Connecticut Valley (Massachusetts), 1725–1770. Refinished, originally Spanish brown. Feet restored. Ex coll. Edward C. Wheeler, Jr. H. 71″, W. 44″, D. 21″.

The two cupboards on this page are a local type, made in or near Deerfield. The scalloped openings, especially when paneled as on 494, seem to be a French influence coming down the Valley from the north. Both cupboards were painted originally, and the basic wood is the so-called hard pine like that used on the early local chests of the Deerfield-Hatfield area (see text, page 170; and figures, page 177). Both also retain their old wrought-iron H hinges.

While these cupboards do not have known histories, a similar painted one at Winterthur was owned by Osmund and Winifred Skinner of Shelburne, a town just west of Deerfield on the Mohawk Trail. Another related cupboard was found just north of Greenfield in Bernardston. While the panels of 494 are more exciting, its base had rotted out and, with the lower shelf of the interior, has been replaced. The pewter tankard was made by Henry Will of New York and the dish by the local pewterer, Samuel Pierce, of Greenfield.

495. Cupboard, pine, Deerfield, 1755–1762. Repainted red, with old Spanish brown interior, with edges of shelves and finials gray-green. From Major Elijah Williams house on the Common. Originally flanked a fireplace and was not a corner cupboard. Williams' wig stand is shown on page 163.
H. 93½″, W. 46⅞″, D. 24″. P.V.M.A.

496. Dresser, white pine, New England, 1750–1800.
Original red paint. H. 87½″, W. 76″, D. 18″.

Dressers, with large, open shelves which stored china, glass, pewter, and other household trappings, were popular in the working area of early homes. This example was made in the last half of the eighteenth century, with paneled doors and old scalloping on the ends by the exposed shelves. The top molding has been cut off the left end, apparently so the dresser could fit into a kitchen corner. At least one large drawer in the closed area is usually found in a dresser. The wrought-iron H hinges and pulls are old. Since this form was a timeless one made into the 1800s, the dating of dressers is conjectural at best.

497 (near right). Folding table
pine top, oak leg, New England,
1725–1800. Old scrubbed finish.
Wall brackets replaced. Top
25″ x 34½″.

498 (far right). Shelves, pine,
probably Deerfield, 1760–1810.
Refinished. H. 73″, W. 85¼″.

499 (below). Corner cupboard,
pine, New England, 1730–1785.
Original paint: red, with interior
of shelves painted blue. Shelves
grooved for plates. Scalloping is
like arches on aprons of early high
chests. H. 79″, W. 46″, D. 16″.

The backless scalloped shelves above (498)
were in the Wells-Thorn house when it
was acquired by the Thorns about 1900.
It is made in the form of a cupboard, with
scalloped shelf supports in the upper sections and a straight base below. Many cupboards were also made without backboards,
since the paneling of the room could serve
this purpose once the cupboard was affixed.

The corner cupboard below (499)
looks a bit moth-eaten in the photograph,
but in person it has a glorious two-tone
combination of red and blue paint. A similar cupboard has an extra flattened arch at
the very top (Wallace Nutting, *Furniture
of the Pilgrim Century*, Framingham, 1924,
no. 233); and perhaps this one had another
eight inches at the top originally, making
it very high.

The folding table (at the left above,
497) is a type that is found in early inventories but rarely in the flesh. Perhaps they
were too insignificant to keep. Its scrubbed
top indicates usage in a kitchen.

500 (left). Hanging wall cupboard, pine, Connecticut, 1780–1810. Original red paint. Door and top ornament missing. H. 27¾", W. 20", D. 8¾".

501 (right). Hanging wall cupboard with watch box in door, white pine, New England, 1725–1770. Traces of original black paint. H. 22¼", W. 22¼", D. 9".

502 (below). Cupboard, white pine, Salem, Massachusetts, 1750–1800. Originally painted red. Scalloping at top replaced. H. 85", W. 67" and 39", D. 15".

Cupboards for varying purposes are shown on these two pages. Opposite, two wall (or hanging) cupboards are at the top. The shelves of 500 are finished off and shaped very well, yet they were originally covered by a paneled door. At the top is the remnant of a hanger that probably extended a foot above the cupboard, with a pierced heart in it. A cupboard of this type is shown in Nutting (*Furniture of the Pilgrim Century*, Framingham, 1924, no. 263).

The other hanging wall cupboard is most unusual in having an arched opening for a watch holder in the paneled door. The butterfly hinges are original, and the cupboard has quite an early appearance.

At the bottom of the opposite page is a fine cupboard which was built in a corner of a Salem house originally. The top probably extended up to the ceiling when built, and the fussy cornice is a modern improvisation. The side scalloping is original, however; and, in spite of what appears to be a high tide line about eight inches off the floor, this cornered cupboard is a grand one—and one of the most interesting examples at Deerfield.

On this page, the wig cupboard at the top is very rare. Behind the tambour sliding doors are compartments for the storage of wigs, and two small drawers below originally held combs, brushes, and other paraphernalia pertaining to tonsorial maintenance. The cupboard is not too surely constructed, and the half-hooded bonnet top presented the maker all sorts of problems with moldings and the shaping of the opening. It is a fine country example, made at some distance from the lights of the big city, and unusual in being made entirely of chestnut.

The china cupboard (or beaufait) at the right resembles a bookcase, but grooves on the three shelves of the upper section indicate it was made to hold plates or dishes. The blue-green color contrasts handsomely with the red interior. A dentiled cornice at the top, plus the shaping of the upper border and inclusion of a pullout slide, are unexpected details of quality. The cupboard was found by Mrs. Flynt near the New Jersey coast.

503. Wig cupboard, chestnut, Connecticut or Rhode Island, 1785–1815. Original red paint. Tambour doors. H. 33¼", W. 22½", D. 10½".

504. China cupboard, maple and tulip, possibly New Jersey, 1775–1810. Original blue-green paint on exterior and red on interior of both sections. Pullout slide above paneled lower doors. H. 83", W. 50", D. 14½".

505. The Frary house is one of Deerfield's best and was added to and changed in typical New England fashion by each generation that lived in it. Built for the Frary family, it was purchased by the Barnards and run as an inn at the time of the Revolution. In 1797, the trustees of Deerfield Academy first met there. Later, Miss C. Alice Baker, a Frary descendent, purchased the house in 1890 and lovingly restored and furnished it with locally found objects. She left it to the Pocumtuck Valley Memorial Association, in which she had been very active, and it was transferred to Historic Deerfield, Inc. in 1969.

506. Headquarters of the Pocumtuck Valley Memorial Association, Memorial Hall was built as the first building of Deerfield Academy and dedicated on New Year's Day, 1799. The designer was probably Asher Benjamin of Greenfield. The third story and wing were added in 1809, and by 1878 the Academy moved to its present site across the Common. George Sheldon was responsible for P.V.M.A. acquiring the building by 1880 and making further alterations to it. Major repairs were made in 1968 (see J. Peter Spang III, "Deerfield's Memorial Hall," *Antiques,* August 1968, pp. 206–209).

IV. CLOCKS

While clocks were mentioned in Boston as early as 1645 in inventories (Lyon, p. 233), they were not widely used in houses in the Colonial period. The earliest clocks were attached to wall brackets, their works exposed (Lyon, figs. 107–109). The tall case that hid the works and weights did not come into general use in the Colonies until well into the eighteenth century. While clocks were imported in great numbers, it was not until after the Revolution that the tall-case clock of American manufacture could be considered at all plentiful—and then only to those who could afford it. Even in Salem, the Reverend William Bentley suggested, in 1786, that public notice of each hour be given: "as there are few clocks & watches in the Town in families, there can be no other certain time of collecting." (*The Diary of William Bentley, D.D.*, Salem, I, 1905, 32). As late as 1806, the Wapping section of Deerfield obtained a clock for the school-house so that clockless people could get to meetings on time.

It was not until mass production and less costly mechanisms developed in the 1800s—spearheaded by the ingenuity of Connecticut clockmakers—that clocks and watches became more generally available to a wider public.

Cases of tall clocks can range from the most lavish examples of the cabinetmaker's art to productions of extreme simplicity. In cities, teams of craftsmen, including clockmakers, cabinetmakers, carvers, and dial painters, would band together to produce one clock, while in more rural areas one person would attempt the entire production himself.

The clock at the right was made by Richardson Minor, a Stratford, Connecticut, maker who started working about 1758. He was a silversmith as well as a clockmaker; these two trades were often combined in many smaller towns. The eight-day brass movement which is well made, is fronted by a brass dial with a calendar window, inset seconds dial, and all framed by brass spandrels, with the signature plate in the arch. The case is a simple one, with a flat top and rounded arch door that repeats the shape of the upper door. While the feet have been cut, the cyma scroll remains at the base. (A similar clock made by Minor, "c.1760," is shown in Penrose R. Hoopes, *Connecticut Clockmakers of the Eighteenth Century*, reprint, New York, 1974, figs. 12 and 36).

507. Tall clock, cherry and white pine; works by Richardson Minor (1736–1797) of Stratford, Connecticut. Old finish; feet cut down. H. 87″, W. 18″, D. 11½″. Case W. 12″, D. 8″. Gift of Eric M. Wunsch.

508 (left). Tall clock by Preserved Clapp, Amherst, Massachusetts, dated 1773. Case, maple with pine backboard, probably Deerfield, c. 1800. Refinished; case probably grained originally. H. 94″, W. 17½″, D. 11″. Case, W. 11¾″, D. 8⅜″.

The two tall clocks on this page are examples of rural clockmaking. At the left is a clock by Preserved Clapp of Amherst, who was born in 1731. The eight-day brass movement lacks the refinement of an urban production, the striking weight having to be wound counterclockwise. This clock was probably made originally to be hung exposed on a bracket. A so-called "wag-on-the-wall" clock by Clapp is known. About the end of the eighteenth century, it was put into its present maple case, a wondrous rural adaptation of the big time, topped off by gilt eagle-and-flame finials. The character of the carved fan, together with the broad fluting of the pilasters, recalls the interior of the desk possibly made by Moses Stebbins (figure 471a, page 234). This clock was owned by the Stebbins family, having been taken to Orlando, Florida, by Lucius Stebbins, an early settler there and a descendant of Preserved Clapp.

Neither the clock nor the case at the right would ever be considered pinups, but the David Blaisdell clock is the earliest at Deerfield. The Blaisdell clan contained many ingenious mechanic craftsmen (see Charles S. Parsons, *Blasdell Clockmakers*, unpublished paper, Goffstown, N.H., 1957). David (1712–1756) was the first of three Davids who made clocks, and five of his sons became clockmakers or metalworkers. Clocks by David are dated from 1735 to 1756 (a dozen dated examples are known). While 509 is not dated, it is considered one of his earliest works. The movement is a heavy brass, one-day pull-up type in an iron frame. It resembles the earlier English lantern clock, having spike feet and standing in the case rather than fitting into it. The dial is brass, but the spandrels and name plate are pewter.

509 (right). Tall clock by David Blaisdell, Amesbury, Massachusetts, 1733–1735. "David Blasdel in Almsbury" engraved on round plate in arch. Case, white pine with original red paint. H. 84″, W. 17½″, D. 9½″.

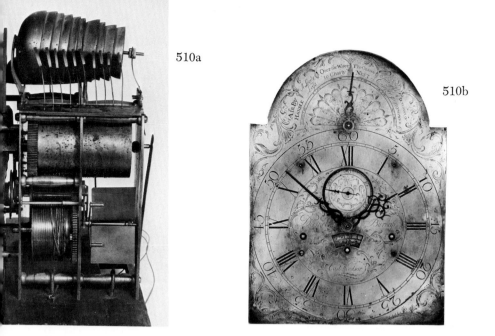

510a

510b

510. Chime clock made by Daniel Burnap (1759–1838), East Windsor, Connecticut, 1790–1794. Case, cherry and pine. Movement with chimes at left (510a), detail of brass dial with airs listed, right (510b).

One of the most interesting of the American clockmaker/ mechanic/silversmith combinations was Daniel Burnap of East Windsor—and later Coventry—Connecticut. He apprenticed to one of the most gifted early clockmakers, Thomas Harland of Norwich, and started work in East Windsor about 1782, moving to Coventry toward 1800 and retiring from the manufacture of clocks by 1810. Most of Burnap's account books and ledgers are at the Connecticut Historical Society, and one of the best books on an individual American craftsman, *Shop Records of Daniel Burnap, Clockmaker,* by Penrose R. Hoopes, was published by the Society in 1958. Not only are all of Burnap's accounts for the making of clocks listed, but his directions for making a chime clock, written in 1779, are given (*ibid.* pp. 118–120). Between 1788 and 1808, Burnap charged for fifty-one clocks and thirteen clock dials. Among these were thirty striking tall clocks, nine moon phase clocks, and six chime clocks. Five of the latter were made between 1790 and 1795, and one in 1802.

The brass movement of Deerfield's Burnap tall clock is remarkable, with ten bells keyed to play six different tunes. These chime clocks provide the only actual "live" music of the eighteenth century. "A Lovely Lass," for instance, was written by the Boston organist, William Selby.

The case is a handsome cherry one, with a rounded pagoda top with lacy fretwork, quarter columns and ogee feet. No less than seven cabinetmakers made cases for Burnap, and they included Samuel Kneeland of Hartford, Simeon Loomis of East Windsor, and Hezekiah Kelly of far-off Norwich, Vermont. Unfortunately, these cabinetmakers cannot be tied in with specific remaining clocks.

To complete the cycle of Burnap's importance, one of his apprentices was Eli Terry (1772–1852), who became the early mass producer of nineteenth-century clocks. One of Terry's earliest clocks had a pagoda-top case (Edwin A. Battison and Patricia E. Kane, *The American Clock 1725–1865,* Greenwich, for Yale University Art Gallery, 1973, no. 5).

510. H. 94″, W. 20¼″, D. 10⅝″

America's most famous clockmaker was Simon Willard (1753–1848), who worked in Roxbury, Massachusetts, after 1780. So successful were his endeavors that, by the early 1800s, a small army of craftsmen had moved to Roxbury; they included apprentice clockmakers, cabinetmakers, gilders, and painters of dials and glass. In 1802, Willard received a patent for an "improved timepiece," the banjo clock, and from that time he concentrated mostly on the manufacture of these simpler, still elegant clocks. It has been estimated that he took a week to construct the mechanism of a tall clock, while he took only a day to make a "patent timepiece" (see John Ware Willard, *Simon Willard and his Clocks,* reprint, New York, 1968). Other craftsmen in the Roxbury–Boston area that did work for Willard included John Doggett, John R. Penniman, and William Fisk.

One of the stubbiest of Willard's tall-case clocks, 512 (at the right) is of the highest, quietest quality. The inlaid case is handsome, and on top is delicate scrollwork. Brass trim, inlays, and carving are also used. These "Roxbury" cases always have a stylish appearance (see Montgomery, no. 148). The brass works are also finely made and feature the anchor recoil escapement and rack-and-snail striking system usually used by Willard. The dial is inscribed for Calvin Allen. While no further details are known, a Calvin Allen, carver, was listed in Boston directories from 1833 to 1842.

Another excellent Federal clockmaker was David Wood of Newburyport. He sold Willard timepieces and is known for his fine shelf clocks (see Fales, *Essex,* nos. 69–70; Montgomery, nos. 169–171). Like Willard, he used imported English dials a great deal. The case of 511 (left) features fan inlays and stringing (both plain and patterned), with no carving.

511 (left). Tall clock by David Wood, Newburyport, Massachusetts, 1795–1815. Dial painted: polychrome and gilt corners, with ship in upper arch. Case mahogany (inlaid) and white pine. Brass finials. H. 90″, W. 19¾″, D. 10″. Case, W. 13¼″, D. 7¼″.

512 (right). Tall clock by Simon Willard, Roxbury, Massachusetts, 1792–1805. Dial painted: polychrome and gilt corners, with two birds in upper arch. "Warranted for Mr. Calvin Allen" on dial. Case mahogany (inlaid) and pine. Brass finials. H. 83¾″, W. 17⅝″, D. 10″. Case, W. 13⅛″, D. 7¼″.

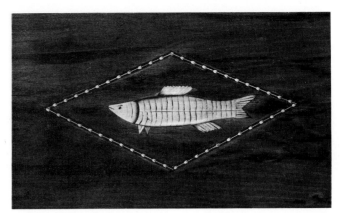

513a. Detail of inlay on base.

The case of this tall clock is important, since it bears the label of William Lloyd, a cabinetmaker of Springfield, Massachusetts. He worked from 1802 to about 1820, and his known works include tables, bureaus, sideboards, and this clock case. His work spanned the Hepplewhite and Sheraton styles and varied considerably in quality and in his use of cherry, mahogany, and maple (Florence Thompson Howe, "The Decline and Fall of William Lloyd," *Antiques*, February 1930, pp. 117–121; Montgomery, no. 400). This clock case is well made in a rural tradition, and its highlight is the inlaid fish surrounded by a diamond of arrow stringing on the base (513a). Inlaid on the chamfered corners are four segmented icicles (or "carrots") of a type used by other Connecticut and Rhode Island cabinetmakers. While the cherry case retains its original mahoganized color, the drilled fret seems more a feature of convenience than of inspiration. The eight-day brass movement has the normal anchor recoil escapement and rack-and-snail striking system. It is unmarked, but script initials "JP" are painted in white on the back of the dial, which has polychrome roses and flowers painted on the front.

513b. Label inside case.

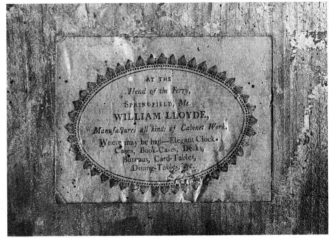

513. Tall clock (maker of works not known); painted dial with roses in arch. Case, cherry (mahoganized and inlaid), labeled by William Lloyd (1779–1845), Springfield, Massachusetts, 1805–1811. H. 94″, W. 20½″, D. 10⅜″. Case W. 13¾″, D. 7¾″.

The two tall clocks on this page were made in rural Massachusetts. George Holbrook (1767–1846) made few tall clocks, finally devoting his efforts to a bell foundry established after 1810. He worked mostly in the town of Wrentham, Massachusetts, as well as in Medway and Brookfield, where he made the clock at the left (514). The eight-day brass movement is ably made and housed in a stylish case probably made nearby in central Massachusetts. Inlaid paterae and fans on the front are complemented by the brass finials, hinges, and trappings on the columns and colonnettes. The entire clock is quite sophisticated and a tribute to Holbrook's abilities (see Palmer, p. 213). The clock was owned by Major David Dickinson (1747–1822) of Deerfield.

The clock at the right was made in Northampton by Isaac Gere (1771–1812). Born in Preston, Connecticut, Gere worked in Northampton from 1793 on. He was a clockmaker, watchmaker, and a silversmith (see Henry N. Flynt and Martha Gandy Fales, *The Heritage Foundation Collection of Silver with Biographical Sketches of New England Silversmiths, 1625–1825*, Deerfield, 1968, p. 225). The cherry case is a dignified, well-made Connecticut Valley example. The eight-day movement has the normal brass plates and wheels, cut pinions, anchor recoil escapement and seconds pendulum. It is powered by double-hung, crank-key-wound weights and has a rack-and-snail striking system. The painted dial is double-mounted on a marked "Osborne's Manufactory" plate. The partnership of T. Hadley Osborne and James Wilson produced clock dials in Birmingham, England, for export from 1772–1778, continuing individually until about 1820 (Penrose R. Hoopes, "Osborne and Wilson, Dialmakers," *Antiques*, September 1931, pp. 166–168). This clock was owned by the Williams and Billings families of Hatfield and Deerfield.

514 (left). Tall clock by George Holbrook (1767–1846), Brookfield, Massachusetts, 1790–1810. Painted moon phase dial, polychrome, with birds in center. Case of mahogany and mahogany veneers (inlaid), and pine. Brass finials with eagles. H. 96″, W. 20″, D. 10″. Case W. 13¾″, D. 7¼″.

515 (right). Tall clock by Isaac Gere (1771–1812), Northampton, Massachusetts, 1795–1810. Painted moon phase dial in gilt and polychrome. Case cherry and white pine. Billings family. H. 97⅜″, W. 20¼″, D. 11⅛″. Case W. 12⅞″, D. 7⅜″.

516. Tall clock, maker
unknown; case cherry
with pine backboard,
Deerfield, 1805–1830.
White, gilt, and polychrome
dial. H. 85½",
hood W. 17½", D. 9½".

517. This Allen sisters' photograph of the 1890s shows
the intersection of the Street (foreground) and Memorial
Street. Behind the hay scales is the house built in 1717
and 1751 for Ebenezer Wells, later lived in by Hezekiah
Wright Strong, and in this century by Dr. and Mrs. Edwin
C. Thorn (see Joseph Peter Spang III, "The Wells-Thorn House
in Deerfield, Mass.," *Antiques,* May 1966, pp. 730–733).

This tall clock was found by Dr. Edwin C. Thorn in
a corn crib at the Zebina Stebbins house in the Wapping section of Deerfield about 1900. This would explain its poor condition and the fact that Doctor
Thorn, an accomplished amateur joiner who made
several carved "Hadley" chests, refashioned the missing bonnet of the top. The case is a good example of
early nineteenth-century local cabinetmaking, with an
inlaid curled-maple oval in the base and maple-faced
feet. The lamb's tongues on the chamfered corners of
the upper section are echoed in the inlaid square and
triangles on the door. Mechanically, it has a one-day
wooden movement of the pull-up type typical of those
produced by pioneer Connecticut clock factories in
the nineteenth century and peddled throughout the
east. A bird on a branch crowns the painted wooden
dial.

Zebina Stebbins (1797–1879) was a miller and
farmer who married Ruby Graves of Sunderland in
1819. The clock could have been made at this time. A
label with her name and that of their son Baxter is
inside the door of the case.

Two clocks with cases labeled by Daniel Clay are preserved at Deerfield. Both bear his earliest 1794 label (518a), and one (519) has the printed date cut off and 1799 written in old ink. Figure 518 was owned by the Stevens family of Greenfield and Warwick, Massachusetts. The case is a simple cherry one, with chamfered and fluted corners more highly developed than those on the Deerfield double chest attributed to Clay (page 222, figure 450). The feet and fretwork at the top, as well as the brass finials, are recent restorations. The case, now refinished, was originally mahoganized.

While the maker of the clock was once thought to be David Wood of Newburyport, Massachusetts, it has an unsigned, eight-day movement. The dial plate is English, and the painted iron dial has a polychrome bird and flowers at the top, floral sprays and a swag in the center, and clusters of grapes in the spandrels. The movement stands nearer the front of the case than normal, and inside the door is a well-worn wooden wedge over the lock to guide the strike weight safely past.

Both Clay clock cases at Deerfield have variations of Gothic side windows on the hoods.

(NOTE: *for references to Daniel Clay, see page 124*).

518a. 1794 label of Daniel Clay. His later label, used after 1800, is shown on page 124, figure 258a.

518. Tall clock, maker unknown. Case, cherry with pine backboard, labeled by Daniel Clay, Greenfield, Massachusetts, 1794–1800. Bracket feet and fretwork restored. H. 95½", W. 20¾", D. 11". Case W. 12⅝", D. 6⅞".

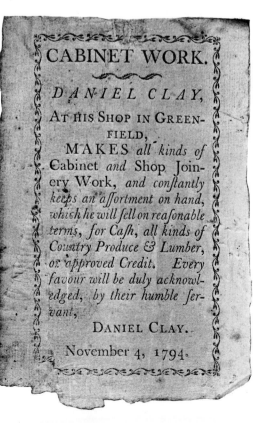

CABINET WORK.

DANIEL CLAY,

AT HIS SHOP IN GREEN-
FIELD,

MAKES *all kinds of* Cabinet *and* Shop Join-
ery Work, *and constantly keeps an assortment on hand, which he will sell on reasonable terms, for Cash, all kinds of Country Produce & Lumber, or approved Credit. Every favour will be duly acknowledged, by their humble servant,*

DANIEL CLAY.

November 4, 1794.

519a

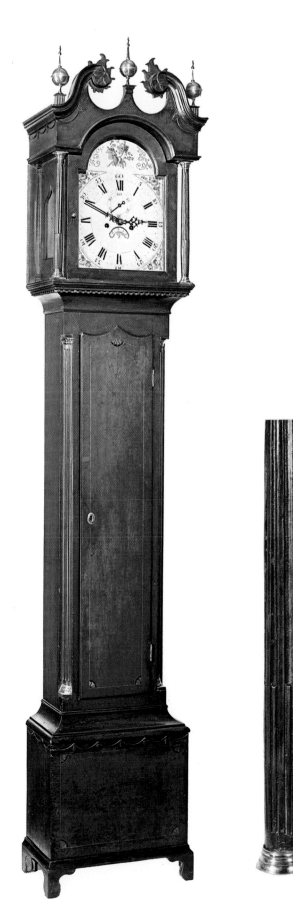

519b

Combining carving on the hood and the quarter columns (and stop-fluting on the colonnettes) with inlays on the base, the tall clock case on this page is the most elaborate example of Daniel Clay's work known. It was made for Jerome Ripley of Greenfield and placed "on the stairs," according to his great granddaughter. It was later owned by his son Franklin, reputedly the first insurance agent in the country, and then by his descendants, the Manning and Greenough families. In addition to Clay's label, there are two others: one about 1911 with Mary Greenough's history of the clock, and one of repairer B. M. Boyce of 49 Union Street, Boston. The eight-day brass movement is unmarked, and a wooden guide above the door lock is similar to that on 518. The double-mounted dial is signed by James Wilson of Birmingham, England (see page 264), and is decorated with polychrome roses at the top and in the spandrels.

519c

519. Tall clock, maker unknown. Case, cherry, inlaid, with pine backboard. Labeled by Daniel Clay, Greenfield, Massachusetts, dated 1799. All original. H. 97½″, W. 20″, D. 10½″. Case W. 13¾″, D. 7″.

520. (left). Shelf clock, maker unknown; case maple and white pine, probably Massachusetts, c. 1780. H. 46", W. 10⅛", D. 5¼".

A predecessor of the Massachusetts wall clock—a type primarily made by the Willards, Samuel Mulliken, and Levi Hutchins —520 has a severely handsome maple case which was painted a light blue-gray color. The eight-day brass movement is similar to one made by Samuel Mulliken of Newburyport, the brass plates giving way to strips and the pendulum (directly hung) located behind the large double-hung weight (see Brooks Palmer, *A Treasury of American Clocks*, New York, 1967, p. 25).

At the right, a Massachusetts wall clock by Aaron Willard (1757–1844) demonstrates how this talented family succeeded in making smaller, simpler clock movements. These ultimately led to the "patent timepiece" of Aaron's brother Simon in 1802. This clock has a thirty-hour brass movement, and the design of the case gives it the appearance of a bracket clock (see Montgomery, nos. 155–156; Lockwood Barr, "The Forerunner of the Willard Banjo," *Antiques*, March 1959, pp. 282–285).

Dwarf tall clocks, later known as "grandmother" clocks unfortunately, are eagerly sought by collectors today. They were expensive and not too many were made, most buyers probably having been content to pay only a bit more for a full-sized clock. Figure 521 (below left) was found by the Potters in Charlemont and has a rurally stylish Federal case, with French feet and urn finials. The moon phase indicator on the brass dial is unusual on such a small clock. The eight-day brass movement has a pendulum only 10½" long.

In the Hingham, Massachusetts area, Reuben Tower and Joshua Wilder made many dwarf tall clocks between 1810 and 1830. A Wilder example (523, to the right) is well made, with eight-day brass works. The entire back of the case is hinged as a full-length door. The dial is painted white, with both swags and scrolls in two shades of green and gilt. Wilder's clocks are usually housed in stylish, well-made mahogany cases similar to this (see Lawrence L. Barber, "Grandmother Clocks," *Antiques*, May 1937, pp. 244–246).

522 (above). Wall clock, by Aaron Willard, Grafton, Massachusetts, 1775–1780. Mahogany case. H. 23½", W. 8¾", D. 3⅝".

523 (below). Dwarf tall clock, by Joshua Wilder (1786–1860), Hingham, Massachusetts, 1808–1825. Case mahogany veneers on pine. H. 44", W. 10¾", D. 5⅝".

521 (below) Dwarf tall clock, maker unknown; case pine (mahoganized), Deerfield area, 1800–1825. H. 41¾", W. 12¾", D. 8". Lucius D. Potter Memorial.

Grace and economy (not necessarily in that order) were two of the most important reasons why Simon Willard's "patent timepiece" of 1802 became so popular. These so-called banjo clocks were produced by many craftsmen including case makers, gilders, and dial painters in Roxbury and Boston. They were a technical triumph on the part of the Willards, and their popularity continues to this day (see John Ware Willard, *Simon Willard and His Clocks*, reprint, New York, 1968, pp. 46–51; and Montgomery, nos. 159–160).

The banjo clock at the left (524) is one of the largest ones known and was made by Aaron Willard, Jr. (1783–1864), who succeeded his father in 1823 and retired in 1850. Owned by Henry Flynt's father, it went out of the family after his death; but, in the tradition of true collectors, the Flynts were successful in retrieving it at a later date.

Though its condition is disheveled, the banjo clock at the right (525) is important to Deerfield. It was owned by the Hoyt family in the Old Indian house. In January 1823, Elihu Hoyt wrote to his wife Hannah from Boston:

> I yesterday put on board Mr. Lucius Tuttles sleigh a *Willard timepiece in a box,* which I expect he will deliver to you . . . I charged him to take good care of it as it is a very tender thing to handle. I hope it will arrive safe.

The letter (Hoyt mss., P.V.M.A.) could refer to 525, if Hoyt kept the clock for his own use. "1 Brass eight day time piece" was listed in his 1833 inventory, its value eleven dollars.

The banjo clock at the lower right (526) was made by Samuel Whiting of Concord, Massachusetts after his partnership with Nathaniel Munroe. The eight-day brass movement has an escapement of the normal anchor-recoil type. The finial, drop, and front are gilt, and the bezel and side brackets are brass. The upper glass is convex, and the reverse-painted lower glass features a building (Mount Vernon?), a ship and a peephole made like the sun.

524. Banjo clock, by Aaron Willard, Jr., Boston, 1820–1835. Case mahogany and pine. Owned by Henry N. Flynt's father, George C. Flynt of Monson, Massachusetts. H. 55½", W. 14½", D. 4¾".

525. Banjo clock, by Aaron Willard, Boston, 1815–1823. Hoyt family, Deerfield. "No. 1710" on dial. H. 29½", W. 10", D. 3⅞".

526. Banjo clock, by Samuel Whiting, Concord, Massachusetts, c. 1817. Case mahogany and pine. Later label of Foster Brothers, Greenfield. H. 42⅛", W. 10", D. 4". Lucius D. Potter Memorial.

527 (left). Connecticut wall clock, maker unknown, 1817–1820. Case mahogany, maple and pine. H. 48″, W. 19½″, D. 6¾″.

528 (above, center). Shelf clock, by Seth Thomas, Plymouth, Connecticut, c.1830 (Eli Terry patent). Case mahogany and white pine. H. 31½″, W. 17½″, D. 5″. Gift of Henry N. Flynt, Jr.

529 (above, right). Shelf clock by George C. Marsh, Bristol, Connecticut, c.1830. Case mahogany and white pine. Owned by George C. Flynt. H. 29½″, W. 16¾″, D. 5″.

At the left is a wall clock with painted glass panels and a looking glass on the door. The building on the lower polychrome panel is Mount Vernon. This clock is nearly identical to a looking glass clock patented by Joseph Ives of Bristol, Connecticut in 1817 (Kenneth D. Roberts, *The Contributions of Joseph Ives to Connecticut Technology*, Bristol, 1970, figs. 7, 8). The movement is stamped brass, with Ives' roller pinions. It has rack-and-snail striking, and the long 41″ pendulum is powered by rectangular cast weights. The clock was owned by the carpenter William Russell, who came to Deerfield in 1806. His daughter Mary married Elijah Nims in 1820 (Sheldon, II, 276); and the clock was purchased from Anna Nims (Russell's great granddaughter) by Dr. and Mrs. Edwin Thorn. It was acquired by the Flynts in 1962 with the Wells-Thorn house.

One of the most popular of all American clocks was the pillar and scroll shelf clock introduced by Eli Terry of Plymouth, Connecticut, after he received a patent in 1816 for thirty-hour brass and wooden clocks. A compatriot (and adversary at times) of Terry was Seth Thomas, who made the shelf clock at the center (528). The works are wooden, and the dial is painted in white, black, and gold with polychrome paints in the scene below. This clock was made after 1829 (see Kenneth D. Roberts, *Eli Terry and the Connecticut Shelf Clock*, Bristol, 1973, pp. 109, 281).

At the right is a shelf clock (529) made by George Marsh of Bristol, Connecticut. Like the Seth Thomas pillar and scroll clock, this shelf clock has a one-day wooden movement, powered by cast weights —the almost universal type of movement used in Connecticut clocks before rolled and stamped brass shelf clock mechanisms were introduced about 1838. The case is fiercely Empire in style, with carved paw feet, front columns, and an eagle at the top flanked by pineapple finials (compare to Kenneth D. Roberts, *Eli Terry and the Connecticut Shelf Clock*, p. 246; see also pp. 242, 245).

This clock (529) was owned by Henry Flynt's father, George Converse Flynt of Monson, Massachusetts. He and his brother, L. C. Flynt, were clock collectors, and over 80 of the latter's clocks were advertised in *Antiques*, July 1925, page 7.

V. LOOKING GLASSES

530. Looking glass, pine, England or Massachusetts, 1700–1740. Old black paint. Removable cresting. Beveled glass, 23¼" x 13¼".

531. Looking glass, walnut and pine, England, 1740–1760. Gilt shell; glass not beveled. 23½" x 11½".

Even angels now tread lightly in the field of the American looking glass. While many Colonial looking glasses were once thought to be of American manufacture, it has been found through records and wood analysis that only a few of the frames were made here before 1790, and that sizeable glass plates were not manufactured in America until well into the nineteenth century (Montgomery, p. 255). While glass plates were imported to the Colonies and frames could have been made here, the trade of importing entire looking glasses was tremendous. Between 1720 and 1728, for example, English trade records show that the value of looking glasses exported to the Colonies was equal to that of all other furniture combined (Downs, xxix).

Looking glasses appear in records in New England from the mid-seventeenth century on. Soon after the *Boston News-Letter* started publication, William Randle, the japanner, advertised "at the Sign of the Cabbinett, a Looking-Glass Shop," in 1715 (Dow, pp. 106–107). Looking glasses "23 to 43 inches long" were advertised in 1717; and, by 1743, "Pier and Sconce Looking-Glasses, Chimney and Pocket Ditto" were sold by Stephen Whiting (Dow, pp. 127–128).

The earliest looking glasses that are found here had heavy bolection-molded frames with elaborate crestings reminiscent of the outlines of cane-back chair tops (530). These crests could be removable. Beveled glass—a mark of quality—was often used. The frame of 530 might have been made in eastern Massachusetts.

The other looking glasses reflect the gentler, curvilinear Queen Anne style, with and without added crestings. Figures 531 and 532 were both owned in southeastern Massachusetts at an early date. Figure 532, from Hanover, has "Hannah" on the backboard. Figure 533, with etched decoration on the glass, was found in the Connecticut Valley and relates to the so-called courting glasses shown on page 276.

532. Looking glass, walnut and spruce, England, 1710–1735. Beveled glass; never had cresting, 36" x 17¼".

533. Looking glass, walnut, England or Continent, 1725–1770. Removable cresting. 16⅝" x 10¼".

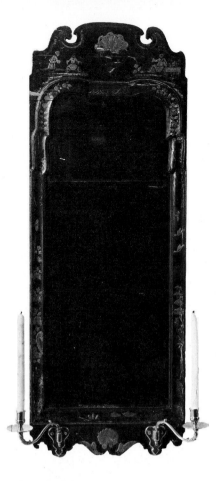

534. Looking glass, green japanned decoration, England, 1710–1725. Original beveled glass. Old candle arms added later. 42″ x 15¾″.

535. Looking glass, green japanned decoration, probably New York, 1735–1760. Beveled glass. Wendell family. Ex coll. Mrs. Anson B. Moran. 39″ x 17⅝″.

536. Looking glass, pine, possibly American, 1735–1785. Red background with black animals, birds, buildings, and flora. Crest and top of frame marked "V." 16¼″ x 9½″.

In the Colonies, japanned furniture was produced in Boston, New York, and Philadelphia, with Boston leading the way (see page 204). Most of the japanned looking glasses found here were imported from England (534), although a few Massachusetts and New York examples have been found. Figure 535 (left) has several inscriptions on its back, including one that states "Heirloom through Hermanus Wendell 1700." The Wendells were a prominent New York family, and this looking glass was lent by a later owner to the famous Girl Scout exhibition in 1929 (Catalogue no. 650). Made of soft pine and painted dark green with raised gilt decoration, the frame makes use of whiting under the paint to fill in the pores of the wood. This technique was used in English japanning, but it occurs only occasionally on New York clock cases and looking glasses, with most American japanners being content to paint the base coat directly on a fine-grained wood. Since the senior and junior Gerardus Duyckincks were the only japanners known to be working in New York from 1735 on, one of them might have decorated this looking glass. A later stamp on the back by Hyman and Bricker in 1907 indicates they resilvered the glass at that time for Mrs. Anson B. Moran, the owner.

The small looking glass above (536) is related to japanned work but does not have raised decoration and is merely painted in black and red. An outdoor theme is featured, with animals, plants, birds, and buildings on the frame (see Downs, nos. 244, 245). Two scrolls are missing from the crest. On the back is a hinged double prop which enables the looking glass to be used on a table, while a brass ring permits it also to be hung on a wall.

537. Looking glass, walnut and gilt (repainted), England, 1750–1765. Eagle finial old but not original. 53″ x 26½″.

538. Looking glass, mahogany and gilt, England, 1755–1785. Phoenix finial original. Glass replaced. 59″ x 28″.

In the 1740s, broken-arch scrolled pediments became popular in English looking glasses (Wills, p. 83), and by 1762, "large gilt Piedmont Glasses" were advertised in Boston (Dow, p. 129). English glassmakers were able to produce large glass plates at this time (Wills, pp. 41–64), and an auction in Boston in 1762 offered "two very handsome Large Looking-Glasses, about Eight Feet in Height" (Dow, p. 129).

On this page are two rather large examples of English looking glasses of the pediment type. Figure 537 is made of walnut veneers on pine, with the formerly gilt decoration incised, carved, and in the case of the pendant flowers, leaves and fruit on the sides, on wired gesso. The eagle finial is a later replacement, phoenixes or flowers in baskets being the expected finials for looking glasses of this type (Wills, p. 83). The incised bowknot at the bottom is

unusual. Unfortunately, the original gilding has been covered by modern imitation bronze radiator paint, a fate that often befalls old gilding.

The mahogany veneered looking glass at the right (538) has its original gilding and finial. It is similar to a looking glass at Mount Vernon that was puchased by Martha Washington in Philadelphia probably in 1783 (Helen Maggs Fede, *Washington Furniture at Mount Vernon*, Mount Vernon, 1966, pp. 30–31). A looking glass at Winterthur with some similarities bears the 1753–1761 label of John Elliott, Sr., who made and imported looking glasses in Philadelphia. A more similar pier glass was owned by Philip Van Rensselaer at Cherry Hill, built in 1768 in the Albany area (Benjamin Ginsburg, "The Furniture of Albany's Cherry Hill," *Antiques*, June 1960, p. 566).

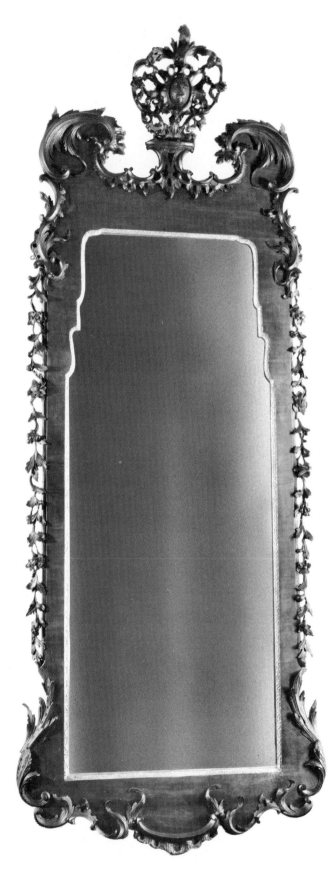

"Peer Glasses" were advertised in Boston newspapers as early as 1735 (see Dow, p. 110). Pier glasses were oversized, vertical looking glasses, while related "chimney glasses" were short but wide, with a horizontal emphasis. This imposing pier glass features extremely able carving, topped by a rococo cartouche. The fruit and leafage at the sides are executed with minute delicacy, and the scrolls at the top and bottom add verve and motion to the frame. While this looking glass was once hoped to be American, microscopic examination of the secondary woods indicates that they are a spruce most likely British in origin.

The looking glass was owned in the downstairs hall of Brooklandwood, a handsome country house built near Brooklandville, Maryland (just north of Baltimore) on 1,400 acres which Charles Carroll of Carrollton provided for his daughter Mary and her husband Richard Caton, who were married in 1787. Due to financial reverses, the Catons were forced to sell the house only a few years after it was finished to Alexander Brown. It was later owned by the Emersons and is now a school.

This looking glass was probably ordered and owned originally by Charles Carroll of Carrollton. Later, he helped the Catons retain another home, now the Carroll Mansion in Baltimore (*Antiques*, March 1968, pp. 322, 324).

539. Pier glass, mahogany, mahogany veneers, and spruce, England, 1750–1765. Detail of rococo carving at right. Owned at Brooklandwood, a country house near Baltimore, Maryland, by Richard and Polly Caton. 90″ x 36″.

539a

540. Looking glass, mahogany and Scots, pine, England, 1750–1765. Original unbeveled glass and gilding. 39″ x 17″.

541. Looking glass, walnut and spruce, England, 1750–1765. Original beveled glass and gilding. 42¼″ x 22″.

542. Looking glass, mahogany and spruce, England, 1755–1785. Found in eastern Massachusetts. 40⅜″ x 22⅝″.

Looking glasses of the types shown on this page are often encountered in New England and were formerly thought to be of American manufacture. The secondary woods, however, point toward an almost certain English origin for all of them. With scrolled ears and a pierced gilt shell, 540 is similar to another looking glass privately owned with a long history in the Boston area. A second similar example was found in New Hampshire (*Antiques*, September 1970, p. 378). Others are at Deerfield.

At the right, 541 is a very well finished looking glass with contrasting areas of gilding and walnut veneers. The plume in the arch at the top is unusual, as are the six pierced trefoils at the bottom and two quatrefoils at the top. This looking glass is quite light and has an American "feel," but the secondary wood of it and 542 is an English spruce.

Many looking glasses with phoenixes in the crests were imported to the Colonies (542; see *Georgian Furniture*, London, Victoria and Albert Museum, 1951, no. 96). Eagles appeared in the crestings later; and a smaller example of this type, made in Boston by Bittle and Cooper in the early 1800s, is one of a number that were finally produced in this country (*Antiques*, May 1968, p. 650).

543. Looking glass, walnut, Flemish or Dutch, 1700–1725. Gold foil at top. 28½″ x 19½″.

544. Looking glass, Scots pine, Europe, 1745–1770. Foil missing. 17″ x 11⅛″.

545. Looking glass, Scots pine, Europe, 1745–1770. In original box. 17¾″ x 13″.

"Dutch Looking Glasses" were advertised in Boston newspapers in 1760 and 1772 (Dow, pp. 95, 128). At the left above, 543 is a Dutch or Flemish looking glass with a prop in the back which allows it to be placed on a table as well as hung on a wall. The upper section, having a portrait of a gentleman on glass, has a gold-colored foil in the background; and this foil also originally lined the smaller moldings of the frame. It was a prototype for a large group of looking glasses made in Holland, north Germany, and Denmark throughout the eighteenth century for export (544, 545). These were later referred to as courting glasses, and many of them were brought back to New England and other coastal towns (Judith Coolidge Hughes, "Courting Mirrors: Another European Export Product?" *Antiques*, July 1962, pp. 68–71). They were usually pegged into their protective shipping boxes (545) and were decorated with painted glass borders and gold "Dutch metal" foil in the small moldings, usually missing today. They were a colorful group of looking glasses, formerly thought to be from China (Kettell, nos. 191–195). The three looking glasses below are also imports from the North Germany–Denmark area, often found in New England. Figure 547 was found in the Deerfield area. The bird cutouts on 548 are especially artful.

546. Looking glass, walnut and gilt, northern Europe, 1725–1755. 31″ x 13¾″.

547. Looking glass, walnut and gilt, northern Europe, 1725–1755. 26¼″ x 11⅞″.

548. Looking glass, walnut and Scots pine, northern Europe, 1725–1755. 29½″ x 13¼″.

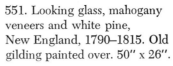

551. Looking glass, mahogany
veneers and white pine,
New England, 1790–1815. Old
gilding painted over. 50″ x 26″.

549. Looking glass, mahogany
and spruce, England, 1750–
1850. Old glass. 44″ x 22″.
Lucius D. Potter Memorial.

550. Looking glass, walnut
and Scots pine, England,
1755–1850. Original glass
and gilding. 40⅜″ x 22⅝″.

The looking glass at the left (549), with its handsome phoenix finial, appears to be a well made Chippendale looking glass (compare with Wills, no. 49). However, the incised lines in the scrolls and cutouts, as well as the leafage at the sides, have a different character, much like that of a similar looking glass made about 1840 by Samuel Hassall, a Yorkshire carver and gilder (Christopher Hutchinson, *Furniture Made in Yorkshire: 1750–1900*, Leeds, Temple Newsam, 1974, no. 10). Certain popular forms continued to be made well after they were originally introduced. Figure 550 may well be later also, with its urn and incised lines. A similar, urnless looking glass was owned in Providence (Nutting, II, no. 2961).

At the right are two American looking glasses. Figure 551 is a large one with an eagle finial. While the frame appears to be Chippendale at first glance, the moldings are later, and festoons of Federalized leafage replace the earlier pendant oak leaves at the sides. White pine is used as a secondary wood, and the old gilding unfortunately has been covered over by imitation bronze radiator paint. This looking glass seems a rural translation of one at Winterthur owned in Dorchester, Massachusetts, and considered American by Downs (no. 262). At the bottom of the frame are two brass mirror knobs with eagle decoration. These were attached to the wall to help support looking glasses in the Federal period.

Below is a small looking glass (one of a pair) labeled by John Elliott of Philadelphia. He was a comb maker as well as a looking glass retailer and manufacturer; and he also sold japanned ware on Market Street between 1808 and 1839. He was located at 82 Market Street from 1811 until 1814, so the looking glass can be dated within these years (see *Antiques*, April 1967, pp. 518–519; and October 1967, p. 565). It is a late survival of the Chippendale style, quite similar to looking glasses labeled by other Philadelphia makers (Montgomery, nos. 221–222).

552, 552a. (below). Looking glass,
mahogany, labeled by John Elliott,
Philadelphia, 1811–1814. One of
a pair. Old glass. 29½″ x 16⅝″.

553. Looking glass, mahogany and pine, possibly Massachusetts, 1795–1805. 60″ x 24″.

554. Looking glass, mahogany and pine, probably New York or Albany, 1795–1810. 60″ x 19½″.

555. Looking glass, mahogany and pine, New York or Albany, 1795–1810. 55″ x 21″.

The looking glasses on this page are graceful transitional forms, with Federal ornament (inlays, urns, and a glass tablet with reverse painting) superimposed on an earlier type of fretwork looking glass with scrolled top. Figure 553 was found in eastern Massachusetts and was once on loan to the Winslow house in Marshfield. It has cutout ears at the top instead of the pendant gilded flowers and leafage usually associated with this type. The inlaid, shimmery four-petaled flower has been found on card tables. Oval inlaid eagles and paterae were also used under the pediments of these looking glasses (Montgomery, no. 216). Another decorative device was the shell, which was favored in New York (Montgomery, nos. 214–215). Figure 554 makes use of this device and is similar to a looking glass owned in Albany (Frances Clary Morse, *Furniture of the Olden Time*, New York, 1902

[1940 edition], pp. 315, 391–392). The sparse floral decoration at the sides is very similar to that on another looking glass owned by the Bushnell family of New Haven, Connecticut (*Antiques*, January 1965, p. 57).

Eglomisé panels were used occasionally in the upper sections of the glass, and 555 contains one with a ruin by a lake in black, white, gray, and gilt. In 1802, John Sandford, the New York carver and gilder, advertised "Enamelled Glass for Prints or Tablets, lettered or plain." He also listed looking glasses, girandoles, picture frames, window cornices, brackets, and fancy furniture, as well as "Needle-Work neatly strained, framed and glazed." He also repaired frames and resilvered glass (Rita Susswein Gottesman [comp.], *The Arts and Crafts in New York: 1800–1804*, New York, 1965, no. 413).

556. Looking glass, walnut and gilt, northern Europe, 1765–1785. 31¼″ x 12½″.

557. Looking glass, pine and gesso with gold leaf, England, 1775–1790. 37½″ x 16½″.

Among the imported looking glasses featured here, 556 is a very handsome type, with well defined gilt moldings, rosettes, and floral sprays. It was made in northern Germany or Denmark and is a later, more developed type than figure 548, page 276. Considerable work has been done in restoring this looking glass.

The imposing looking glass at the right has gilding which complements the warm peach color of the marble frame (558). The classical urns, sprays, and swags are well defined in gesso and wire. Looking glasses of this type are called Bilbao mirrors, after the Spanish port on the Bay of Biscay. Perhaps some were shipped through this port once, although a Portuguese or more likely a northern European origin has been suggested for them (see Montgomery, no. 229).

The two looking glasses below are English. Figure 557 (left) is made of gesso and wire on pine, its gilding intact. The sprays of leaves and flowers, topped off by a fluted and beaded urn with three ears of wheat, all surround the oval frame which had become so popular in the newer classical styles. This looking glass was owned by the Bryant family of South Deerfield and given to Miss C. Alice Baker for the Frary house (compare with Wills, no. 147).

When Thomas Sheraton's *The Cabinet Dictionary* appeared in 1803, a "mirror" was defined as "a circular convex glass in a gilt frame, silvered on the concave side, by which the reflection of the rays of light are produced" (p. 271). A looking glass was still a looking glass. At the right is a mirror with two girandoles (or sconces) attached. This form, usually with an eagle at the top, was introduced in France and England about 1800, and few were made here (see Montgomery, nos. 233–234; Wills, no. 163; and Fales, *Painted*, no. 197).

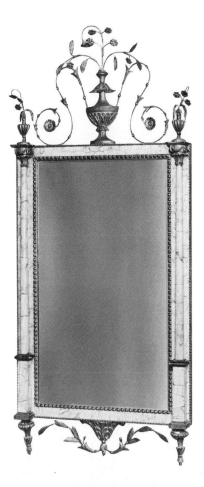

558. Looking glass, marble, gesso, and gilt, Bilbao type, Europe, c. 1800. Ex coll. Mr. and Mrs. Ellerton M. Jetté. 50″ x 23″.

559. Girandole mirror, pine, gesso, and gilt, probably England, 1805–1820. 36″ x 22″.

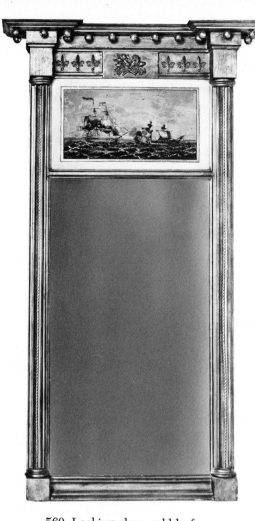

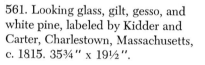

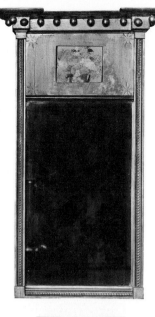

560. Looking glass, gold leaf, gesso, and white pine, probably Boston, c. 1815. Polychrome naval engagement. 43½" x 25⅜".

561. Looking glass, gilt, gesso, and white pine, labeled by Kidder and Carter, Charlestown, Massachusetts, c. 1815. 35¾" x 19½".

562. Looking glass, white pine (later paint), labeled by Smith and Norton, Northampton, Massachusetts, c. 1820. 30⅜" x 17½".

On these two pages are looking glasses of the columnar, or so-called tabernacle, type which became very popular in America after 1800. Usually featuring upper panels with scenes painted in reverse on glass, these looking glasses were well gilt and often had balls nailed under the cornice.

The large looking glass above (560) is a type popular after the War of 1812, celebrating the victory of the *United States* over the *Macedonian* in October, 1812. Many looking glasses depicting naval victories reflected the new wave of nationalism that swept America in the early 1800s.

Columnar looking glasses were made in cities and towns, and they are frequently found with labels. The firm of John Kidder (1753–1835) and Joseph Carter, who joined the partnership about 1811, made 561 above. Another example of their work is shown in Helen Comstock, *The Looking Glass in America: 1700–1825*, New York, 1968, nos. 80, 81. The frame, with its hollowed colonettes and single twist, is more run-of-the-mill than 560; and the painted rowboat scene is from mythology. The original scene of 562 has vanished, the frame is even less elaborate, and it has been daubed over with imitation bronze radiator paint, but it bears the label of Smith and Norton of Northampton.

On the next page, the large pier glass contains a wealth of classical decoration, with urns, swags, paterae, leafage, and even an eagle—all features which were used in England (Wills, nos. 159, 160). The upper panel is painted wood rather than glass. (A similar example formerly in the same collection is shown in Luke Vincent Lockwood, *Colonial Furniture in America,* New York, I, 1926, 397). The remnants of a label are on the backboard—in undecipherable condition with only "C," "Glass," and part of an oval left.

A small "Hitchcocky" looking glass is on the next page (565), and above it is a picture with a patterned, single-twist gilt frame bearing the label of Nathan Ruggles of Hartford engraved by Abner Reed. Ruggles, a looking glass maker, worked by himself and in partnerships in Hartford from 1803 until his untimely death in 1835 (see Montgomery, no. 213; "Ruggles and Dunbar: Looking Glass Manufacturers," *Bulletin,* the Connecticut Historical Society, April 1960, 56–60; Annual Report, the Connecticut Historical Society, 1961, pp. 25, 32).

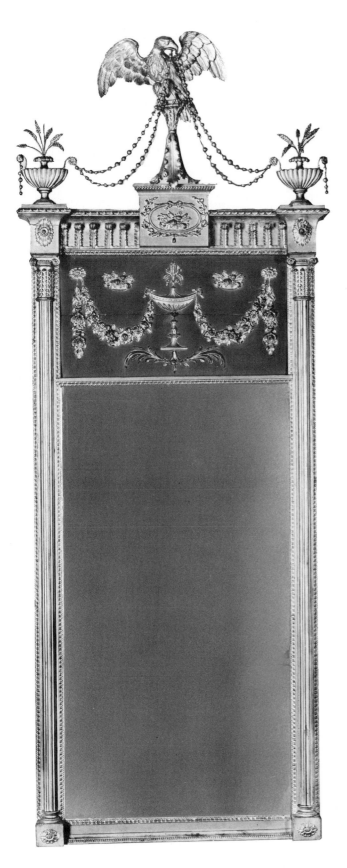

564. Needlework picture, "Liberty Guided by the Wisdom of '76." Frame labeled by Nathan Ruggles, Hartford, 1806–1817. 564a, detail of label. 23″ x 25″.

563. Pier glass, gold leaf, gesso, and pine, possibly New York or Albany, 1800–1810. Upper panel blue ground with gilt decoration. 80″ x 31⅜″. Gift of George A. Cluett, Jr.

565 (right). Looking glass, mahogany and white pine, New England, 1825–1835. Ebonized pillars with stenciled decoration in bronze powder, 26⅜″ x 12½″.

VI. MISCELLANEOUS FORMS

566 . Pipe box, cherry and
pine drawer bottom, New England,
1750–1800. H. 20″, W. 6¾″, D. 5″.

567 . Pipe box, pine,
Connecticut Valley, 1780–1810.
Dark brown stain. H. 24″, W. 7″, D. 6½″.

In the collections of Historic Deerfield, Inc. and the Pocumtuck Valley Memorial Association are many smaller miscellaneous wooden objects that include boxes of all types, spinning and wool wheels, and musical instruments. There is not room to include them all in this book, but a sampling of some of the best is given here.

Above are two pipe boxes. Made to hold pipes in their upper sections and tobacco or other accoutrements in the drawer below, these boxes could be extremely simple or quietly elaborate. With a nice Queen Anne rounded arch on the front and a simply fluted fan on the drawer, 566 rises well above the ordinary. The other pipe box (567) is made of pine and not carved, but the scalloping on its sides and especially the front dividers gives it a feeling of verve and motion. Pipe boxes were also made of mahogany and walnut, and they often are microcosms reflecting delicious bits of the styles in vogue. They could be

hung on walls or placed on the tops of desks or tables.

In the P.V.M.A. library is a highly interesting letter from Purley Torrey, a Worcester cabinetmaker, to Christopher Arms of Deerfield in 1828, about Torrey taking on Christopher Arms, Jr., as an apprentice. In a most paternal manner, Torrey enumerated the terms of the young man's training, especially his off-hours. In addition to tending fires and running errands, the youth would be expected to attend Bible class on Sundays and could not go out in the evenings unless Torrey knew where he was going. "I do not mean to keep him as close as though he was in a cloister, but I do mean that he shall not go and come when he pleases and where he pleases without giving any account or feeling himself accountable to me." In addition to his training. Torrey also felt responsible for his "moral character, habits of industry and temperance." Christopher, Jr. became a civil engineer.

568. Hanging candle box, pine, New England, 1780–1825. Old black paint. Sliding top; nailed construction. H. 19½″, W. 9½″, D. 3″.

569. Hanging salt box, white pine, probably Connecticut, 1760–1795. Original Spanish brown paint. H. 10″, W. 7⅛″, D. 5″.

570. Hanging watch box, pine, Connecticut, 1760–1810. Original blue-gray paint. Chip decoration on top. H. 11½″, W. 5½″, D. 2½″.

Various boxes are shown above, all with their old paint. The elaborately carved salt box in the center (569) is a continuation of an earlier type of chip carving that was popular in the Friesland section of Holland as well as in Scandinavia. The technique used in this country was not as crisply executed as in foreign examples (see *Antiques*, May 1934, p. 171; and June 1925, pp. 312–315). Boxes and spoon racks are found with this decoration, and one of the latter,

dated 1783, has many similarities to this salt box (Kettell, no. 123). A busk from Massachusetts dated 1823 (privately owned) shows the technique continued well into the 1800s. Chip carving is used more sparingly on the charming blue watch box above.

The medicine chest (below) is dovetailed and bears the handsome label of Thomas Weld, an apothecary "at the north side of the Market," Boston. He was listed there only in the 1807 Directory.

571. Medicine chest, white pine, made for Thomas Weld, Boston, c. 1807. Painted black-brown. Label above (571a). Inside compartmented; original iron hinges. H. 6½″, W. 18½″, D. 11″.

572. Medicine chest, mahogany with tulip in drawer bottoms, made by John Needles, Baltimore, 1810–1830. Sold by Edme Ducatel & Sons. Labels above (572a). Original bottles. H. 10″, W. 11½″, D. 11½″.

Baltimore to England to Deerfield seems a lengthy triple play, but that is the history of the medicine box above. It was found in England in this century and brought to Deerfield. It was made by one of the best of the Empire cabinetmakers of Baltimore, John Needles (1786–1878), who worked there between 1810 and 1853. This medicine chest has his earliest label, used until about 1830 (see Charles F. Montgomery, "John Needles, Baltimore Cabinetmaker,"

Antiques, April 1954, pp. 292–295). The bottles and mortar and pestle inside are original. Cloth tabs are used on the drawer fronts, since there was no clearance for brass knobs there.

Below, as a final interior view of Deerfield, is the garret of the Wells-Thorn house. A Cromwellian chair from Salem, a banister back chair with a carved top rail, and a paneled Massachusetts chest represent even more of the vast treasures at Deerfield.

573

574. No work on Deerfield would be complete without a look at the Street. In the view above, taken about 1900 by the Allen sisters, the Sheldon-Hawks house (left) and Cowles house (right) help the magnificent elms frame the north end of the Street. About sixty years later, Samuel Chamberlain took the view below, showing the other end, with the Wilson Printing and Hoyt houses on the west side. A few minor signs of the twentieth century can be seen. Yet the Street still serves as the connecting link of time—between the houses, the people, and their possessions.

Hampshire County once included all of western Massachusetts. By 1770, Berkshire County was incorporated, taking the westernmost area of the Colony but leaving to Hampshire County the rich area of the Connecticut Valley. Later, even this swath was divided into three counties. In 1811, the northern part (including Deerfield) became Franklin County, with Greenfield the county seat; and in 1812, the southern part became Hampden County, with Springfield its chief town. Hampshire County remained, with Northampton still the seat of a county that had been decreased considerably over the years.

In March 1796, when the house joiners and cabinetmakers of the county met at Hatfield, Hampshire County still included the entire Connecticut Valley of Massachusetts. Other cabinetmakers in Hartford had already issued a list of cabinet work prices in 1792 (Lyon, pp. 267–270; see also Montgomery, pp. 19–26). Since Hampshire County was more rural and work less specialized among artisans, the joining of two major groups of craftsmen is logical.

In 1796, the Federal style was about to make its way up the Connecticut Valley. The Hatfield list still featured the older forms, with high chests and turn-up beds noted. Woods were not described in detail, but cherry and pine are mentioned specifically.

Two versions of the results of the meeting were printed (see Montgomery, p. 488). Since the prices agreed upon applied to products of both journeymen and masters throughout the Connecticut Valley of Massachusetts, the first portion of the 1796 broadside, containing all the references and descriptions of cabinetwork, is given here. The second (and longer) portion dealing with house work is not. This is copied from the original at the Historical Society of Pennsylvania, brought to the Flynts' attention by Charles F. Montgomery.

AT a general Meeting of the House-Joiners and Cabinet-Makers in the County of Hampshire, held at Hatfield, on the second day of March, 1796,—when they agreed on the following prises of WORK, viz.—

CABINET WORK

	Dol.	Cts.
PLAIN Desks, 3 feet long, 5 drawers, in the head, plain feet	12	50
ditto, with swell'd feet,	13	33
ditto, with 8 drawers in the head,	16	66
Book Case, square head,	6	0
ditto, scroll head,	10	0

Cases with Drawers

	Dol.	Cts.
Low Case, 5 drawers,	9	17
High Case with 8 drawers, square head,	15	0
ditto, with scroll head,	20	0
ditto, with columns and cock beed,	25	0
Plain Bureau, 3 feet long,	8	33
ditto, with swelled feet and columns,	10	0
Plain Clock Case, with scroll head,	15	0
Pine Chest, with 3 drawers,	5	0
ditto, with 2 drawers,	4	50
ditto, with 1 drawer,	3	33
Plain Chest, dovetail'd,	2	0
ditto, rabbitted,	1	66
Dining Tables, per foot,	1	50
Plain Breakfast, ditto,	4	17
ditto, with streatches and drawer,	5	0
Stand ditto, 3 feet diameter,	4	66
Plain square Card Table,	4	0
Circular ditto,	7	0
Kitchen Table,	3	0
Candle Stand, 17 inches diameter	1	50
Creek Bedstead,	1	33
Cord, ditto,	1	66
ditto, for sack bottom,	3	0
ditto, with long posts, 8 square,	5	0
ditto, to turn against the wall,	4	0
ditto, with case and pannel door,	9	17
Common pine Cradle,	1	66
Cherry ditto, with top,	4	66
Common plain Coffin,	1	66
Smallest size,	0	66
Other sizes in proportion.		
Sleigh Frame,	6	0
Plain Sleigh Box, with screws,	7	0
(Trimings for Drawers, excluded.)		

(end)

576. Armchair, maple, Hampshire County, Massachusetts, 1720–1780. Refinished; originally painted Spanish brown or Indian red. Feet cut down. Similar to the child's chair shown on page 22, figure 18. Owned by Bates family of Conway. Gift of Mr. and Mrs. John Staub. H. 43½", W. 21¾", D. 20".

577. Chest with two drawers, white pine, possibly made by William Mather in Whately, Hampshire County, 1790–1805. Originally painted red; refinished. Brasses replaced. See page 185, figure 386. H. 45½", W. 37½", D. 19".

THE

CABINET-MAKER'S GUIDE:

OR

RULES AND INSTRUCTIONS

IN THE ART OF

VARNISHING, DYING, STAINING, JAPANNING, POLISH-
ING, LACKERING AND BEAUTIFYING

**WOOD, IVORY, TORTOISE-SHELL
AND METAL.**

WITH

OBSERVATIONS ON THEIR MANAGEMENT
AND APPLICATION.

A New Edition, with considerable Additions.

INCLUDING

AN APPENDIX,

CONTAINING SEVERAL VALUABLE TABLES.

———

LONDON:
PRINTED FOR KNIGHT AND LACY,
PATERNOSTER-ROW.

GREENFIELD, MASS.

Re-printed by Ansel Phelps, and for sale by him, at his
Bookstore,—also by West & Richardson, Cummings,
Hilliard & Co. Boston; and Wilder & Campbell,
New-York.

1825.

578. Title page of G. A. Siddons' *The Cabinet-Maker's Guide*, published in London and reprinted in Greenfield in 1825. Courtesy, Joseph Peter Spang III. 6¼" x 3¾".

Photograph Credits

Numbers refer to figure numbers.

THE MISSES MARY and FRANCES ALLEN, Deerfield, Massachusetts:
153, 517, 574

E. IRVING BLOMSTRANN, New Britain, Connecticut:
10

AL DAIGLE, Greenfield, Massachusetts:
543, 545

GINSBURG and LEVY, INC., New York City:
30, 474

H. M. MANUGIAN, South Norwalk, Connecticut:
146, 237, 242, 295, 302, 303, 417, 438, 461, 509, 530

RICHARD MERRILL, Saugus, Massachusetts:
215, 223, 369, 382, 426

AMELIA F. MILLER, Deerfield, Massachusetts:
424

MEYER STUDIO, INC., Wethersfield, Connecticut:
403

TAYLOR and DULL, INC., New York City:
10, 28, 69, 72, 74, 77, 89–91, 98, 101, 103, 115, 118, 126, 133, 209, 213, 239, 250, 259, 262, 265, 268, 272, 276, 277, 277a, 284, 284a, 304, 308, 309, 315, 318, 319, 321, 322, 347, 354, 356, 360, 376–378, 380, 389, 421, 427, 427a, 428a, 434, 436, 439, 441a, 452–454, 457a, 462–464b, 475, 478–480, 481a, 481c, 482, 486, 494, 507, 508, 510, 511, 513–515, 521, 523, 528, 535, 539, 542, 551–552a, 564, 564a, 569, 573

ARTHUR VITOLS, HELGA PHOTO STUDIO, New York City:
1–9, 11–27, 29, 31–66, 68, 70, 71, 73, 74a–76, 78–88, 92–97, 100, 102, 104–114, 116, 117, 119–125, 126a–132, 134–145, 147–152, 154, 156–208, 210–212, 214, 216–222, 226–236, 238, 240, 241, 243–249, 251–258, 259a–261, 263, 264, 266, 267, 269–271a, 273–275, 276a, 278–280, 282, 283, 285–294, 296–301, 305–307, 310–314, 316, 317, 320, 323–346, 348–353, 357–359, 361–368, 370–375, 379, 381, 383–388, 390–402, 404–412, 415, 416, 418–420, 422, 423, 425, 428, 428b–430a, 435, 437, 440, 441, 442–447, 449–451, 454a–456, 458–460a, 464c–469, 471–473a, 476, 477, 481, 481b, 483–485, 486a–493, 495–501, 503, 504, 512, 513a, 513b, 516, 518–520, 522, 524–527, 529, 531–534, 536–538, 540, 541, 544, 546–550, 553–563, 565–568, 570–572, 576–578

Index